On the Dynamics of
Growth and Debt

On the Dynamics of Growth and Debt

Casper van Ewijk

CLARENDON PRESS · OXFORD
1991

Oxford University Press, Walton Street, Oxford OX2 6DP
Oxford New York Toronto
Delhi Bombay Calcutta Madras Karachi
Petaling Jaya Singapore Hong Kong Tokyo
Nairobi Dar es Salaam Cape Town
Melbourne Auckland
and associated companies in
Berlin Ibadan

Oxford is a trade mark of Oxford University Press

Published in the United States
by Oxford University Press, New York

British Library Cataloguing in Publication Data
Data available

Library of Congress Cataloging-in-Publication Data
Ewijk, Casper van.
On the dynamics of growth and debt / Casper van Ewijk.
p. cm.
Includes bibliographical references (p.   ) and index.
1. Debts, Public. 2. Economic development. I. Title.
HJ8015.E95 1991 336.3′ 4—dc20 91–17462
ISBN 0–19–828346–6

Set by Pure Tech Corporation, Pondicherry, India.
Printed in Great Britain by
Bookcraft (Bath) Ltd., Midsomer Norton, Avon

To Emma, Roelof, Arend, and Sven

Acknowledgements

In the course of preparing this book I benefited from discussions, comments, and encouragement from a number of people.

First of all, I am greatly indebted to Professor Theo van de Klundert. Each chapter has benefited from his critical comments, which often inspired me to do further research and to improve vital points of the argument.

This book has also benefited from discussions with colleagues at the University of Amsterdam. In particular, I wish to thank Rob de Klerk who read and commented on many parts of it.

I am indebted for very helpful comments to Peter Skott, S. K. Kuipers, and two anonymous referees, and to Frederick van der Ploeg who stimulated me to accomplish this work.

Mrs P. Ellman greatly helped me with my grammar and found many errors in earlier drafts of the manuscript. Of course, all errors and omissions in this final version are mine.

Finally, I want to thank Roelof, Arend, and Sven and, above all, Emma for giving me the time and encouragement to finish this book.

Contents

List of Symbols

For ease of reference, the most important variables used throughout this book are listed below. The overdot is used to represent time derivatives ($\dot{x} = dx/dt$), and expected variables are indicated by the subscript e, i.e. x_e = expected value of x.

All stock and flow variables are in real terms, and expressed as a ratio to capital stock, unless stated otherwise.

a corporate debt
b public debt
C aggregate consumption
e net external creditor (+) or debtor position (-)
f balance of trade
g government expenditure
h utilization rate
i net investment
K capital stock (absolute, volume)
m (base) money
M (base) money (absolute, nominal)
l employment (in efficiency units)
l_s labour supply (in efficiency units)
n growth of labour supply (in efficiency units)
p inflation
P price level
r real interest rate
R nominal interest rate

S total savings
T total taxes
u rate of unemployment
V net worth
w wage income
W real wage rate
y net production
Y production (absolute, volume)
z wealth
α risk aversion coefficient
γ_i fiscal reaction coefficient ($i = 1, \ldots 4$)
δ pay-out of profits
ξ time preference
ϑ_x adjustment coefficient ($x = i, g, \pi, \ldots$)
θ pay-out ratio
ν money growth
π profit rate
η discount rate
ρ growth rate of production
σ risk premium
τ_i tax rate ($i = 1, 2, 3$)

1

Introduction

Economic development in the past decades has been characterized by large shifts in the distribution of debt and wealth: on a country scale within the private sector and between the government and the private sector, and on a world scale among developed countries and between developed and less-developed countries. These shifts have exerted a pervasive influence on long-term movements in economic growth. Even the seemingly steady growth of the 1960s was associated with significant shifts in financial positions. Behind the façade of continuing high growth there was a gradual deterioration of the financial position of firms, leading to historically high levels of debt financing at the beginning of the 1970s.[1] This fragile financial structure may have been one of the reasons why firms were unable to absorb the shocks of the 1970s smoothly and why, as a result, investment collapsed more than might have been expected on cyclical grounds alone.

One of the most dramatic features of recent development is the surge in public debt after the early 1970s in nearly all the major industrial economies. Initially the rise of debt seemed to be a 'normal' cyclical reaction to the recession, but when the slow-down of economic growth was prolonged the increase in debt became structural. As a consequence of the rising interest payments the deficits were increased further, which had to be financed too, thereby leading to a further rise in debts. This debt–interest spiral became acute in the 1980s when real interest rates rose to historically high levels while economic growth remained very modest. This had important consequences, not only for the financing of the government budget, but also for the feasibility of monetary and fiscal

[1] See e.g. Taggart (1986) who gives evidence for the USA.

policy. The fear of ever increasing debt and interest payments
has proved to be an effective impediment to 'Keynesian' demand management policies.

The accumulation of debts and assets across sectors of the
economy and its relation to dynamics of growth is the main
concern of this book. The analysis will start from a disequilibrium model of growth inspired by the (post-) Keynesian
theories of growth. This theoretical framework allows us to
investigate the dynamics of growth simultaneously with the
evolution of the distribution of income and wealth between
different sectors (or 'classes') of the economy. Our main interest is in the adjustment processes following from disequilibrium, rather than in the characterization of equilibrium.

In particular we are interested in the dynamics ensuing from
the government budget constraint (hereafter abbreviated as
GBC), and, from a policy perspective, in the possibilities of
influencing the stability of the economic system by choosing
a proper policy regime. A necessary condition for stability is,
of course, that the debt–interest spiral does not accelerate,
but converges to a stable situation. Whether or not this occurs
depends on the interrelationships between debt accumulation
and the determination of growth and distribution in the private sector.

This theoretical starting-point is different from the conventional analysis of the GBC dynamics. Following the provoca-
tive contribution of Blinder and Solow (1973) there has been
a wave of modelling of the dynamics of public debt (cf. Tobin
and Buiter 1976, Turnovsky 1976, Christ 1978, 1979, Tobin
1982, Rau 1985 to mention only a few). Nevertheless, despite
the intrinsically long-term nature of debt accumulation practically all these studies start from IS/LM type of models. In
our opinion the IS/LM model, however, does not offer a very
suitable framework for this analysis. This model is designed
for the analysis of short-term equilibrium and therefore refers
to a basically stationary economy, i.e. an economy in which
all the important exogenous variables are supposed to be
fixed. As the accumulation of debt is a very slow process
which takes decades rather than years, it seems natural to
start the analysis from a growth model which gives special
attention to medium-term and long-term economic dynamics.

1.1 Background

For an impression of the importance of growth and distribution for the dynamics of public debt it is useful to take a glance at the developments during the past decades. After some twenty-five years of steady decline in the post-war period public debt started rising again in the early 1970s in nearly all the major industrial economies. On the average gross public debt of OECD countries increased from 39.3 per cent of national income in 1975 to 59.2 per cent in 1987. After this peak growth of debt appears to have levelled off leading to a slightly falling trend of debt as a percentage of national income (see Fig. 1.1).

Large borrowing by the government is, of course, not a new phenomenon, but in history this was usually associated with

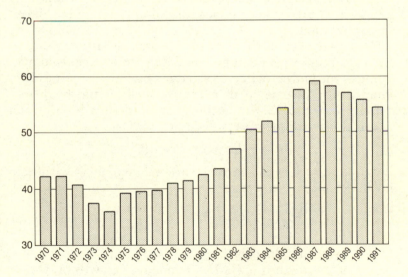

Note: For the period until 1987 this figure based on Tanzi and Lutz (1990), who give the aggregate for the thirteen OECD countries for which the statistical information is available. The series is completed by OECD estimates and projections given in *Economic Outlook* of June 1990.

FIG. 1.1 Gross public debt in the OECD (percentage of GDP)

war financing or other specific circumstances. After World Wars I and II debt ratios of more than 100 per cent were in fact quite common in countries that had participated in these wars. However, for peacetime the recent rise in debt is unprecedented.

To a large extent this is due to a dramatic change in the dynamics of debt accumulation after the mid-1970s. Before this breaking-point the economy was characterized by high growth and low, often even negative, real interest rates. During this period it was therefore fairly easy to manage the high post-war debts. For example, thanks to the high growth rates and low interest rates the United States federal debt fell from 127 per cent in 1946 to less than 30 per cent in the early 1970s even with hardly any budgetary restraint. But this favourable situation changed drastically in the 1980s when the real interest rates rose to historically high levels. As a result the accumulation of debt has gained a strong momentum of its own, which can be kept under control only by severe budgetary restriction.

The importance of the growth rate and the interest rate to the dynamics of debt can be seen by the following decomposition of the budget deficit. Neglecting money financing (seigniorage) the change in debt (B) is equal to the budgetary deficit, which consists of the primary deficit ($G - T$) and nominal interest payments (RB):

$$dB/dt = (G - T) + RB.$$

If we measure debt as a ratio to national income(Y) we obtain for the change of this ratio:

$$\frac{d(B/Y)}{dt} = \frac{G - T + RB}{Y} - \frac{B}{Y}\left(\frac{dY}{dt}\frac{1}{Y}\right).$$

Finally, denoting the debt ratio as $b = B/Y$ and dividing nominal income growth in inflation (p) and real growth (ρ) we get the convenient equality:

$$\frac{db}{dt} = \frac{G - T}{Y} + (R - p)b - \rho b.$$

This equation clearly shows the crucial importance of the real interest rate ($R - p$) and the real growth rate ρ. If the growth rate exceeds the interest rate debt reduction is fairly easy and does not even require a primary surplus. This was on the average the case in the pre-1980 period. During this period Ponzi-games (i.e. financing debt service by issuing new debt) could be played without great harm. However, if the growth rate falls short of the interest rate the dynamics of debt change dramatically. This happened in the 1980s at a time when governments had already accumulated sizeable debts as a result of the prolonged primary deficits during the 1970s. When real interest rates increased sharply after 1980 this put a large burden on the government's budget. Together with the low growth rates this caused an unprecedented surge in public debt. It can be observed that it took considerable time, on average for the OECD countries until 1987, before governments had effectively reduced their primary deficits and created the surpluses necessary to stop the debt–interest spiral.

1.2 Disequilibrium growth theory

This book is concerned with dynamics of debt accumulation from a long-term point of view. The economy to be considered is (post-) Keynesian in the sense that it is characterized by disequilibrium rather than equilibrium, by uncertainty rather than full information, by market failures rather than perfect markets, and by heterogeneous 'classes' rather than a representative agent.

One of the valuable propositions of post-Keynesian macro-economic theory is the notion that on average a higher fraction is saved out of profits than out of wages. At the macro-economic level this implies that aggregate savings are linked to the distribution of income over wages and profits. Whereas this proposition of differential saving is considered to be true by most macroeconomists (Malinvaud 1986: 110), it is neglected by most conventional models which assume a uniform rate of saving for all agents and for all types of income. This is unwarranted, especially in a theory which endeavours to analyse the long-term dynamics of debt and wealth. Moreover, it conceals the role of distribution effects in the determination of the income–expenditure equilibrium which may

—as we shall see—become very significant in case of a large government debt.

In (post-) Keynesian theory individual behaviour is in general considered to be rule-guided rather than to be derived from rational discretionary optimization. This can be motivated by the impossibility of gathering all information necessary for a continuous process of discretionary optimization. Rule-guided behaviour can therefore be explained in terms of bounded rationality due to incomplete information (cf. Sawyer 1989). A related argument is that it is not the availability of information which is the main problem (it is immense), but rather the limited capacity to process all information, i.e. the limited speed of learning (e.g. Moss 1984). This approach is especially relevant for areas where information is costly in comparison with the benefits of this information in terms of a better decision. When information is readily available and where the objectives are well defined, a discretionary optimization procedure seems more appropriate. In the bounded rationality approach rules are thus conceived as cost-saving devices.

A more fundamental problem arises when the economy is characterized by true, 'Keynesian' or 'Knightian'[2] uncertainty. In that case calculation of the time- and risk-discounted optimum is not possible at all, i.e. information is not only costly, but non-existent. Keynes thought this especially relevant with respect to decisions on saving and investment: 'The whole object of the accumulation of wealth is to produce results, or potential results, at a comparatively distant, and sometimes at an *indefinitely* distant, date. Thus the fact that our knowledge of the future is fluctuating, vague and uncertain, renders wealth a peculiarly unsuitable subject for the methods of the classical economic theory' (Keynes 1973: 113). This may explain why, especially for decisions on debt and savings, agents seem to be inclined to rely on certain rules or norms of 'proper' financial behaviour.

[2] Keynesian and Knightian uncertainty are often lumped together under the title 'Keynes–Knightian' uncertainty. Hoogduin (1987: 53) has pointed out that this is not justified: 'Whereas Knight mainly focuses on the distinction between numerically measurable and not numerically measurable probabilities, Keynes stresses the slight amount of knowledge on which probabilities often have to be based.'

Although we do not reject the principle of discretionary optimization in general it seems appropriate at least for the purpose of our analysis to assume rule-guided behaviour for some kinds of decisions. This is especially true for consumers for whom optimization is seriously restricted by informational costs and liquidity constraints. The same holds for government behaviour which is hampered by bureaucracy and various political and institutional constraints. In our analysis fiscal policy will therefore be described by certain well-defined 'regimes' in terms of specific targets, rather than derived from the optimization of some aggregate welfare function.

The stress laid on rules does not mean that behaviour is fixed for ever. It is evident that in the long term these rules somehow entail an economic assessment of costs and benefits. Therefore the rules have to be evaluated at times, and, if necessary, changed. For example, if a change in the state of the economy causes the government's budget to fall into an accelerating spiral of debt and interest payments, it is evident that the government will have to reconsider its budgetary regime. Rules are thus always contingent on the state of the economy. Which regime performs best in which state is therefore a main theme of this book.

1.3 A sequential analytical approach

For the analysis of the macroeconomic dynamics we have adopted a sequential analytical approach. According to this method the analysis is divided into different levels corresponding to the different lengths of the periods (cf. Malinvaud 1980, Kuipers 1981). At each level a different type of disequilibrium is considered, and therefore different kinds of adjustment processes. Malinvaud (1980) distinguishes three periods: the short period, the medium period, and the long period. The medium period is conceived as a (continuous) sequence of short-period ('momentary') equilibria, and the long period as a sequence of medium-period equilibria. Each of these levels can thus in principle be investigated independently of the other levels. In this book these periods are defined as follows.

The short period is characterized by income–expenditure disequilibrium. In this period capacity is assumed to be given, and prices to be rigid. The dynamics are then governed by volume signals rather than price signals. This level encompasses the traditional Keynesian and Kaleckian income–expenditure approach.

On the medium-period level income–expenditure equilibrium is taken for granted and attention shifts to the development of demand and capacity. At this level of analysis capacity, prices and expectations are assumed to be endogenous, but with imperfect adjustment to the true, or desired, values. The central question is now whether medium-period dynamics leads to a steady (warranted) growth where expectations of demand and profits are continuously fulfilled.

Finally, in the long period both income–expenditure equilibrium and warranted growth are presupposed. Now wages and prices are assumed to be perfectly flexible. The analysis then concentrates on technical change, on labour-market disequilibrium and wages, and on the accumulation of debt and wealth. The central question is whether the system tends to a 'golden age' with a constant rate of unemployment and a constant distribution of income and wealth.

Our analysis concentrates on the medium period and the long period. In some respects these levels are different from the levels distinguished by Malinvaud and Kuipers. Malinvaud concentrates on the short-period and medium-period levels and largely neglects the long period, although he recognizes that 'growth models . . . should be introduced in any satisfactory theory of medium-term evolution' for reasons of analytical clarity and robustness (Malinvaud 1980: 11). Kuipers extends Malinvaud's analysis to the long period, but he disregards the accumulation of financial assets.

Method

The models used in this book are in general simple non-linear models. It is our endeavour to construct models that are consistent not only in the neighbourhood of equilibrium but also for positions further away from equilibrium. This is necessary to determine the global dynamics of the system.

This is relevant unless one believes that the economy is always in or close to its ('natural') equilibrium. A complication of non-linear systems concerns the uniqueness of equilibrium. Our analysis shows that even fairly simple and natural non-linear systems may produce multiple equilibria. In economic terms this means that the actual evolution of the economy becomes critically dependent on its initial position. Moreover, it is no longer certain that after a shock the system will always return to its original equilibrium. It might well tend to another equilibrium, or develop into an unstable process which does not lead to a new equilibrium at all.

Because of the complex nature of non-linear dynamic systems, it is necessary to keep the models simple. The dynamics of two-dimensional systems of differential equations (quadratic functions) is reasonably well established, but even three-dimensional (cubic) systems soon become hard to deal with mathematically. As our main concern is the theory and not the technique of modelling non-linear systems, we shall construct our models in such a way that, even if they cannot always be solved explicitly, they remain transparent from an economic point of view. The dynamics of the models will be examined as far as possible by analytical means and in most cases illustrated by numerical simulations.

1.4 Outline of the book

Chapter 2 begins with a brief review of alternative theories of differential saving, and then as a first step in the analysis investigates the consequences of the introduction of the government budget constraint in a generalized Pasinetti–Kaldor model. It will be shown that this model in its 'classical' post-Keynesian form yields a highly unstable dynamic system, which can produce a stable 'two-class' solution only under very special, unrealistic assumptions.

In order to develop a more sophisticated macroeconomic model Chapters 3 and 4 make a digression on the long-term determinants of growth on the basis of a microeconomic model of a representative firm. Following our main interest, this model concentrates on the long-term relationships between profits, finance, and the growth of the firm. Chapter 3 develops a basic model for a fully equity-rationed firm. It is shown that this firm faces a trade-off between growth and risk. This 'growth–risk' frontier is the basis for the determination of the optimum rate of growth. Chapter 4 relaxes the assumption of full equity rationing and introduces an imperfect equity market. Consequently the conflict of interests between managers and shareholders must be taken into account. Furthermore, this chapter introduces costs of growth and examines the consequences for the growth strategy and the adjustment process.

These two chapters on the growth of the firm provide the microeconomic background of investment behaviour in the long-period model considered in Chapters 6 and 7. They may, however, be skipped without losing the thread of our analysis of the macroeconomic dynamics.

After this digression we return to the macroeconomic level and complete our model for the closed economy. This model will be used to investigate the dynamic relationships between growth, income distribution, and the financial positions of the government, firms, and the social classes distinguished. Particular attention is given to the stability of the system for alternative fiscal and monetary regimes. Chapter 5 concentrates on the medium period and Chapter 6 on the long period.

In Chapter 7 the analysis will be generalized for the open economy. It is shown that for a (small) open economy the dynamics of the government budget constraint is closely linked to the dynamics ensuing from the balance of payments constraint. This chapter will be concluded by some considerations with respect to economic policy in the presence of external and internal disturbances.

2

Pasinetti Paradoxes and the Government Budget Constraint

2.1 Introduction

This chapter examines the long-term dynamics of public debt in a two-class post-Keynesian model. Our concern is twofold. In the first place we are interested in the dynamics arising from the government budget constraint when analysed on the basis of a post-Keynesian model where the distribution of income between wages and profits is the key mechanism for savings–investment equilibrium. This point of departure of our analysis is radically different from most other macroeconomic investigations of the dynamics of public debt which adopt the IS/LM framework in which income distribution plays no (explicit) role at all.[1]

Secondly, we wish to examine the consequences for the consistency of the post-Keynesian model when the government budget constraint is introduced. As is well known, Pasinetti's model, as well as more general models based on it, is subject to rather stringent conditions which must be satisfied for an interior 'two-class' solution to be feasible.[2] If these conditions are not satisfied, one of the social classes will disappear in the long run, and what is more serious, the distribution of income over workers and *rentiers* will no longer operate as a mechanism ensuring equilibrium between savings and investment. The possibility of such an 'anti-

[1] Among the classical papers on this subject are Christ (1968), Blinder and Solow (1973), and Tobin and Buiter (1976).

[2] The debate was initiated by the famous article of Pasinetti (1962) and its discussion by Samuelson and Modigliani (1966). There have been many attempts to generalize Pasinetti's model and to criticize the conclusions of Samuelson and Modigliani with reference to their 'anti-Pasinetti land', see e.g. Laing (1969), Chiang (1973), Pasinetti (1974, 1983), Baranzini (1975), Fazi and Salvadori (1981), Darity (1981), O'Connell (1985).

Pasinetti' state led Samuelson and Modigliani (1966) to conclude that a more general theory of income distribution is
required, based on the principles of the neo-classical marginal
productivity theory. We shall re-examine this conclusion
with reference to the generalized post-Keynesian model to be
developed in this chapter.

The chapter is built up as follows. First, there is a brief
review of several alternative views on differential savings
(section 2.2). This discussion of differential savings provides
the starting-point for our modified post-Keynesian model
(sections 2.3–2.6). The basic difference from traditional post-
Keynesian models concerns the inclusion of the government
sector. In most other respects it follows the 'classical' post-
Keynesian model, assuming constant propensities to save, a
fixed technique of production, a given ('natural') rate of
growth, etc. Some of these assumptions will be relaxed in
section 2.7 when wealth and interest effects are introduced
in the saving function and the technique of production is
related to factor prices. However, the analysis stays confined
to the evolution of debt and wealth in a steady state world
with a given 'natural' rate of growth. The dynamics of investment and income distribution, the role of money, and the
international aspects are considered in later chapters.

2.2 A bird's eye view of differential saving

One of the basic propositions of post-Keynesian theory is that
savings–investment equilibrium is ensured by shifts in the
distribution of income between profits and wages. According
to Robinson (1965) excess demand for goods causes sellers'
markets to emerge with rising prices and profit margins, and
correspondingly falling real wages. As the (marginal) propensity to consume out of profits is supposed to be less than the
propensity to consume out of wages, this shift in income
distribution reduces aggregate demand and thus restores
equilibrium between aggregate demand and supply. In the
opposite case of excess supply, buyers' markets will arise,
leading to falling profits and rising real wages, and thus to a
rising demand.

Other authors have suggested that there also exists a direct link between profits and (planned) investment (e.g. Eichner 1976, Harcourt and Kenyon 1976). Building on Kalecki's mark-up hypothesis they argue that rapidly growing firms will set higher profit margins than similar firms with a low rate of expansion because they have a larger need for investment funds.[3] Thus in this theory also, investment generates (part of) its own savings.[4]

Life-cycle hypothesis

It is obvious that this post-Keynesian distribution mechanism hinges on the proposition that the (marginal) propensity to save is higher for profits than for wages. In this respect it evidently builds on the classical theories of Ricardo and Marx, according to which workers consume the whole of their income, while capitalists (and *rentiers*) save the larger part of their income.

It needs little argument that this class-related explanation of differential saving is at variance with mainstream (micro) economic theory which takes the representative individual as the unit of analysis, and denies the existence, or relevance, of social classes. For some time it was thought, and claimed, that the life-cycle theory of saving had finally rejected the idea of differential saving. As, for any individual, saving is

---

[3] Under the proposition that under monopolistic competition substitution between products is a slow process, Eichner (1976) shows that firms can temporarily raise their revenues by increasing the price of their products, but, of course, at the expense of returns in later years. Given this intertemporal trade-off in revenues, it is attractive for firms to raise their profit margin up to the point where the implicit costs of this 'internal' method of finance are equal to the costs of external finance. If one further assumes that the firm faces an upward-sloping supply curve of external finance, it is obvious that the optimum profit margin is positively associated with the volume of investment. Note that the underlying trade-off between short-term and long-term price effects on demand is very similar to the well-known J-curve effect of the balance of payments.

[4] There is no reason to assume that these savings are sufficient, unless one presupposes full internal financing, which is not very convincing. This theory is therefore less general than Robinson's mechanism sketched above. Moreover, this mark-up mechanism applies exclusively to investment; if excess demand arises from sources other than investment, such as government expenditure or exports, this mechanism fails completely.

just deferred consumption, there is, according to this theory, no reason to assume that consumption is systematically higher for one group than for another group. Whether income is high or low, individuals aim at an optimal spread of consumption over their lifetime. In fact, a shift in distribution from wages to profits may even produce a (temporary) *reverse* effect on savings: a rise in profits increases the income of the pensioned people, who consume their full income or even dissave, while the fall in wages affects the younger people who are still saving for their own old age. This shift in the intergenerational distribution of income thus gives rise to a 'perverse neoclassical savings function' (Marglin 1984: 45).

However, this representation of the life-cycle model has proved to be too simple. It neglects the existence of liquidity constraints and of intergenerational transfers, gifts, and bequests. If these aspects are taken into account as well, the life-cycle model can be shown to be fully consistent with differential saving, and even to give a justification for it. Differences in time preference or attitude towards inheritance across individuals or groups can be shown to produce a divergence between wealthy people who plan for inheritance and have high propensities, and people who are liquidity constrained and do not save (except for obligatory savings schemes). In Appendix 2.1 this is shown more formally on the basis of a simple two-class life-cycle model with a class of 'workers' who save for old age only, and a hereditary class of *rentiers* who have a high propensity to save and leave bequests to their children.

Macroeconomic view

Contrary to the above negative (microeconomic) view on differential saving is the much more positive standpoint of most macroeconomists. According to Malinvaud (1986: 110), 'the prevailing [macroeconomic] view is definitely in favor of the truth and significance of the proposition'. Therefore it is, in his view, necessary to reconsider the significance of differential saving and to work on a justification from the mainstream point of view. Malinvaud distinguishes three possible (complementary) explanations for the proposition that the marginal propensity to save is less for wages than for profits:

1. Pure distribution effect: Wage-earners generally face stronger liquidity constraints than profit-earners, so that they react more strongly to changes in their actual income than profit-earners. Moreover, because profits have a higher variability than wages, a wage change is considered to be more permanent and thus has a stronger effect on consumption than the opposite change in profits.
2. Retained earnings: Because of the 'corporate veil' and perturbations in the stock market valuation of shares, a change in corporate retained earnings is generally valued less than a similar change in wages or distributed profits.
3. Differential taxing: When profits are more heavily taxed than wages a shift from wages to profits leads to higher aggregate savings.[5]

At this stage it is important to note that these explanations of differential saving all relate to differences in the type or source of income. No attention is paid to the fact that differences in savings propensities may also arise from different attitudes amongst the recipients of the income, i.e. amongst different social classes. In this respect they are in contrast to the classical explanation discussed above.

Kaldor and Pasinetti revisited

A similar conflict in the explanation of differential saving is found within the post-Keynesian school between Kaldor and Pasinetti. While Pasinetti adheres to the classical proposition that differences in savings propensities should be related to social groups with different attitudes towards savings, Kaldor explicitly rejects this idea and regards 'the high savings propensity out of profits as something which attaches to the nature of business income' (1966: 310). Thus, in contrast to Pasinetti who attributes the higher propensity of *rentiers* to save to 'a stronger tendency for people in the higher income

---

[5] This is true only if subjects do not see through the '*government veil*' i.e. people are assumed not to adjust their savings fully to the change in government savings as stated by the 'Ricardian equivalence' theorem (Barro 1974).

brackets (normally wealth owners) to plan for inheritance' (1983: 100), Kaldor explains the higher savings out of profits from the necessity of corporate firms 'to plough back a proportion of the profits earned . . . in order to ensure the survival of the enterprise in the long run' (1966: 310). In a formal manner the alternative saving functions may be modelled as:

$$S = s_1(y - \pi) + s_2\pi \qquad \text{(Kaldor);} \qquad (2.1a)$$

$$S = s_w(y - \pi + z_1\pi) + s_c(1 - z_1)\pi \qquad \text{(Pasinetti);} \qquad (2.1b)$$

where $0 \leqslant s_1 < s_2 \leqslant 1$ and $0 \leqslant s_w < s_c \leqslant 1$, and

z_1 = share of workers in total wealth,
π = rate of profit,
s_1, s_2 = savings propensities from wages and profits,
s_w, s_c = savings propensities of workers and capitalists,
S = aggregate saving (ratio to capital stock),
y = production (ratio to capital stock).

Throughout the following all stock and flow variables are expressed as ratios to capital stock. As there are no other assets than capital total wealth equals unity, and the share of capitalists $(1 - z_1)$. The savings propensities are treated as constants, or, in any case, as independent from the interest rate. The first equation relates savings propensities to wages $(y - \pi)$ and profits π, whereas the second equation relates them to the income of workers, including their share in profits $(y - \pi + z_1\pi)$, and the income of *rentiers* $(1 - z_1)\pi$. For convenience we assume that $s_w = s_1$ and $s_c = s_2$ and use s_1 and s_2 for s_w and s_c below.

In the short run, when the distribution of wealth is given, these functions are not essentially different from a macro-economic point of view. In both cases aggregate savings are positively associated with the share of profits; only the slope is different.

$$\frac{\mathrm{d}S}{\mathrm{d}\pi} = (s_2 - s_1) \qquad \text{(Kaldor);} \qquad (2.2)$$

$$\frac{\mathrm{d}S}{\mathrm{d}\pi} = (1 - z_1)(s_2 - s_1) \qquad \text{(Pasinetti).}$$

However, despite this short-term similarity there is an important difference between these two saving equations from a long-term point of view. Because savings add to wealth one must in the long period take account of the evolution of the distribution of wealth as well. This has led Pasinetti (1962) to his famous signalling of a logical 'slip' in Kaldor's model, because it allows for the savings of workers but disregards the accumulation of wealth ensuing from them. Therefore, Pasinetti considered his function as a 'repaired' version of Kaldor's.

Kaldor did not accept Pasinetti's model as an improved version of his own model. Nor did he agree with the 'schizophrenic' interpretation of his savings function suggested by Meade (1963) and Samuelson and Modigliani (1966). According to this interpretation workers have different savings propensities with regard to wages and to profits. As mentioned above, Kaldor argues that the higher savings propensity out of profits must be explained by the fact that changes in retained earnings are not fully reflected in the consumption decisions of shareholders. Unfortunately, Kaldor never worked out this view convincingly.[6]

A generalized savings function

There have been many attempts to integrate Kaldor's idea of undistributed profits with Pasinetti's long-term model in order to obtain a 'general' post-Keynesian model (e.g. Chiang 1973, Darity 1981, Marglin 1984). These attempts generally lead to a mixed savings equation like:

$$S = s_1(y - \pi + \theta\pi z_1) + s_2\theta\pi z_2 + (1 - z\theta)\pi, \qquad (2.1c)$$

where θ = fraction of profits distributed $(0 \leqslant \theta \leqslant 1)$,
  z_1 = share of workers in total capital,
  z_2 = share of *rentiers* in total capital,
  z = $z_1 + z_2$.

---

[6] It is often suggested that Kaldor's *'neo-Pasinetti theorem'* is an elaboration of this idea. However, the mechanism underlying this theorem is entirely different from the post-Keynesian income distribution mechanism. Instead of wages and profits it attributes a central role to the valuation of shares in maintaining income–expenditure equilibrium. A more positive account of this theorem is given in Skott (1989).

The first term denotes savings by workers from wages and their share in distributed profits ($\theta\pi z_1$), the second term indicates savings by *rentiers*, and the final term retained earnings. Usually it is assumed that $z = 1$, which means that workers and *rentiers* own the whole capital stock. Although this is not strictly necessary, as will be seen below, we shall for the moment follow this common proposition. This generalized function (2.1c) is 'Kaldorian', as the effective savings rate of workers is different for wages and profits, s_1 and θs_1 respectively, while at the same time it is 'Pasinettian', as it distinguishes two classes with different propensities to save, s_1 and s_2. If all profits are distributed ($\theta = 1$) and $z = 1$, this equation reduces to the simple Pasinetti equation (2.1b). If, alternatively, savings propensities are identical for both classes ($s_1 = s_2 = s$) we obtain a quasi-Kaldor function where the propensities to save out of wages (s_1') and profits (s_2') are equal to:

$$s_1' = s$$

$$s_2' = s + (1 - s)(1 - \theta).$$

Whenever profits are not fully distributed ($\theta < 1$) this result implies that $s_2' > s_1'$.

There exist, however, some fundamental problems with regard to this generalized function that often seem to go unnoticed. These problems arise from the ambiguous interpretation of the fraction of profits distributed θ. Basically, there are two alternative interpretations: one relating to different returns on financial assets and capital stock, and the other relating to retained earnings.

1. According to the first interpretation, θ measures the ratio between the rate of return on the financial wealth of workers and *rentiers* and the real profit rate. As has been suggested originally by Laing (1969) and elaborated by Pasinetti (1974, 1983) the reward on financial assets of workers (and *rentiers*) is generally lower than the return on capital. The parameter θ might then be interpreted as the relation between the interest rate and the profit rate. However, if one adopts this interpretation of θ, the question arises where the difference between total profits and distributed profits remains. In fact, this interpretation is only consistent if one allows for a third

class, namely the capitalists, who organize the production and to whom accrue the undistributed profits. In that case, however, it can no longer be automatically assumed that the shares of workers and *rentiers* in total wealth sum up to unity. On the contrary, one should also allow for the accumulation of wealth by the capitalists (hence $z < 1$). If this is not recognized properly one falls into a 'slip' similar to the one Pasinetti blamed Kaldor for.

2. The second interpretation of equation 2.1c is that workers and *rentiers* do indeed own the entire capital stock, and that profits have a smaller impact on consumption because only a fraction of profits is distributed to the shareholders. This interpretation is more in accordance with Kaldor's views and fits in with Malinvaud's second ('corporate veil') explanation above. However, it is not right in that case to conceive of θ as the fraction of distributed profits as Chiang (1973), Darity (1981), and Marglin (1984) do, for this would imply that shareholders do not receive any capital gains at all, or, alternatively, that capital gains have no effect on their consumption. Retained earnings are thus simply assumed to vanish. This is clearly unwarranted with reference to modern society where most of the savings of workers and *rentiers* consist of claims to pension funds and life assurance. These institutions will be able to see through the corporate veil, although it is true that it may take some time before they adjust their premiums or allowances accordingly.

It is evident that the mere existence of retained earnings does not provide a sufficient justification for the proposition of differential saving. Some other factors have to be taken into account as well. One might follow Malinvaud and add liquidity constraints and informational imperfections to the model. Because this approach stresses disequilibrium and market imperfections as the principal cause of differential or 'forced' savings, it seems more appropriate in the short period than in the long period.

As our main interest is the long-term evolution of savings and wealth, in the subsequent section another approach will be used to explain, following Pasinetti, differential saving in terms of different attitudes towards saving between social classes. However, we do not agree with Pasinetti's view that the propensity to save is a purely psychological concept which has to do with the attitude towards provisions for old age and inheritance only (Pasinetti 1983: 100). In this respect we have sympathy for the arguments of Kaldor that differences in savings propensities also arise from the institutional organization of the economy. The basic error of Kaldor's model is, however, that it rejects the idea of social classes altogether and conceives the corporate sector as an anonymous and non-owned Moloch who absorbs retained earnings without ever giving anything back in return. As we have seen this view is unwarranted. Even in modern society a 'class' of managers and owners can be distinguished with a distinct role in the economic system and with a different attitude from the workers towards saving. For workers savings concern primarily deferred consumption and provision for old age, and for the better-off employees maybe for inheritance as well. For the class of owners and top managers saving is, however, also a means for maintaining and, if possible, increasing their power and status. They save for the intrinsic benefits of wealth as well.

Although there is some mobility between different groups, it is supposed to be sufficiently low to be neglected, at least within the time-span of a few generations, which may be thought of as a relevant time-horizon for the dynamics of growth and debt analysed in this book. Therefore the subsequent analysis adopts a classical savings function with two different classes, workers who receive interest on their savings and a corporate class of owners and managers who appropriate profits after payment of interest to the workers. As the interest rate is in general lower than the profit rate, this conception allows for differential rewards on savings by workers and on the wealth of the owners of the capital stock. As all profits, after payment of interest, accrue to the corporate class there are no vanishing retained earnings.

This two-class division enables us to examine the role of income distribution in economic dynamics. For the purpose of our analysis it is not necessary to generalize this approach to an economy with more heterogeneous groups or individuals; although this may be interesting for its own purpose, it does not basically change our analysis of the role of income distribution because our conception of distribution is a two-dimensional one too, namely the division in wages and profits.

2.3 The Pasinetti paradox

As was shown above the Pasinetti and Kaldor savings equations are not essentially different from a short-term point of view. However, in long-term equilibrium when the distribution of wealth too is endogenous, these functions yield remarkably different results:[7]

$$\pi = \frac{i - s_1 y}{s_2 - s_1} \qquad \text{(Kaldor)}; \qquad (2.3a)$$

$$\pi = \frac{i}{s_2} \quad \text{and} \quad z_1 = \frac{s_1}{i} \frac{s_2 y - i}{s_2 - s_1} \quad \text{(Pasinetti)}. \qquad (2.3b)$$

As we have mentioned as investment (i) is expressed as a ratio to capital stock it represents the growth of capital stock as well. The result (2.3b) for Pasinetti's model has raised much controversy as it suggests that the long-term profit rate is independent of saving by workers. This is known as the 'Pasinetti paradox'. The intuition behind this result is that, if the steady state exists, the wealth of *rentiers* should grow at the same pace as the wealth of workers, which again must grow at the same rate as production. As the growth of *rentier* capital is given by $s_2\pi$ and the growth of production is equal to i, one obtains equation 2.3b.

Whether the steady state is feasible is however not certain. It is well known that the solutions for both the Kaldor and the Pasinetti models are subject to quite stringent boundary conditions arising from limits for the distribution of income.[8] First, it is obvious that profits cannot fall below zero. In addition Pasinetti's model requires that the wealth of *rentiers* should not be negative in long-term equilibrium. It is often assumed that there is also a lower boundary for the share of

---

[7] These equations are obtained by solving the conditions for flow equilibrium $i = S$ and stock equilibrium $dz_1/dt = s_1(y - \pi + z_1\pi) - iz_1 = 0$.

[8] The stringency of the boundary conditions was raised originally by Tobin (1960) with respect to Kaldor's model and by Samuelson and Modigliani (1966) for Pasinetti's model.

wages (the 'inflation barrier').[9] In the present model, where a considerable part of workers' income may consist of interest income, it seems, however, more appropriate to specify a lower boundary to *total* income by workers rather than to wages only. Denoting the minimum income share of workers by χ, the boundary conditions become:

$$0 \leqslant \pi \leqslant (y - \chi)/(1 - z_1); \qquad (2.4)$$

$$0 \leqslant z_1 \leqslant 1.$$

Solving these conditions by substituting for π (eq. 2.3a–b) we find:

$$s_1 y \leqslant i \qquad\qquad \text{(Kaldor)}; \quad (2.4')$$

$$s_1 y \leqslant i \leqslant \{\chi s_1 + (1 - \chi) s_2\}\, y \quad \text{(Pasinetti)}.$$

These inequalities bring out that, although the lower boundary is the same for both models, the upper boundary for the Pasinetti model is quite restrictive, particularly if the savings propensities s_1 and s_2 are not very different, whereas the Kaldor model yields no upper boundary at all.

These results concern an economy with only two sectors or classes. If we add a third sector by introducing the government it may be expected that these conditions become even more restrictive. This will be the principal theme in the remainder of this chapter.

2.4 A generalized model with government

The introduction of the government sector has several important consequences for the post-Keynesian model. In the first place it adds a new possible cause of differential saving, namely different tax rates for wages and profits. If profits are taxed at a higher rate than wages, a redistribution from wages to profits will increase aggregate savings even if there is no difference in the propensities to save. This was also noted by Malinvaud (1986) (see section 2.2). Secondly, it complicates

---

[9] This term was first introduced in Robinson (1965). A similar process was described earlier by Kalecki (1954: 48).

the long-term dynamics of the model as the accumulation of public debt must be taken into account as well.

The model is set up as follows. Besides the government sector there exist two classes: workers who receive wages and interest on their accumulated savings, and capitalists who receive the profits after payment of interest to the workers. In order to avoid the complications connected with the valuation of shares workers are supposed not to own shares.

The government sector finances its deficit by issuing loans to the private sector. There is no money in this model. Taxes are levied at fixed rates on wages, interest income of workers, and net earnings of capitalists. Government expenditure consists of (exhaustive) consumption only and is supposed to be a constant fraction of total production.

In all other respects our model follows the 'classical' post-Keynesian model: the rate of growth is determined by the 'natural' rate of growth (n), the technique of production is fixed, and distribution of income between wages and profits always adjusts to ensure savings–investment equilibrium. Then expressing all stock and flow variables as ratios to capital stock, the static part of the model can be written as follows:

$$i + g + rb = S + T; \tag{2.5}$$

$$S = s_1\{(1 - \tau_0)(y - \pi) + (1 - \tau_1)(a + b)r\}$$
$$+ s_2(1 - \tau_2)(\pi - ar) \quad 0 \leqslant s_1 \leqslant s_2 \leqslant 1; \tag{2.1d}$$

$$T = \tau_0(y - \pi) + \tau_1(a + b)r + \tau_2(\pi - ar)$$
$$0 \leqslant \tau_1, \tau_2, \tau_3 \leqslant 1; \tag{2.6}$$

$$\pi = r + \phi i \qquad\qquad \phi \geqslant 0; \tag{2.7}$$

$$i = n. \tag{2.8}$$

Equation 2.5 states the familiar condition for income–expenditure equilibrium taking account of interest payments on government debt (g denotes government expenditure, b public debt). The savings equation 2.1d differs from the simple

Kaldor and Pasinetti equations (2.1*a* and *b*) in two respects. First, it distinguishes between the profit rate on capital (π) and the rate of return on financial wealth (r), and secondly, it takes account of (differential) tax rates on wages, interest income, and net corporate earnings, τ_0, τ_1, τ_2 respectively. The (fixed) savings propensities are denoted by s_1 for the workers and s_2 for the capitalists. Throughout the following it is assumed that workers save less than capitalists: $s_1 < s_2$.

Equation 2.6 defines total taxes T. Equation 2.7 represents the steady state condition with respect to the profit rate and the interest rate. This equation allows for a difference between the profit rate and the interest rate. The $\pi - r$ gap is related to the rate of investment reflecting, for example, the existence of adjustment costs. Another way to look at this equation is to rewrite it as an investment function $i = (\pi - r)/\phi$ which can be interpreted in terms of Tobin's q approach. Finally, equation 2.8 states the condition for growth equilibrium according to which i must be equal to the given ('natural') rate of growth, which is assumed to be exogenous.

These equations together form the static part of the model. It can be solved for given stocks of debt of firms (a) and public debt (b). Over time these stocks change, however, due to the budget constraints for the government and the firms sector. For the corporate sector the change in debt is equal to the excess of investment over savings, thus in absolute terms:

$$dA/dt = - s_2(1 - \tau_2)(\pi - ar)K + iK,$$

where A and K denote absolute debt and capital stock. If debt is expressed as a ratio to capital stock the impact of the growth of K must also be taken into account. If it is further noticed that a constant capital–output ratio implies that the growth rate of production (ρ) is equal to the investment capital ratio, thus:

$$\rho = i,$$

we can obtain for the change in the debt ratio:

$$\dot{a} = - s_2(1 - \tau_2)(\pi - ar) + (1 - a)\rho, \qquad (2.9)$$

where $\dot{a}$ denotes the time derivative da/dt. By analogy we obtain for the government budget constraint:

$$\dot{b} = g - T + rb - \rho b, \tag{2.10}$$

where $\dot{b} = db/dt$. This equation states that, in the absence of money financing, the change in the debt ratio of the government is determined by the primary deficit ($g-T$), interest payments rb, and the 'real erosion' of debt due to production growth, ρb.

Statics

As mentioned above savings–investment equilibrium is ensured by the distribution of income over wages and profits. Solving the static part of the model (eq. 2.1d to 2.8) yields the following condition for the interest rate:[10]

$$r = \frac{n + g - (1 - c_0)y - (c_0 - c_2)\phi n}{(c_0 - c_1) + (c_1 - c_2)(1 - a) - c_1 b}, \tag{2.11}$$

where

$$c_j = (1 - \tau_j)(1 - s_1); \quad \text{for } j = 0, 1;$$

$$c_2 = (1 - \tau_2)(1 - s_2).$$

For the sake of brevity the symbol c_j is introduced representing the rate of consumption per category of income. Note that the denominator of (2.11) represents the effect of the interest rate on aggregate savings (dS/dr). Throughout the following analysis it is assumed that $dS/dr > 0$; that is, the analysis is confined to the case with a normal, positive, Cambridge relation between profits and savings, thus:

$$(c_0 - c_1) + (c_1 - c_2)(1 - a) - c_1 b > 0. \tag{2.12}$$

In the case of a 'reverse Cambridge effect' ($dS/dr < 0$) a rise in profits and the interest rate in response to excess demand would lead to even lower savings and thus to a further increase in demand. A reverse Cambridge effect will thus have a destabilizing effect on the income–expenditure dynamics.[11]

---

[10] For the moment it is not necessary to explain how this condition is ensured, we simply assume that it is. The determination of growth will be dealt with extensively in Chs. 3 and 4. In Chs. 5 and 6 we shall discuss how the 'natural growth' equilibrium is achieved.

[11] This assumes that the interest rate varies with the profit rate according to eq. 2.7. As this equation concerns long-term equilibrium this condition is not generally true in the short period. Note that the partial effects of π

As can be seen from (2.12) a normal Cambridge effect requires at least one of the following inequalities to be satisfied: $c_0 > c_1$ or $c_1 > c_2$ (provided that $a < 1$) or $b < 0$, which implies that:

1. capitalists have a higher propensity to save than workers ($s_2 > s_1$);
2. profits are taxed at a higher rate than wages ($\tau_2 > \tau_0$);
3. interest income of workers is taxed more heavily than wages income ($\tau_1 > \tau_0$);
4. the government is a net creditor ($b < 0$).

In each of these cases a shift from wages to profits leads to an increase of aggregate saving. For the last possibility ($b < 0$), which is of course not very likely in practice, this can be explained as follows. When the state is a net creditor a rise in the interest rate leads to a shift of income from the private sector to the state. As government expenditure is assumed to be fixed, the ensuing fall in private sector consumption implies an increase in aggregate saving. Conversely, if the state is a net debtor the higher interest rate leads to a higher private sector income and thus tends to *lower* savings.[12] If this destabilizing effect of public debt is strong relative to the stabilizing impact of the simultaneous shift from wage-earners to profit-earners, this may give rise to a reverse Cambridge effect. There is thus a maximum beyond which public debt should not grow, thus from equation 2.12:

$$b < \frac{1}{c_1} \{(c_0 - c_1) + (c_1 - c_2)(1 - a)\}.$$

and r on savings are: $\partial S/\partial \pi = s_2(1 - \tau_2) - s_1(1 - \tau_1)$; $\partial S/\partial r = -\{s_2(1 - \tau_2) - s_1(1 - \tau_1)\} a - s_1(1 - \tau_1)b$. As both π and r normally respond positively to excess demand it can be seen that the profit rate is generally stabilizing while in this model the interest has a destabilizing (positive) impact on demand. Therefore it depends on whether r or π reacts more strongly whether short-period equilibrium is stable or not. But even if the condition for short-period stability is less restrictive than condition 2.17, this long-period condition will sooner or later become relevant for the system's stability.

[12] While the case of the state as a net creditor is not very likely, a similar effect may in the short run arise due to pension funds. It is well known that these funds, which in practice belong to the greatest investors, are very reluctant to pass changes in their returns to their contributors. As a result a rise in property income does not lead to an equivalent rise in disposable private income, and thus to an increase in aggregate savings. This is of course only true if individuals do not look through the 'pension fund veil'.

If debt exceeds this upper limit the Cambridge effect will be reversed causing income–expenditure equilibrium to become unstable.

Unfortunately, the model described above gives no neat solution for the steady state. Solving the differential system for $\dot{a} = 0$ and $\dot{b} = 0$ it yields a cubic equation with three possible roots. In order to grasp the basic features of the model we shall therefore examine two simplified cases: first, a quasi-schizophrenic Kaldorian version, where differential saving arises from differences in tax rates. And secondly, a Pasinetti version with different savings propensities for capitalists and workers. In both cases for simplicity it is assumed that the profit rate is equal to the interest rate ($\phi = 0$).

2.5 A Pasinetti paradox for public debt

The schizophrenic interpretation of Kaldor's savings equation by Samuelson–Modigliani and others, according to which differential saving is due to different attitudes of individuals towards wage income and profit income, is generally rejected (cf. Kaldor 1966, Pasinetti 1983). However, if one recognizes that taxes may also cause differences in effective propensities to save this version of Kaldor's model may become relevant again. As known, wages and profits are treated differently in most tax systems. If profits are taxed at a higher rate than wages there will exist a positive Cambridge relation even if workers and capitalists have the same savings propensities. In this section we will analyse a simple quasi-schizophrenic Kaldorian model with

I. $s_1 = s_2 = s$ (uniform savings propensities);
II. $\tau_0 < \tau_1 = \tau_2$ (lower taxes on wages than on profits and interest).

Steady state

Denoting the uniform savings rate by s the model yields the following unique steady state solution.[13]

---

[13] The solution for $\dot{a} = 0$ and $\dot{b} = 0$ yields a second solution at an infinite interest rate and an undetermined debt ratio a. This solution is neglected as it makes little sense economically.

$$r = \frac{n\{n + g - \tau_0 y - s(1 - \tau_0)y\}}{(1 - \tau_1)n + (\tau_1 - \tau_0)(1 - s)n - (1 - \tau_1)s(y - g)}, \quad (2.13)$$

$$a = 1,$$

$$b = -\frac{n - s(y - g)}{(1 - s)n}.$$

This solution implies the following remarkable results:

1. wealth of capitalists vanishes in the long run ($a = 1$);
2. the size of public debt is negatively associated with government expenditure;
3. the size of public debt is independent of the tax rates.

This last result may be regarded as a 'Pasinetti paradox' for public debt. Apparently, steady state equilibrium for debt is such that the direct impact of a change in one of the tax rates on the budget is precisely offset by their indirect impact through the change in the interest rate, and thereby in the burden of debt and the deficit.

Dynamics

The dynamics can be discussed with reference to the phase diagram (Fig. 2.1), which shows the $\dot{a} = 0$ and $\dot{b} = 0$ loci in the (b, a) plane. The peculiar shape of this diagram is due to the fact that, because workers and capitalists in this Kaldorian model have the same net saving rate with respect to profits, $\dot{a}$ and $\dot{b}$ are independent of the net debt of capitalists (a). The $r = \infty$ locus represents the upper boundary for debt implied by the condition for a positive Cambridge effect (eq. 2.12). Only the region below this boundary is relevant.

The $\dot{b} = 0$ locus is found at the level of b where $g - T - (n - r)b = 0$. The $\dot{a} = 0$ condition is found to be satisfied if $a = 1$, thus if capitalists have vanished, or if $n - s(1 - \tau_2)r = 0$. This latter condition is represented by the horizontal $\dot{a} = 0$ locus in the figure. As this condition is independent of the $\dot{b} = 0$ condition, it must be concluded that there will in general exist no interior solution with positive wealth of capitalists. Any point of the horizontal $\dot{a} = 0$ locus is associated with a non-steady public debt (in our example ($\dot{b} < 0$). As a corollary the unique equilibrium is represented by the point (S) on the $\dot{b} = 0$ locus where $a = 1$. In our example this equilibrium can be seen to be stable, locally as well as globally, for any starting-point below the $r = \infty$ boundary.

The exact conditions for local stability of solution S can be established by linearizing the system around its steady state solution (a_s, b_s)

$$\begin{bmatrix} \dot{a} \\ \dot{b} \end{bmatrix} = J \begin{bmatrix} a - a_s \\ b - b_s \end{bmatrix}, \qquad (2.14)$$

where the elements of the J-matrix are given by:

$$j_{11} = -n + s(1 - \tau_1)r,$$

$$j_{12} = -s(1 - \tau_1)(1 - a)\partial r/\partial b,$$

$$j_{21} = 0,$$

$$j_{22} = -n + (1 - \tau_1)r + \{(1 - \tau_1)b - (\tau_1 - \tau_0)\} \partial r/\partial b,$$

where $\partial r/\partial b$ is determined by equation 2.11. Solution S is locally stable if the real parts of the eigenvalues, evaluated in S, are negative, or by the Routh–Hurwitz conditions if the trace of the Jacobian matrix J is negative and its determinant positive, thus:

$$\text{Tr}(J) = j_{11} + j_{22} < 0,$$

$$\text{Det}(J) = j_{11} \cdot j_{22} - j_{12} \cdot j_{21} > 0. \qquad (2.15)$$

Since $j_{21} = 0$ the conditions reduce simply to $j_{11} < 0$ and $j_{22} < 0$, which implies:

$$n > 0, \qquad (2.16)$$

$$n - s(1 - \tau_1)r > 0$$

In terms of the figure this means that the equilibrium S is stable whenever it is below the horizontal $\dot{a} = 0$ locus, and unstable if it lies above this locus. After substitution for r and taking account of the condition for a positive Cambridge effect this condition (2.16) can be solved into:[14]

---

[14] Substitution of r (eq.2.13) in the condition 2.16 yields: $n > 0$ and $n\{ n - s (1 - \tau_1)y\}/\{(1 - \tau_1) n + s(1 - \tau_1)(g - y) + (1 - s)(\tau_1 - \tau_0) n\} > 0$. As a positive Cambridge effect in the steady state requires (eqs. 2.12 and 2.13) $n - s(y - g) - n(1 - s)(\tau_1 - \tau_0)/(1 - \tau_1) > 0$, it can easily be seen that both the numerator and the denominator of the above equation must be > 0, hence eq. 2.16′

$$n > \mathrm{MAX}\left\{ s(1 - \tau_1)y,\, s(1 - \tau_1)\,\frac{y - g}{(1 - \tau_0) - s(\tau_1 - \tau_0)} \right\} \quad (2.16')$$

This inequality requires the growth rate (and government expenditure) to be sufficiently high in relation to the rate of saving.

A remarkable consequence of these conditions, when they are superimposed on the solution for government debt (2.13), is that any stable equilibrium must be characterized by a negative government debt. In case of positive growth this implies that there must be a permanent excess in the government budget. This is, of course, not very likely in practice.

2.6 Different savings propensities

These rather discomforting results are not exclusive to the Kaldor variant discussed above, but are obtained for other versions of the general model as well. As an alternative we

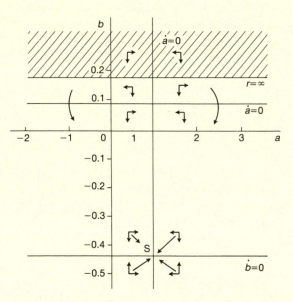

Note: This figure is based on the following numerical values: $n = 4\%$; $y = 0.4$; $\phi = 0$; $s_1 = s_2 = s = 0.1$; $\tau_0 = 0.15$; $\tau_1 = \tau_2 = 0.2$; $g/y = 0.16$.

FIG. 2.1 Phase diagram for the quasi-schizophrenic Kaldor model

shall now consider a Pasinetti variant where differential saving is caused by different savings propensities of workers and
capitalists. Tax rates are now assumed to be uniform. This
model is thus characterized by:

I. $s_2 > s_1$ (higher propensity to save of capitalists);
II. $\tau_0 = \tau_1 = \tau_2 = \tau$ (uniform tax rates).

Steady state

Under these propositions the model has two steady state
solutions: a two-class 'Pasinetti' solution and a dual 'anti-
Pasinetti' solution where the capitalists have disappeared. It
may be noted that this second solution is 'anti-Samuelson–
Modigliani' as well in the sense that income distribution is
still an effective mechanism for ensuring savings–investment
equilibrium, no longer indeed through redistribution between
capitalists and workers but now through redistribution between workers and the state. These solutions are:

Solution (I): the Pasinetti state

$$r = \frac{n}{(1-\tau)s_2},$$ (2.17a)

$$b = -\frac{s_2}{1-s_2}\frac{g-\tau y}{n},$$

$$a = 1 - \frac{s_2}{n}\frac{(1-s_2)x - (1-s_1)(g-\tau y)}{(1-s_2)(s_2-s_1)}.$$

Solution (II): the dual state

$$r = \frac{n}{1-\tau}\frac{x}{x-(1-s_1)(g-\tau y)},$$ (2.17b)

$$b = -\frac{x-(1-s_1)(g-\tau y)}{(1-s_1)n},$$

$$a = 1,$$

where $x = n + g - \tau y - s_1(1-\tau)y$. With respect to the first solution we can observe that:

1. income distribution exhibits the familiar Pasinetti feature that the interest rate (= profit rate) is determined by
   the growth rate and the net savings rate $(1-\tau)s_2$;

2. public debt is negatively associated with government expenditure (for any $n > 0$), just as in the Kaldorian model discussed above;
3. the size of public debt is independent of savings of workers.

According to the dual solution, where capitalists have disappeared, the interest rate as well as the debt ratio do depend on the savings propensity of workers.

Boundary conditions

These results are again subject to several boundary conditions (eq. 2.18 below). For the first (Pasinetti) solution the boundary conditions with respect to the wealth of capitalists $a \leqslant 1$ and the income of workers $y - \pi + ar \geqslant \chi$ are:

$$n - s_1(1 - \tau)y - (g - \tau y) \geqslant 0, \tag{2.18a}$$

$$n - (1 - \tau)\{s_1\chi + s_2(1 - \chi)\} \geqslant 0,$$

respectively. These conditions are satisfied if growth is sufficiently high. For the dual solution, on the contrary, the inflation barrier $(y - \pi + ra \geqslant \chi)$ requires growth to be low:

$$n + (g - \tau y) - (1 - \tau)\{1 - (1 - s_1)\chi\}y \leqslant 0. \tag{2.18b}$$

Dynamics

The dynamics of this model can be made up from the phase diagram (Fig. 2.2) which draws the $\dot{a} = 0$ and $\dot{b} = 0$ loci in the (b, a) plane. Note that $\dot{a} = 0$ is also satisfied for any point on the $a = 1$ line as well. The condition of a positive Cambridge effect is again represented by the $r = \infty$ locus; only the area below this boundary is relevant. Apart from the singularity point $(a = 1, b = 0)$ the system has two solutions, one at $a = 0.3$ (Pasinetti state) and the other at $a = 1$ (dual state). In both cases public debt is negative. As can be seen from the diagram the second solution is locally (not globally) stable; the first solution (at $a = 0.3$) is characterized by a saddle-point configuration and is thus unstable. As to the adjustment trajectory we can distinguish the two cases:

1. If the system starts from a point below the separatrix S–S, it will tend to the anti-Pasinetti state (II). During this adjustment process the share of wealth of capitalists shrinks asymptotically to zero.
2. If the starting-point is above the S–S locus, but below the $r = \infty$ boundary, public debt will grow for ever, pushing up the interest rate further and further, and leading to an ever greater wealth of capitalists (path T–T in the figure).

Note that for any feasible starting-point with a positive public debt ($b > 0$) the system can never reach the stable solution (II).

The conditions for local stability are obtained from the linearized system (2.19) evaluated in its steady state solution (a_s, b_s) :

$$\begin{bmatrix} \dot{a} \\ \dot{b} \end{bmatrix} = J \begin{bmatrix} a - a_s \\ b - b_s \end{bmatrix} \qquad (2.19)$$

where the elements of the J-matrix are:

$$j_{11} = -n + s_2(1 - \tau)r - (1 - \tau)(1 - a)s_2 \, \partial r / \partial a,$$

$$j_{12} = -s_2(1 - \tau)(1 - a) \, \partial r / \partial b,$$

$$j_{21} = -(1 - \tau)b \, \partial r / \partial a,$$

$$j_{22} = -n + (1-\tau)r + (1 - \tau)b \, \partial r / \partial b,$$

where $\partial r / \partial a$ and $\partial r / \partial b$, are again determined by equation 2.11. The resulting stability conditions are given in Table 2.1 together with the other constraints for this model. The derivation of these results is given in Appendix 2.2.

Fig. 2.3 may provide some help to interpret these results as it shows all possible combinations of μ and λ. For simplicity the boundary conditions with respect to the minimum share of workers have been neglected. The characteristics of both solutions in each of the six regions in this graph are summarized in Table 2.2. On the basis of these results we can conclude that:

1. There is no feasible Pasinetti state which is both stable and satisfies the boundary conditions; the first solution in each region is either characterized by a negative wealth of capitalists ($1 - a < 0$), or by instability, or a reverse Cambridge effect.

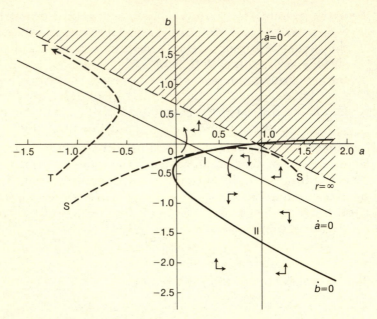

Note: This figure is based on: $y = 0.4$; $n = 0.04$; $\tau = 0.2$; $g/y = 0.21$; $s_1 = 0.05$; $s_2 = 0.3$.

FIG. 2.2 Phase diagram for the Pasinetti variant

2. In contrast, the dual solution may satisfy the stability conditions as well as the boundary conditions, but only when μ and λ lie in zone I or II, i.e. if

TABLE 2.1 *Stability conditions*

	Solution I: Pasinetti state	Solution II: dual state
Local stability	$(\mu + \lambda)(\mu - \dfrac{1 - s_2}{s_2 - s_1} \lambda) > 0$	$(s_1\mu + \lambda)(\mu - \dfrac{1 - s_2}{s_2 - s_1} \lambda) < 0$
Positive Cambridge effect	$\mu + \lambda > 0$	$s_1\mu + \lambda > 0$
Boundary conditions: $a < 1$	$\mu - \dfrac{1 - s_2}{s_2 - s_1} \lambda < 0$	
$y - \pi + ra > \chi$	$\lambda(s_2 - s_1)vy > 0$	$\lambda + \mu - (1 - s_1)v < 0$

Note: $\mu = g - \tau y$, $\lambda = n - s_1(1 - \tau) y$, and $v = (1 - \tau)(1 - \chi)$.

$-\lambda/s_1 < \mu < \lambda(1 - s_2)/(s_2 - s_1)$. These regions are however quite restrictive: if, for example, the rate of growth falls below $s_1(1 - \tau)y$ the model can never satisfy these conditions. Further, note that in the stable regions I and II public debt is always negative.

Thus, any stable long-term equilibrium, if it exists at all, is characterized by the disappearance of capitalists ($a = 1$) and a net creditor position of the government ($b < 0$). This conclusion is the same as the conclusion reached for the Kaldor variant above.

These unsatisfactory results in the two simplified variants considered above are not really changed for more general examples. Numerical simulations for the general model, within a wide range for the parameters, did not yield any stable solution with positive government debt and positive interest rate. Apparently the 'classical' post-Keynesian model, even in its hybrid version above, is too restrictive to yield satisfactory results when the government budget constraint is superimposed on to it. It is therefore necessary to modify the model and relax some of its rigidities. In the first place, one may introduce a more flexible savings function including interest and wealth effects. Further, one should drop the assumption

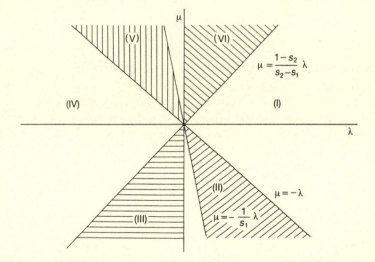

FIG. 2.3 Long-term characteristics of the Pasinetti variant

TABLE 2.2 *Characteristics of the Pasinetti model*

Zone			Solution I			Solution II	
	b	1-a	Cambridge effect	Stability (+ = stable)	b	Cambridge effect	Stability (+ = stable)
I	−	+	+	−	−	+	+
II	−	+	−	+	−	+	+
III	+/−	+	−	+	−	+	−
IV	+	−	−	−	+	−	+
V	+	−	+	+	+	−	+
VI	+/−	−	+	+	+	−	−

of a given rate of growth and also government behaviour should be modelled more carefully. Finally, one cannot truly discuss the short- and long-term dynamics of private and public debt without introducing a monetary sector in the model. These latter modifications will be discussed in later chapters. By way of a preview of the consequences to be expected we shall now, in the final section of the present chapter, examine the implications for our 'classical' post-Keynesian model if a more sophisticated savings function and a variable technique of production are introduced.

2.7 Interest and wealth effects

While maintaining the basic structure of our model we shall now introduce interest and wealth effects in the savings equation and make the technique of production dependent on the factor prices (represented by π). Again choosing linear relations the equations for the savings of workers S_1 and capitalists S_2 and the production technique (y)[15] become:

$$S_1 = s_{1o} + s_1\{(1 - \tau_0)(y - \pi) + (1 - \tau_1)(a + b)r\}$$
$$+ s_{1r}(1 - \tau_1)r - s_{1z}(a + b),$$

$$S_2 = s_{2o} + s_2(1-\tau_2)(\pi + ar) + s_{2r}(1 - \tau_2) - s_{2z}(1 - a),$$

[15] Note that y is the reciprocal of the capital output ratio (K/Y) for which it is assumed that $K/Y = (1 - \beta\pi)/y_0$. The relation between the choice of technique and the cost of capital has been linearized for simplicity.

$$S = S_1 + S_2, \tag{2.1e}$$

$$y = y_0 / (1 - \beta\pi), \tag{2.20}$$

where s_{jo} denotes autonomous saving of class j ($j = 1, 2$), s_{jr} the interest effect and s_{jz} the wealth effect on saving. All other equations remain the same. For the steady state the model again gives three possible solutions.

Unfortunately the price of greater flexibility of the model is, as always, a loss of transparency. As it is not rewarding to examine this model analytically we shall present some numerical exercises. In general, it has become clear from the numerical simulations that this model yields 'normal' solutions for a wide range of parameter settings. This is apparently due to the mitigating influence of interest effects on saving and the choice of technique. However, inclusion of the wealth effects seems to worsen the stability of the model.

Dynamics

Fig. 2.4*a* shows the phase diagram for a 'Pasinettian' set of parameters with uniform tax rates and different saving rates for workers and capitalists. As the figure brings out this model has two solutions in the relevant region where $a < 1$, one of which is stable and the other is not. The stable solution (A) is characterized by a positive public debt ($b/y = 1.39$) and a positive (real) interest rate ($r = 1.4$ per cent). Moreover, this solution satisfies the boundary conditions for any reasonable minimum boundary for the income of workers.

Whether the system actually tends to this stable solution depends on its initial position. Particularly if the system starts with a large initial public debt it may develop into an unstable process of continuously growing public debt and falling debt of capitalists (the C–C path in the figure). If public debt is even so large that the starting-point is above the $r = \infty$ boundary the system is subject to a reverse Cambridge effect as well.

Adjustment process

Next imagine that the system is in its stable equilibrium (A) and that government expenditure is raised from 0.24 to 0.25.

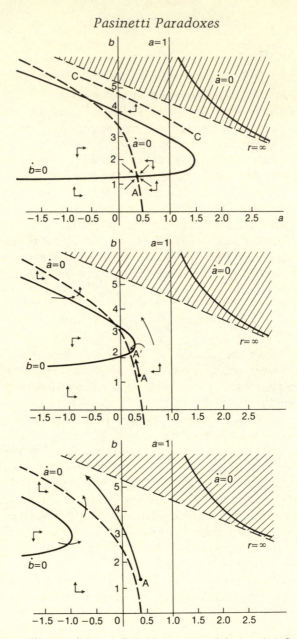

Note: $n = 4\%$; $s_1 = 0.1$; $s_2 = 0.4$; $\tau_0 = \tau_1 = \tau_2 = 0.2$; $y_0 = 0.4$; $\beta = 0$; $\phi = 1$; $s_{1r} = s_{2r} = 2$; $s_{1o}, s_{2o}, s_{1z}, s_{2z} = 0$; $g/y = 0.24, 0.25, 0.26$.

FIG. 2.4 Phase diagram for the modified model

As Fig. 2.4*b* brings out the system moves to the new equilibrium (*A'*) with a higher *b* and lower *a*. If, however, government expenditure is raised further to 0.26, the stable solution in this example disappears and the system becomes entirely unstable, whatever its initial position. This is shown in Fig. 2.4*c*.

Fig. 2.5 shows the adjustment trajectories following the increase in government expenditure from 0.24 to 0.25 and 0.26 respectively on a time axis. If government expenditure is raised to 0.25 the simulated time path shows a slow and gradual rise in public debt (*b*) and the interest rate (*r*) and a fall in debt of capitalists (*a*) to their new steady state values. This is shown by the solid curves. In the second case, when *g* is raised to 0.26 the adjustment process (dashed line) also happens to be slow and gradual for many years. However, after several decades this gradual process changes quite abruptly into an accelerating process with a sharply rising interest rate and a polarizing distribution of wealth. These results bring out clearly that the basic destabilizing force arises from the accumulation of debt by firms and the government. Through its effect on the distribution of income a

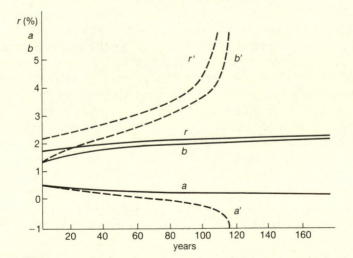

FIG. 2.5 The adjustment process

rising debt tends to increase consumption and to decrease savings. This causes the rate of interest to rise, thereby worsening the budgetary position of the government and firms even further. As the figure shows this may lead to an unstable process of accelerating growth of debt and rising interest rates.

Minimum growth rate

These exercises reveal that the system may yield a stable steady state equilibrium as long as government consumption g does not exceed a certain limit. Instead of looking for the limit of g, one may also establish a boundary below which the growth rate n should not fall for a stable equilibrium to exist. For example, if $g = 0.25$ there is a stable solution as long as the growth rate does not fall below 3.4 per cent. Thus for $n = 4$ per cent, as in the example above, it does indeed possess a stable solution. However, when $g = 0.26$ the critical value for n rises to 6.3 per cent. As this exceeds the growth rate in our example the system becomes inevitably unstable.[16] As in general the given system is more stable as the gap between the actual and the critical growth rate is larger, we can use this minimum growth rate as a measure of the stability of the system. A high critical growth rate points to an unstable system, and a low critical rate to a stable system.

How is this critical rate influenced by the parameters and the policy variables of our model? Table 2.3 gives the partial effects of each parameter on the critical growth rate. If a parameter has a negative impact on the minimum growth rate it can be regarded as having a stabilizing effect on the system. A positive impact on the critical rate corresponds to a destabilizing impact. The numerical results reported in the table corroborate our observations above. Government expenditure (g) and the wealth effects (s_{1z}, s_{2z}) turn out to have a strong destabilizing impact on the system. All other variables appear to mitigate the intrinsic instability of the system, including the substitution coefficient of production technique

---

[16] In Ch. 5 it will be shown that this critical growth rate corresponds to the bifurcation point of a catastrophe manifold.

TABLE 2.3 *Partial effects on the minimum growth rate necessary for stability*

Parameter	Effect on n
τ_0	-3.66
τ_1	-0.18
τ_2	-0.32
s_1	-1.75
s_2	-0.30
s_{1o}	-2.36
s_{2o}	-2.81
$s_{1r}{}^a$	-3.99
$s_{2r}{}^a$	-4.73
s_{1z}	4.68
s_{2z}	6.06
g	4.35
β	-0.002
ϕ^a	-6.00

Note: These effects have been calculated with reference to the steady state given in Fig. 2.4. One should be careful to compare the magnitude of these effects because an equal change in each variable may entail very different impacts in absolute amounts.

[a] In order to make these effects more comparable to the other effects they have been multiplied by 100 as they are attached to the interest or growth rate.

β. If one recognizes that the cumulative growth of debt is the basic source of instability in this model, the stabilizing impact of the tax rates and saving rates is straightforward since these parameters increase savings and thereby lower the interest rate. Similarly, a higher interest elasticity of demand has a beneficial impact on the system's stability as it mitigates the effect of debt on the interest rate.

The destabilizing impact of the wealth effect on saving is remarkable as in most other investigations of the dynamics of public debt it proved to be an essential stabilizing factor (cf. Blinder and Solow 1973, Tobin and Buiter 1976, Christ 1979, Rau 1985, and also Asada 1987). This contrary result is a consequence of our focus on long-term growth equilibrium. Most other investigations concentrate on a short-term

Keynesian world with price rigidity and without growth. In that case a high wealth effect is favourable because it reinforces the positive effect of debt on demand and thereby production, thus increasing tax receipts and reducing the budget deficit. In our model, however, production is fixed at capacity level. The stimulus of demand due to the wealth effect then leads to a rise in the interest rate, thereby increasing the burden of debt, rather than to a rise in income. There is thus a sharp distinction between the impact of the wealth effect on the dynamics in the short term and the long term. We shall return to these matters in Chapter 5 and 6 when we deal in more detail with the medium-period and long-period dynamics.

2.8 Conclusion

This chapter has examined the dynamics of long-term asset accumulation on the basis of a simple two-class post-Keynesian model including a government sector. This model is built on two central relationships: the relation between income distribution and aggregate savings which ensures momentary savings–investment equilibrium, and the relation between the budget constraints and the growth of wealth (or debt) which determines the long-term dynamics of the model.

Our discussion of differential saving revealed that the mere existence of retained earnings is not a sufficient explanation of a higher propensity to save out of profits than out of wages. Therefore, we developed a synthesis between Kaldor's view that differences in savings propensities must be explained from the nature of business income, and Pasinetti's standpoint that savings propensities should be attached to social groups or classes.

Introduction of the government budget constraint in the post-Keynesian model reveals that this model in its 'classical' form is too restrictive to yield acceptable solutions for long-term equilibrium. It was found that a stable solution, if it exists at all, is always characterized by the disappearance of one class (the 'capitalists') and by a negative public debt. This is, of course, not very likely in practice.

The model considered so far—although certainly attractive for its transparency—is too simple to give an appropriate account of the dynamics of public debt in a two-class model. The assumption of an exogenous growth rate and the neglect of the monetary sector is especially unsatisfactory. In the ensuing chapters we shall therefore develop a more sophisticated model with endogenous growth and a proper representation of medium-term dynamics.

Appendix 2.1 A life-cycle model of differential saving

This appendix shows that the life-cycle approach of saving can be fully consistent with the Cambridge savings equation if two distinct classes (workers and capitalists) are introduced with different attitudes towards saving and bequests. The model is a simple overlapping generations model with two classes (workers and capitalists) and two generations of each class (young and old) living at any one time. Following Pasinetti 1983 we assume that workers save only for their old age, whereas capitalists save for inheritance too. Choosing suitable dimensions the budget constraints for each group can be written as:

young workers $\qquad W = C_{wy} + Z_{wo}(+\,1);$

pensioned workers $\qquad (1 + r)Z_{wo}/(1 + n) = C_{wo}/(1 + n);$

young capitalists $\qquad (1 + r)Z_{cy} = C_{cy} + Z_{co}(+\,1);$

old capitalists $\qquad (1 + r)Z_{co}/(1 + n) = C_{co}/(1 + n) + (1 + r)Z_{cy};$

where C_{ij} = consumption of group i, j;

$\quad\;\; Z_{ij}$ = Wealth of group i, j (beginning of period);

$\quad\;\; n$ = population growth;

$\quad\;\; r$ = interest rate;

$\quad\;\; W$ = wage;

$\quad\;\; i$ = w, c for workers and capitalists respectively;

$\quad\;\; j$ = y, o for the young and the old respectively;

$\quad X(+\,1) = X$ in the next period.

Young workers receive wage income only. Pensioned workers consume the whole of their capital saved in the foregoing period. Young capitalists receive an inheritance at the beginning of the period. The amount of this inheritance is decided by the pensioned capitalists. For simplicity we assume that the wage component in their income is negligible. The rate of interest is assumed to be equal to the profit rate. Further, employment is assumed to be given by the number of young workers. Capital stock is determined by savings in the past. Then choosing capital stock equal to unity we obtain:

$$Y = W + r,$$

$$1 = (Z_{wo} + Z_{co})/(1 + n),$$

where production Y is determined by the stock of capital. Now define with respect to consumption behaviour:

$$C_{wy} = c_w W,$$

$$C_{cy} = c_1(1 + r)Z_{cy},$$

$$C_{co} = c_2(1 + r)Z_{co}.$$

The consumption rates $c_w, c_1,$ and c_2 are determined by the intertemporal optimum for each group. These rates are not necessarily constant; they may or may not depend on the interest rate. The optimization procedure is well known in literature (cf. Baranzini 1982) and does not need to be repeated here.

Let us first consider the short-term solution for aggregate consumption C:

$$C = c_w W + (1 + r)Z_{wo}/(1 + n) + c_1(1 + r)Z_{cy} + c_2(1 + r)Z_{co}/(1 + n).$$

After substitution for $W, Z_{co},$ and Z_{cy} we get:

$$C = c_w(Y - r) + c_c(1 + r) + (1 + r)(1 - c_c)Z_{wo}/(1 + n),$$

where $c_c = c_1(1 + c_2) + c_2$ is the average consumption rate of the capitalist class (young and old). Since Z_{wo} is predetermined, the effect of a shift in income distribution in favour of profits (r) is given by:

$$dC/dr = - (c_w - c_c) + (1 - c_c)Z_{wo}/(1 + n) + X_r,$$

where the first two terms on the right-hand side represent the distribution effect of a change in r, and X_r measures the intertemporal substitution effect (the effect on c_w and c_c). Note that the distribution effect is negative, i.e. a normal Cambridge effect of profits on savings, if, and only if:

$$c_w > c_c + (1 - c_c)Z_{wo}/(1 + n).$$

The overall effect depends on both the distribution effect and the substitution effect X_r, the outcome of which is not certain a priori. It is evident that this condition is more likely to be fulfilled if the share of workers in total wealth is smaller, and thus the income of pensioned workers is less relative to the income of capitalists. In the extreme case with $Z_{wo} = 0$ this condition reduces to the familiar Cambridge condition $c_w > c_c$. However, for the other extreme, i.e. a single-class model without capitalists (therefore $Z_{wo}/(1 + n) = 1$), the distribution effect is certainly negative, entailing a reverse Cambridge effect for any $c_w < 1$. Hence we can conclude that for a normal Cambridge effect workers should own not too large a share of total wealth.

Now consider the long run. In steady state equilibrium with constant $n, r,$ and W the amount of wealth per person must be constant as well, hence:

$$Z_{wo} = Z_{wo}(+1) \quad \text{and} \quad Z_{co} = Z_{co}(+1).$$

Substitution in the budget constraints for workers and capitalists yields:

$$Z_{wo} = (1 - c_w)W,$$

$$1 + r = (1 + n)/(1 - c_c).$$

This latter result is remarkable as it implies that this model is also subject to the Pasinetti paradox; that is, the profit rate depends exclusively on the growth rate and the savings propensity of capitalists. Again, this conclusion is of course valid only for $Z_{co} > 0$; if $Z_{co} = 0$ this model yields an anti-Pasinetti dual solution, just as in the more traditional Pasinetti models.

If these results are substituted in dC/dr above we obtain

$$dC/dr = - (1 - c_c)\{n + c_w - (1 - c_w)Y\}/(1 + n) + X_r,$$

and hence a normal Cambridge distribution effect ($dC/dr < 0$) if :

$$n > (1 - c_w)Y - c_w.$$

The rate of growth (and thus the rate of investment) should thus be sufficiently large in relation to the savings of workers. This condition is not surprising as the share of workers in total wealth is less as they provide less of the savings necessary for investment.

Appendix 2.2 Dynamics of the Pasinetti variant of the model with government

This appendix determines the conditions for local stability of the Pasinetti variant of the model with a government sector in section 2.6.

Solution I

Linearization of (2.9) and (2.10) gives:

$$\begin{bmatrix} \dot{a} \\ \dot{b} \end{bmatrix} = J \begin{bmatrix} a - a_s \\ b - b_s \end{bmatrix}$$

After substitution for r (eq. 2.11) the coefficients of the J-matrix are:

$$j_{11} = -s_2(1 - \tau)(1 - a)\partial r/\partial a,$$

$$j_{12} = -s_2(1 - \tau)(1 - a)\partial r/\partial b,$$

$$j_{21} = (1 - \tau)b\partial r/\partial a,$$

$$j_{22} = (1 - s_2)n/s_2 + (1 - \tau)b\partial r/\partial b,$$

and the Routh–Hurwitz conditions:

$$\text{Tr}(J): -s_2(1 - \tau)(1 - a)\partial r/\partial a + (1 - s_2)n/s_2 + (1 - \tau)b\partial r/\partial b < 0,$$

$$\text{Det}(J): -(1 - s_2)(1 - \tau)(1 - a)\partial r/\partial a > 0.$$

After substitution for a and $\partial r/\partial a$ the second condition yields:

$$\{(1 - s_2)x - (1 - s_1)(g - \tau y)\}/x > 0,$$

where $x = n + g - \tau y - s_1(1 - \tau)y$. Now consider $\text{Tr}(J)$. After substitution for a, b, $\partial r/\partial a$, and $\partial r/\partial b$ we find:

$$n - \frac{n}{s_2} \frac{(1 - s_2)x - (1 - s_1)(g - \tau y)}{x} > 0.$$

Next define $v = g - \tau y$ and $\mu = n - s_1(1 - \tau)y$ which implies $x = v + \mu$. It can then be assessed that these conditions together require:

$$(v + \mu)\left(v - \frac{1 - s_2}{s_2 - s_1}\mu\right) > 0.$$

Solution II

For the second solution where $a = 1$ we find $j_{12} = 0$ which reduces the Routh–Hurwitz conditions to $j_{11} > 0$ and $j_{22} > 0$. After substitution for r and $\partial r/\partial b$ these conditions yield:

$$n > 0 \quad \text{and} \quad \frac{(1 - s_2)x - (1 - s_1)(1 - \tau)y}{x - (1 - s_1)(g - \tau y)} > 0,$$

which is satisfied if in terms of v and μ defined above:

$$n > 0 \quad \text{and} \quad (s_1v + \mu)\left(v - \frac{1 - s_2}{s_2 - s_1}\mu\right) < 0.$$

These results are presented in Table 2.1 in the text.

3

Finance, Risk, and the Growth of the Firm

3.1 Introduction

In contrast to the 1960s and 1970s during which the Modigliani–Miller 'irrelevance of finance' view reigned, it is nowadays widely recognized that the investment decision cannot be regarded as separated from the decision how to finance it. One important consequence of the imperfection of financial markets is that the opportunities for risk sharing are limited. The equity market in particular is far from perfect; some authors even consider equity typically to be rationed (cf. Greenwald and Stiglitz 1988a, 1988b). Consequentially, if firms have only limited recourse to issues of new shares, they must manage risks on their own. This implies that when deciding on production and investment they should take good account of the consequences of these decisions for the financial position and risk posture of the firm.

This chapter develops a microeconomic framework for the long-term explanation of investment concentrating on the financial constraints. Our starting-point is the growth strategy of a representative corporate firm. The central question of the present analysis is what growth rate a firm will choose when it takes full account of the consequences of sustaining this growth rate for its financial position and its risk posture in the long run. We shall take account of the conflict of interests between the managers and the owners of the firm (shareholders). As a first approximation we shall consider a fully equity-rationed firm, i.e. a firm which has no access to the equity market at all. This assumption will be relaxed in the next chapter when we consider some extensions of our basic model.

This chapter is organized as follows. After a concise overview of post-Keynesian and 'managerial' theories of investment (section 3.2), we shall in section 3.3 develop a basic model for a small firm without access to the equity market. It will be shown that this firm faces a trade-off between the rate of growth and its risk posture (section 3.4). Section 3.5 establishes the optimum growth rate on the basis of this growth–risk frontier and the managerial preferences towards growth, risk, and profitability. In the next chapter the assumption of full equity rationing will be relaxed by the introduction of the (imperfect) equity market. Attention will then also be paid to the costs of growth and to the adjustment process.

3.2 Theory of investment

Despite the prominent place that is given to investment in (post-) Keynesian theory there has always existed a certain reluctance to give an appropriate account of the determinants of this variable. Joan Robinson (1965: 244) even explicitly refuses to develop a theory of investment: 'there is no way of reducing the complexities of the inducement to invest to a simple formula. We must be content with the conclusion that, over the long run, the rate of accumulation is likely to be whatever it is likely to be.' In a similar vein Asimakopulos (1986: 89) argues: 'The possible relations between finance, investment and saving in the post-Keynesian approach are thus complex . . . No general statement about their relationship which does not recognize (the particular historical) circumstances can adequately represent the post-Keynesian position.'

This opinion, although understandable, is unsatisfactory as it frustrates the development of an appropriate investment theory. We shall therefore take a more positive stand and look for the basic ideas on investment in post-Keynesian theory. It is possible then to distinguish three basic approaches:

1. the 'internal savings' approach, which links investment to the flow of retained profits;
2. the 'investment opportunities' approach, which concentrates on the limited availability of profitable investment projects;
3. the 'managerial' approach, which explains the restraint on investment from the organizational and marketing efforts necessary to sustain a certain rate of growth.

1. Internal savings

The first approach builds on the classical and Marxian 'surplus' theories of saving and investment, according to which accumulation takes place primarily through reinvestment of current profits. This idea was taken up by Kalecki (1937, 1943) and later elaborated by Wood (1975) and Eichner (1976). A very strict variant is found in Pasinetti (1981) who assumes that growth in each sector is financed purely by internal savings. Kalecki (1937, 1943) allows for the possibility of debt financing in addition to internal savings. However, by assuming that firms aim at a constant rate of indebtedness, Kalecki also finds a fixed relation between investment and internal savings. If investment is raised above this target rate, the rate of indebtedness will rise, and thus the risk as well. On the basis of this 'principle of increasing risk' Kalecki (1937) proposed the following expression for investment:

$$I = (1 - d)S + \zeta,$$

where I = investment, S = internal savings, d = ratio of debt to net worth, and ζ measures the effect of a shift in the marginal rate of return schedule.

This is elaborated by Wood (1975), who establishes a 'finance frontier' for corporate firms, representing the maximum rate of investment given the net returns of the firm and its targets for the pay-out of net returns (θ) and the degree of external financing (ε), thus: [1]

$$I \leqslant \frac{1 - \theta}{1 - \varepsilon} (\pi - a.r)K,$$

where π = profit rate, r = interest rate, a = ratio of debt to capital stock, ε = fraction of investment financed externally, and K = capital stock. The main weakness of this model, and of Kalecki's, is that the target variables θ and ε are assumed to be fixed. Although Wood is right that in the short term firms tend to rely on given norms for their financial policy, it seems unwarranted to consider these norms as exogenous in the long run too. Wood's analysis therefore seems to be

---

[1] For expository reasons we have neglected depreciation.

suited more to the short or medium term than to the long term.

2. Investment opportunities

The second approach takes just the opposite point of departure and concentrates on investment opportunities as the limiting factor of the firm's growth. Following Keynes it is assumed that the evolution of a well-developed financial system has separated the investment decision from the *ex ante* saving and finance decisions. As is well known, this 'separability' theorem was later formulated rigorously by Modigliani and Miller (1958), who showed that the method of finance is irrelevant to the cost of capital and therefore to the investment decision as well.

The focus thus shifts from financial constraints to demand and profitability as the basic limiting factors of investment (cf. Robinson 1962, Kaldor 1957, Kaldor and Mirrlees 1962[2]). According to Robinson (1965: 51) internal finance may hold back investment at best temporarily: 'It is a large and rapid rise in the rate of investment, not a high rate of investment which the finance limit prevents.'

3. Managerial theories of growth

Managerial, or 'corporate', theories of growth[3] concentrate on the constraints on the growth of individual firms due to the managerial and marketing efforts necessary to keep up a cer-

---

[2] In his early growth models Kaldor (1957, 1961) divides investment into a demand-related ('acceleration') component and a profit-related component. Kaldor motivates the latter component with reference to Kalecki's principle of increasing risk. He does not elaborate this financial aspect further. In his 'new' model (Kaldor and Mirrlees 1962) Kaldor introduces his well-known 'pay-back period' criterion for investment; this 'rule of thumb' implies that investment is related to the (undiscounted) prospective returns within a certain time-horizon.

[3] Seminal contributions to the managerial theory of growth have been made by Baumol (1959), Penrose (1959), Marris (1964), and Williamson (1966). Although these contributions are certainly non-neo-classical, they are not usually labelled as post-Keynesian. Nevertheless we have included them in our survey of post-Keynesian investment theory because this approach has much in common with the post-Keynesian approach, especially the

tain growth. This approach thus emphasizes the costs of growth. The core of the theory of corporate growth is a concave 'growth–valuation' frontier representing the trade-off between the valuation of the firm (q) and its growth rate (ρ) (Fig. 3.1). Because shareholders desire maximization of the market value of their shares they would prefer growth rate ρ^* corresponding to the highest possible valuation q^*. However, managers may have different interests. In particular, this theory assumes that they are more interested in the expansion of the firm than in profits *per se*. As a consequence they will generally select a higher growth rate than desired by shareholders, thus $\rho > \rho^*$. How large the difference between ρ and $\rho*$ will be depends on the preferences of the management, on their discretionary power *vis-à-vis* the shareholders, and on the costs of growth determining the curvature of the q–ρ frontier.

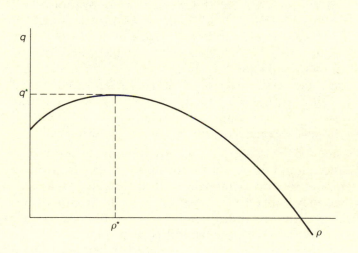

FIG. 3.1 Growth–valuation frontier

emphasis on institutional and behavioural factors. Furthermore several post-Keynesian authors have adopted this approach in order to provide a microeconomic foundation for the traditionally macroeconomic-orientated post-Keynesian theory (cf. Eatwell 1971, Wood 1971, 1975, Eichner 1976).

For the motivation of the q–ρ frontier two approaches can be distinguished, one emphasizing the internal, managerial costs of growth, and the other concentrating on the external, marketing costs of growth.

1. According to the internal approach the growth of firms is constrained by the limited capacity of the management and the time and effort necessary to find, train, and absorb new managers. Sometimes this constraint is conceived as an absolute limit on the capacity to grow (cf. Penrose 1959, Slater 1980, Moss 1984), while other authors assume managerial costs to rise or the efficiency to fall as the firm expands faster (cf. Williamson 1966, Uzawa 1969, Baker 1978, Odagiri 1981).

2. The external approach explains the negative growth–profitability relation by the costs for advertisement and R. & D. necessary to shift the demand curve for the firm's products. This idea, which was put forward by Marris (1964), has been elaborated by Solow (1971), Auberada (1979), and Seoka (1985). In technical terms these authors include the 'stock of goodwill' in the demand function for the firm's products and explain the growth of goodwill from the amount of marketing effort. Lintner (1971) extended Marris's model to an uncertain environment, and showed that a positive association between growth and the variability of profits may also impose a constraint on the firm's growth rate.

These models of corporate growth provide an interesting microeconomic background for investment behaviour. However, as in the 'investment opportunities' approach discussed above, they concentrate on the real costs of growth and pay little attention to the financial aspects. Managerial theories appear to follow the separability approach of finance and investment too. This is unsatisfactory, particularly for a theory which stresses market imperfections and conflicting interests between shareholders and managers.[4]

---

[4] It may even be questioned if the separability theorem is not inconsistent with the idea of conflicting interests between managers and shareholders. As is known, this separability theorem is valid only in a Modigliani–Miller world with perfect capital markets and in the absence of bankruptcy costs and tax subsidies. It is, however, difficult to see how with perfect capital

3.3 A basic model of finance and growth

In the presence of imperfect financial markets it is important to recognize that the firm is the typical legal and organizational entity for production and investment.[5] The firm is the nexus of investment and finance decisions; investment projects do not exist on their own, they exist only when embedded in an organizational entity.[6] Only in a perfect Modigliani–Miller world, without liquidity constraints, irreversibilities, information costs, (re)organization costs, and costs of bankruptcy, would it be permissible to abstract from the organizational and legal structure. However, in such a world firms would not exist either and every investor would run her own project.

If firms are acknowledged as the basic organizational entities, one also must take account of potential conflict of interest between managers and shareholders. In their pioneering article on the agency theory of the corporate firm Jensen and Meckling (1976) distinguished between the interests of the 'inside owners' of the firm (the managers), and the 'outside owners' (the investors without a direct role in the management). Managers are thought to be more interested in perquisites such as 'the physical appointments of the office, the attractiveness of the secretarial staff, a larger than optimal computer to play with . . . etc', than in the pecuniary benefits

markets the firm's strategy can ever diverge from the interests of shareholders; any discrepancy between the actual and the potential maximum would immediately lead to intervention by the shareholders. Since Jensen and Meckling's (1976) seminal contribution on agency theory it is now widely accepted that once the assumption of 100% control by the shareholders is relaxed, one must also take account of the consequences of the finance decision for the 'ownership structure' of the firm and hence for the cost of controlling the management ('agency costs').

[5] In this connection it may be noticed that the focus of financial theory has shifted from market equilibrium to the finance decisions of individual firms. In their introduction to a recent special issue on corporate finance of the *Journal of Financial Economics,* Jensen and Warner (1988: 19) report 'the expansion of financial economists' interests from financial markets to research on behaviour within corporations'.

[6] With respect to the modern theory of finance some authors make a distinction between agency theory and transaction cost theory; agency theory conceives the firm as a nexus of contracts, whereas the transaction cost approach concentrates on the governance of production and finance (cf. Williamson 1988).

which are reflected in the present value of the firm alone. As a result inside owners (the managers) aim at a lower efficiency, and thus a lower valuation, than outside shareholders. This is one way to conceive the conflict of interests between managers and shareholders. In the analysis following we shall, however, adopt the conception of the managerial theories according to which the conflict arises because managers are interested in the expansion of the firm rather than profits.

In this section we shall develop a microeconomic model of growth starting from the strategy of an individual, managerially led firm. We shall concentrate on the financial constraints. As a first step, we assume that the firm has no access to the equity market at all; it is thus fully equity rationed. Investment must therefore be financed by internal savings or external debt. It is evident that for this firm 'every production decision is a risk decision' (Greenwald and Stiglitz 1988*b*: 252). Because the supply of internal finance is limited by current profits, it can be shown that there is a crucial relationship between the rate of expansion and the risk posture of the firm. In essence, this relationship—as we shall see—is similar to Kalecki's principle of increasing risk.

The model

In order to concentrate on the financial aspects we shall consider the following elementary model of a small (corporate) firm. The firm is a price-taker on both the input and the output markets. It operates in a 'steady state' environment: Technical change is purely labour augmenting and (real) wage growth is equal to productivity growth, so that the profit rate and relative prices are constant. The interest rate, time preference, etc. are constant as well. Production is characterized by constant returns to scale and diminishing marginal productivities of capital and labour, hence in ratios to capital stock:

$$y = y(l); \quad y > 0; y' > 0; y'' < 0; \tag{3.1}$$

where l is employment (in efficiency units) and y' and y'' denote the first and second derivatives. Both production factors can be adjusted instantaneously and without cost.

As we wish to concentrate on the internal constraints on growth, the supply of loans is assumed to be perfectly elastic at the given interest rate; there exist no liquidity constraints and no credit rationing. As far as the firm holds positive stocks of financial assets these yield the same interest rate as the firm's debt, so that we can treat debt (a) as a net variable. Then, taking account of different treatment of profits, interest, and inflationary changes in the tax system, the budget constraint for the firm can be written as:

$$\dot{a} = -y + Wl + Ra + \delta + (i + \psi) + \tau_\pi(y - Wl - \psi)$$

$$(-\tau_r R - \tau_p p)a - a(i + p), \tag{3.2}$$

which states that the change in debt $\dot{a}$ is equal to the payments of wages Wl, interest Ra, pay-out of profits to shareholders δ, gross investment $i + \psi$ (ψ = depreciation) and taxes on profits and interest payments less income from production y and less the impact of nominal growth on the debt ratio, $a(i + p)$. The tax rates τ_π, τ_r, τ_p refer to profits, nominal interest, and inflationary changes of debt respectively. This somewhat complex equation reduces considerably if we define the profit and interest rates net of taxes, thus:

$$\pi = (1 - \tau_\pi)(y - Wl - \psi), \tag{3.3}$$

$$r = (1 - \tau_r)R - (1 - \tau_p)p. \tag{3.4}$$

Further, noting that in the steady state production growth is equal to growth of capital ($\rho = i$), the budget constraint can be rewritten as:

$$\dot{a} = -(\pi - \delta) + ra + (1 - a)\rho. \tag{3.5}$$

In steady state equilibrium ($\dot{a} = 0$) this equation implies that the debt ratio must satisfy:

$$a = \frac{\rho - (\pi - \delta)}{\rho - r}. \tag{3.6}$$

Confining our argument for the moment to the case where retained profits as well as the growth rate exceed the interest rate $(\pi - \delta) > r$ and $\rho > r$ [7] we can distinguish the following cases:

[7] As we will see the optimum growth rate will always exceed the interest rate ($\rho > r$) if ($\pi - \delta$) > r. In order to ease our argument the explanation of the model is confined to this situation. The analysis is, however, also valid for the case with ($\pi - \delta$) < r. When discussing the optimum growth rate in s. 3.6 we shall return to this case.

net creditor: $a < 0$　　if $(\pi - \delta) > \rho > r$;

net debtor:　$0 < a < 1$ if $\rho > (\pi - \delta) > r$;

insolvency:　$a > 1$　　if $\rho > r > (\pi - \delta)$.

These results are obvious: if retained profits persistently exceed investment the firm becomes a net creditor in the long run. If retained profits are less than needed for investment the firm must continuously raise external funds and will thus become a net debtor. If, moreover, the rate of interest exceeds the retained profits $(r > (\pi - \delta))$ the rate of indebtedness will rise above unity, leading to insolvency of the firm.

Equation 3.6 implies that, for $(\pi - \delta) > r$, a higher growth rate is associated with a higher debt ratio. At a given pay-out rate a higher indebtedness is thus the price that has to be paid for a higher growth rate in the long term. This relation between growth and debt is illustrated in Fig. 3.2. Notice that $\lim_{\rho \to \infty} a = 1$, which means that there exists no absolute financial limit on the growth rate. Further, this figure brings out that $a \to -\infty$ if the growth rate ρ approximates to r.

The profit rate has, of course, a negative effect on the debt ratio: if π is higher, less external finance is needed entailing a smaller debt ratio in the long run. The influence of the interest rate is ambiguous: if the firm is a net debtor (i.e. if $\rho > \pi - \delta$) a higher interest rate implies a higher steady state debt ratio; but if the firm is a net creditor $(\rho < \pi - \delta)$ a higher interest rate raises the income of the firm and thus leads to a *lower* debt ratio (*in casu* a larger credit position) in the long term. This is illustrated by the shift in the curve in Fig. 3.2.

3.4 Growth–risk frontier

This simple relation between the rate of indebtedness and growth offers a good point of departure for the analysis of the long-term strategy of the firm. In the absence of perfect equity markets it is evident that there exists a positive association between the financial risk of a firm and the rate of indebtedness. The reasons are well known. A large indebtedness implies that a large part of net earnings has to be spent on fixed debt service, so that the remaining flow of earnings

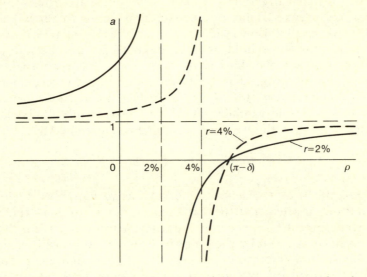

Note: This figure is based on the following numerical values: $\pi = 0.10$; $\delta = 0.05$; and $r = 0.02$ or 0.04 (in both cases $(\pi - \delta) > r$).

FIG. 3.2 Growth and debt

becomes more sensitive to the volatility of the profit and the interest rate. A high indebtedness thus enhances the risk of illiquidity and, in the event, the risk of bankruptcy as well. As we do not pursue a fully fledged assessment of the risk posture of a firm, we shall adopt a simple device to introduce financial risk in the present model, basically following the certainty equivalent approach of Lintner (1971). As mentioned above, we concentrate on borrowers' risk; it is assumed that lenders are willing to supply funds unlimitedly at a given rate of interest.

Now let the profit rate and interest rate be stochastic variables with known mean π and r and variances $\text{var}(\pi)$[8] and $\text{var}(r)$. Given the budget constraint, shocks in these variables must be reflected either in distributed profits δ or in net

---

[8] The variance of the profit rate depends on the probability distribution of the wage rate, technical change, and the prices of input and output (P). If the technique of production and the rate of depreciation are constant, the variance of π is given by: $\text{var}(\pi) = y^2 \text{var}(P) + l^2 \text{var}(W) - 2yl\, \text{covar}(P, W)$. This

investment, or in the growth of debt $\dot{a}$. As it is well established empirically that corporate dividends are sticky[9] we shall treat this variable as a constant in the short term. Further, we shall follow Kalecki (1937) and Wood (1975) and assume that firms hold on to a given target for the rate of indebtedness in the short term, thus $\dot{a} = 0$. This is motivated by the observation that firms only periodically reconsider their financial strategies.[10] Consequently, if a and δ are constant there is only one variable left which must absorb all shocks, namely the growth rate; thus according to equation 3.5:

$$\tilde{\rho} = \frac{1}{1-a}(\tilde{\pi} - \delta - \tilde{r}a), \tag{3.7}$$

where the tilde (~) denotes the stochastic variables.[11] This equation implies that all variance of net returns is transmitted into the variance of ρ. Some empirical support for this hypothesis is given by the empirical investigation of Fazzari, Hubbard, and Petersen (1988) which indicates that variations in net return can explain a significant part of variations in the investment–capital ratio. This is especially true for firms with high retention and low dividends. For mature, high dividend firms the relation between the variance in investment and net returns may be looser, as dividends may absorb part of the variability. In formal terms we obtain for the variance of the growth rate:

expression shows that the variance on π is not dependent of the choice of technique. As a corollary, the optimum technique of production will be dependent on the probability distribution of P and W. Although a further analysis of this effect of uncertainty on the choice of technique is certainly interesting, it would, however, make the present analysis unnecessarily complex and distract us from our main concern. Therefore it will be neglected subsequently, so that var(π) can be treated as a given and independent parameter.

[9] The classic contribution in this field of research is, of course, Lintner (1956).

[10] Apart from this economic motivation for a rigid debt ratio, this assumption also has a considerable technical advantage because a varying debt ratio would create complicated autoregressive processes which, unfortunately, cannot be reduced to a manageable ('Markov process') form on the analytical level.

[11] This result is similar to Lintner (1971), who also assumes a positive association between variations in profits and investment, but different from e.g. Baker (1978), who assumes that dividends absorb the shocks in the firm's earnings.

$$\text{var}(\rho) = \frac{1}{(1-a)^2} \{ \text{var}(\pi) + a^2 . \text{var}(r) - 2a . \text{covar}(\pi, r)\}. \quad (3.8)$$

As the debt ratio depends on the growth rate (eq. 3.6) this result implies that there exists a unique relation between the growth rate and the risk posture of the firm, measured by the variability of the growth rate. This relation will be called the *growth–risk frontier*. As Fig. 3.3 brings out this growth–risk frontier generally has a positive slope, reflecting the fact that the risk increases as the growth rate is pushed up.

However, this general result is not valid when the growth rate approximates to the real interest rate. In this region risk is *negatively* associated with the growth rate. This is because the firm is then a creditor, which has invested its wealth for the larger part in financial assets rather than in capital goods (note that $a \to -\infty$ if $\rho \downarrow r$, see also Fig. 3.3). As a result of this one-sided composition of the portfolio the benefits of diversification decline and the risk rises again when ρ tends to r. This region with a negatively sloping growth–risk frontier is,

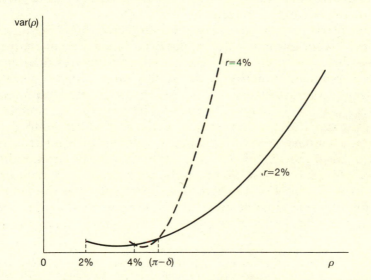

Note: This figure is based on the following numerical values: $\pi = 0.10$; $\delta = 0.05$; $\text{var}(\pi) = 0.006$; $\text{var}(r) = 0.005$; $\text{covar}(\pi, r) = 0.002$; $r = 0.02$ and 0.04.

FIG. 3.3 Growth–risk frontier

however, not very interesting as it will prove to be non-eligible for any risk-averse firm.

It may be noted that the positive association between $var(\rho)$ and ρ is also an essential element in the analysis of Lintner (1971). He does not, however, motivate this relation on the basis of theoretical considerations, but on the basis of an observed relation between these variables in practice: 'Empirically there is evidence that larger retention undertaken to raise expected or average growth also leads to greater variability in the growth rates realized' (Lintner 1971: 190).

3.5 Growth and valuation

In case of imperfect equity markets a conflict may arise between the firm's strategy as selected by the managers and the interest of shareholders. This conflict of interests can be modelled in many different ways. As mentioned above, Jensen and Meckling (1976), for example, explain the divergence in interests between managers and shareholders by the desire of managers for non-pecuniary rewards (perquisites) at the expense of the current profits of the firm. In the present analysis we shall, however, follow the managerial theories of growth and assume that managers aim at maximum expansion of the firm in contrast with shareholders who desire maximum market value. This may be motivated by the well-documented empirical observation that managerial rewards (including the non-pecuniary rewards such as status and perquisites) are related to the size of the firm rather than to its profitability (cf. Odagiri 1981). More precisely, we assume that managers maximize the discounted sum of future sizes of the firm.[12] How the size must be measured is, however, ambiguous. We shall consider two alternatives: the volume of production

---

[12] See Williamson (1966), Auberada (1979), Seoka (1985) for a similar assumption. As an alternative hypothesis it is sometimes assumed that managers aim at maximum (steady state) growth. As growth is generally easier as the initial size is smaller, this hypothesis, however, tends to give rise to unfortunate results. Solow (1971) and Auberada (1979) showed that the growth-maximizing firm yields either the same growth rate as the size-maximizing firm (if initial size is given), or gives rise to an infinitesimally small optimum initial size (if initial size is free).

(Y) and the magnitude of capital stock (K). For the moment we concentrate on the latter. Then the optimization problem at time zero is

$$\text{Maximize}_{\rho,\, l,\, \delta} \quad PV(K) = \int_0^\infty K(t)\exp\{-\int_0^t \eta(\tau)d\tau\}dt, \qquad (3.9a)$$

subject to $dK/dt(t) = \rho(t).K(t);\ l(t) \geqslant 0;\ K(t) \geqslant 0,$

where rate of discount (η) is an endogenous variable dependent on the financial position of the firm. This will be worked out subsequently. The growth rate ρ, labour intensity l, and pay-out δ are control variables; capital stock and the debt ratio are state variables. Since there are no adjustment costs with respect to capital and debt the firm can freely choose its initial capital stock subject to:

$$K(0) = \frac{1}{1 - a(0)}V_o, \qquad (3.10)$$

where V_o is the given initial amount of net worth ($V_o > 0$). As the initial value and the ultimate value of the state variables are free it can be shown that this problem is similar to the problem of choosing a once and for all constant growth rate ρ that maximizes (for a proof see Appendix 3.1):

$$v = \frac{1}{V_o}\int_0^\infty K(0)\exp\{(\rho - \eta)t\}dt, \qquad (3.9b)$$

subject to $K(0) = V_o/(1 - a)$ and $K(0) > 0$, and the steady state budget constraint $a = \{\rho - (\pi - \delta)\}/(\rho - r)$ (eq. 3.6). The valuation ratio of managers $v(= PV(K)/V_o)$ is now defined as the ratio of the discounted size of capital stock and the given initial net worth V_o.

The important question to be answered now is what holds back managers in their desire to maximize the size of the firm *ad infinitum*. Given the budget constraint it is obvious that a higher growth rate implies either a higher debt ratio, or a lower pay-out to shareholders. A higher debt ratio is not attractive to managers as it raises the financial risk for the firm, and thus the risk for the management as well. But it is evident that the alternative of cutting the pay-out to shareholders may also affect the position of the management. If shareholders become discontented with the firm's policy,

they have the ability to intervene and even to dismiss managers. Therefore, managers must take account of the interests
of shareholders too.

   This chapter will concentrate on the first constraint, i.e. the
increasing financial risk as growth is higher. The other constraint, the necessity of keeping shareholders satisfied, is considered in the next chapter. For simplicity the representative
firm in the present chapter is assumed to be a relatively small
firm, which is owned by a small, steady group of shareholders
(for example a family). The pay-out of profits is for the moment taken to be a fixed proportion of total profits.

Financial risk

For the incorporation of risk we follow—with slight modifications—the 'certainty equivalent' method of Lintner (1971).
Given an exponential utility function $U(x) = -x^{\alpha}$ the certainty equivalent $\hat{\rho}$ of a stochastic, normally distributed,
growth rate $\tilde{\rho}$ is given by:

$$\hat{\rho} = E(\tilde{\rho}) - \tfrac{1}{2} \alpha \operatorname{var}(\rho). \tag{3.11}$$

Assuming a constant E $(\tilde{\rho}) = \rho$ and a constant var $= (\rho)$ the
present value PV of a variable $x(t)$ is given by:

$$PV\{x(t)\} = x(0) . \exp[\{\rho - \tfrac{1}{2} \alpha \operatorname{var}(\rho) - \xi\}t], \tag{3.12}$$

where ξ indicates the rate of time preference. This expression
can be reduced by taking time preference ξ and risk premium
$\tfrac{1}{2} \alpha \operatorname{var}(\rho)$ together in the risk-adjusted discount rate η, thus:

$$\eta = \xi + \tfrac{1}{2} \alpha \operatorname{var}(\rho). \tag{3.13}$$

Now our model is complete and can be solved. After substitution for $K(0)$ and assuming convergence of the integral, the
optimization problem (3.9b) can be reduced to:

$$\underset{\rho,\, l}{\text{Maximize }} v = \frac{1}{\eta - \rho} \frac{\rho - r}{\pi - \delta - r} \tag{3.14}$$

subject to $\eta = \xi + \tfrac{1}{2} \alpha \operatorname{var}(\rho).$ (eq. 3.13);

$$\pi = (1 - \tau_\pi)(y - Wl - \psi) \qquad \text{(eq. 3.2)};$$

where var(ρ) is a function of the debt ratio (eq. 3.8) and y is given by the production function $y(l)$ (eq. 3.4). The growth rate ρ and employment l are control variables; the wage rate W, the pay-out rate δ, and the interest rate r are given.

Note that this procedure is only valid if $\rho < \eta$ for all ρ. If there exists some $\rho \geqslant \eta$ the optimization problem (3.9b) becomes subject to the 'growth–stock paradox'; that is, if the integral does not converge the valuation rate v becomes infinite for a range of instrument settings, so that no unique optimum can be determined.[13] As in the present model the risk premium var(ρ), and thus η, rises faster than ρ when $\rho \to \infty$, so that

$$\lim_{\rho \to \infty} (\rho - \eta) = - \infty,$$

it can be concluded that this model may produce a finite optimum without the growth–stock paradox.[14]

The basic considerations regarding the optimum growth rate can be discussed with reference to the scheme of the causal relationships shown in Fig. 3.4. A higher growth rate has a positive effect on v through its effect on the future scale of the firm, and on the initial scale as well (as a result of the higher debt ratio). On the other hand, a greater indebtedness also affects the risk posture of the firm, thus raising the discount rate. For low growth rates the positive effects outweigh this latter negative effect, but beyond some point the negative effect of ρ on the risk will become dominant. This

---

[13] As Lintner (1971) has shown, this paradox hinges on the assumption of a constant rate of discount over time. Lintner rightly argues that this is unrealistic because in reality uncertainty increases as the future becomes more distant. As an alternative he shows that if ρ behaves as a random walk, so that its variance increases linearly with time, the growth–stock paradox is excluded for any ρ. Although his solution is elegant, it is too complex to handle in more elaborate models. Moreover, Lintner seems unaware that if η increases with time, the constant growth path no longer corresponds to the dynamic optimum. Therefore a more general formulation of the optimization problem is necessary. Because of these complexities we shall follow common practice, and assume that the parameters of the $\eta - \rho$ relation are such that $\eta - \rho > 0$ for all (ρ, l).

[14] This is obtained from eqs. 3.6, 3.8, and 3.13.

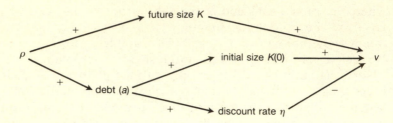

FIG. 3.4 Scheme for the optimum growth rate

is corroborated by the v–ρ frontier in Fig. 3.5 which is based on a numerical simulation of equation 3.14. Just like the growth–valuation frontier in conventional corporate models, this ρ–v frontier initially slopes upward for $\rho > r$ but falls when growth rates become high.[15] However, in our model this is caused by increasing risk whereas in corporate theories it is usually attributed to the declining profitability as ρ increases.

Optimum growth rate

The first-order conditions for an optimum (written in a convenient fashion) are:

$$\frac{\partial v}{\partial l} = \frac{\partial v}{\partial \pi} \cdot \frac{\partial \pi}{\partial l} = 0, \tag{3.15}$$

$$\frac{\partial v}{\partial \rho} = v\left\{ \frac{1}{\rho - r} - \frac{1}{\pi - \rho}\left(\frac{\partial \pi}{\partial \rho} - 1 \right) \right\} = 0. \tag{3.16}$$

The first condition yields the familiar marginal productivity rule for instant profit maximization $\delta\pi/\delta l = 0$, which implies:

$$y' - W = 0. \tag{3.17}$$

---

[15] This ρ–v frontier should not be confused with the growth–valuation frontier in most other managerial theories of growth, where valuation refers to the valuation of shareholders.

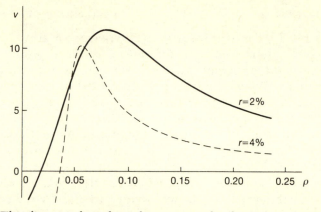

Note: This figure is based on the numerical values given in Fig. 3.3 and $\alpha = 10$; $\xi = 0.15$; and $r = 0.02$ or 0.04.

FIG. 3.5 Growth and valuation

The second condition can after some manipulation be reduced to the following expression for the optimum growth rate ρ^*:[16]

$$\rho^* = r + \{(\pi - \delta) - r\} \sqrt{\left\{\frac{\text{var}(r) + 2(\xi - r)/\alpha}{\text{var}(\pi) + \text{var}(r) - 2\text{covar}(\pi, r)}\right\}} . \quad (3.18)$$

This result implies that $\rho^* > r$ whenever $(\pi - \delta) > r$, and $\rho^* < r$ otherwise. More interesting is however how the growth rate depends on its determinants. This can be made up from the partial derivatives of ρ^*:

$\partial\rho^*/\partial\pi > 0,$

$\partial\rho^*/\partial r > 0,$ if $a > -(1-a)^2\{(\pi - \delta) - r\}$;

$\partial\rho^*/\partial\alpha < 0$; $\partial\rho^*/\partial\xi > 0,$ if $a > 0$ and $(\pi - \delta) - r > 0$;

$\partial\rho^*/\partial\,\text{covar}(\pi, r) > 0$; $\partial\rho^*/\partial\text{var}(\pi) < 0,$

                     if $a > 0$ and $(\pi - \delta) - r > 0$;

---

[16] Eq. 3.16 actually gives two solutions for ρ, but the lower solution corresponds to a minimum. It may be noted that the solution (3.18) is also valid for the case with $(\pi - \delta) < r$. In this case the growth–risk frontier is characterized by $\text{var}(\rho) \to \infty$ if $\rho \to -\infty$ and $\text{var}(\rho) \to \text{var}(r)$ if $\rho \to r$. As risk is still a concave function of ρ, the model will also in this case generally yield an interior solution for ρ. In this case the optimum for ρ will be less than the real interest rate, $\rho^* < r$.

$\partial \rho^* / \partial \text{var}(r) < 0,$　　　　　　if $a > 0$ and $(\pi - \delta) - r > 0.$

Most results confirm intuition. The optimum growth rate is positively associated with the rate of retained profits $(\pi - \delta)$ and the time preference ξ.[17] The sign of the interest rate is ambiguous. When the firm has a net creditor position[18] and the rate of retained profits is close to the interest rate a rise in the interest rate may lead to a *higher* growth rate. Elsewhere the effect of r is negative as usual. As profits become more volatile (var(π) higher) the firm will choose a lower growth rate. The same happens when the volatility of the interest rate goes up, except when the firm is a net creditor; in the latter case the firm will reduce its risk by reducing its net creditor position and thus by choosing a *higher* growth rate. An increase in the covariance between π and r, which lowers the risk, always leads to an increase in the growth rate. Finally, managers will choose a higher growth rate as their time preference (ξ) is greater or as the risk aversion (α) is lower.

All these effects have been discussed for the normal case in which net retained profits exceed the interest rate. If $(\pi - \delta) < r$, a higher growth rate is, as we have seen, associated with a lower steady state debt ratio. It is obvious that many of the above effects may then change direction (see eq. 3.18).

Production maximizer

If managers measure the firm's size by its production rather than by its capital stock the results will be slightly different. The production maximizing firm (YMF) maximizes the size of discounted future production in relation to initial net worth, thus absent the growth–stock paradox:

$$\underset{\rho,\, l}{\text{Maximize }} v_{\text{YMF}} = \frac{y}{\eta - \rho} \frac{\rho - r}{\pi - \delta - r}. \tag{3.14'}$$

[17] Note that eq. 3.18 implies that the optimum debt ratio is independent of π and δ: $a* = 1 - \{\text{var}(\pi) + \text{var}(r) - 2\text{covar}3\,(\pi,\, r)\}^{1/2} / \{\text{var}(r) + 2\,(\xi - r)/\alpha\}$. It varies positively with time preference ξ and the covariance between π and r and negatively with the interest rate and the variance of π.

[18] The firm is a net creditor ($a > 0$) if $r > \xi - \frac{1}{2}\alpha - \{\text{var}(\pi) - 2\,\text{covar}\,(\pi,\, r)\}$.

The first-order condition with respect to ρ is identical to the condition for the capital maximizing firm (KMF) (eq. 3.16 above), and thus yields the same result for the optimum growth rate as above (eq. 3.18). However, the condition with respect to the choice of technique is different and becomes:

$$\frac{v}{y}\,y' + \frac{\partial v}{\partial \pi}\,\frac{\partial \pi}{\partial l} = 0.$$

Since $(v/y)y' > 0$ and $\partial v/\partial \pi > 0$ this condition can be seen to require $\partial \pi/\partial l < 0$; this means that the production-maximizing firm always chooses a more labour-intensive technique and a higher production–capital ratio than the KMF. As a corollary the marginal productivity of labour will be less than the wage rate $(y' - W < 0)$, and the optimum profit rate lower than the maximum profit rate. Moreover, since the growth rate varies with the profit rate (eq. 3.18) it can be concluded that the YMF also chooses a lower growth rate than the KMF. Thus in summary:

$$l_{\text{YMF}} > l_{\text{KMF}}; \quad \pi_{\text{YMF}} < \pi_{\text{KMF}}; \quad \rho_{\text{YMF}} < \rho_{\text{KMF}}.$$

Aside, it may be noticed that the choice of technique has become interdependent with the growth strategy of the production-maximizing firm; all factors affecting the growth–risk trade-off thus influence the choice of technique as well.

In order to get an impression of the differences between the YMF and the KMF, Table 3.1 presents some numerical results for the optimum values $\rho^* \cdot l^*$ and π^* for different wage rates and interest rates, assuming a Cobb–Douglas production function $y = l^\beta$. These results confirm our theoretical findings for the KMF and the YMF. Although the differences are quite small, it can be seen that the YMF chooses a higher l and a lower π, and consequentially a lower ρ than the KMF. These results also show that the technique of production of the YMF is dependent on the interest rate, while it is independent for the KMF. Further, these numerical results indicate that the labour intensity, the profit rate, and the growth rate fall as the wage rate rises. As in our theoretical analysis above, the impact of the interest rate on the growth rate does indeed depend on the financial position of the firm. If the firm is a net debtor a higher interest rate reduces the growth rate, but

TABLE 3.1 *Numerical results for the KMF and the YMF (in brackets) for r = 4% and r = 10%*

W	r(%)	$\pi^*(\%)$		I^*		$\rho^*(\%)$	
		KMF	(YMF)	KMF	(YMF)	KMF	(YMF)
0.8	4	22.0	(22.0)	0.64	(0.68)	14.9	(14.9)
	10	22.0	(21.8)	0.64	(0.72)	10.8	(10.8)
1.2	4	8.5	(8.2)	0.17	(0.23)	4.4	(4.1)
	10	8.5	(8.1)	0.17	(0.24)	5.2	(5.0)
1.6	4	4.4	(4.2)	0.06	(0.09)	1.2	(1.0)
	10	4.4	(4.2)	0.06	(0.09)	3.4	(3.3)
2.0	4	2.6	(2.5)	0.03	(0.04)	− 0.2	(−0.3)
	10	2.6	(2.5)	0.03	(0.04)	2.6	(2.6)

Note: $\beta = 0.7$ and all other numerical values as in Fig. 3.3. At these parameters the debt ratio is 0.36 (if $r = 4\%$) and − 0.18 (if $r = 10\%$)

when it has a net creditor position and the profit rate is low relative to the interest rate it may induce a higher growth rate.

3.6 Conclusion

In this chapter, starting from a basic model of a fully equity-rationed firm, a unique relation has been established between the growth and the financial risk of the firm. On the basis of this growth–risk frontier we have obtained the optimum growth rate as a function of retained profits, the interest rate, and the risk ensuing from the variability of profits and the interest rate, given the time preference and risk aversion of the managers.

Unlike most conventional models of corporate growth the present model does not require a negatively sloped growth–profitability frontier. In stressing increasing risk rather than the declining rate of return our analysis builds on Kalecki's 'principle of increasing risk' rather than on Keynes's proposition of a falling marginal efficiency of investment. This does not mean, however, that the growth–profitability relation is inconsistent with the present approach. On the contrary, this frontier and the growth–risk frontier are natural counterparts in the determination of the growth of firms. Therefore in the next chapter the consequences of incorporating the growth–profitability frontier in the present model will be investigated.

The model considered in this chapter was also restrictive in two other important respects: in the first place it neglected the possibility of raising funds by floating shares; secondly, the analysis was limited to the steady state, and it neglected the adjustment process. The next chapter will extend the analysis on these points as well.

Appendix 3.1 Dynamic optimum

This appendix shows that the time path obtained under the restriction of a once and for all constant growth rate corresponds to a true dynamic optimum if the initial values of a and K are free and if prices and preferences are constant over time. A general formulation of the optimization problem is:

$$\text{Max } v = \int_0^\infty K(t) . \exp\left\{-\int_0^t \eta(\tau)d\tau\right\} dt. \tag{A.1}$$

Since $K(t) = V(t)/|1 - a(t)|$

and $dV(t)/dt = V(t)/\{(\pi - \delta) - a(t)r\}/\{1 - a(t)\}$

(where π, δ and r are constant over time), equation A.1 is equivalent to:

$$\text{Max } v = \int_0^\infty \frac{V_0}{1 - a(t)} z(t)dt, \tag{A.2}$$

subject to $z(0) = 1$ and:

$$dz(t)/dt = \left\{\frac{(\pi - \delta) - a(t)r}{1 - a(t)} - \eta(t)\right\} z(t), \tag{A.3}$$

where z is a state variable and a the control variable. Suppressing the time subscripts the Hamiltonian is:

$$H = \frac{V_0}{1 - a} z + \lambda\left\{\frac{(\pi - \delta) - ra}{1 - a} - \eta\right\} z,$$

subject to $z \geqslant 0$; $z(0) = 1$; $a < 1$. $\tag{A.4}$

The first-order conditions are:

$$\frac{dH}{da} = \frac{V_0}{(1-a)^2} z + \lambda \left\{ \frac{(\pi - \delta) - r}{1-a} - \eta_a \right\} z = 0,$$

$$\frac{dH}{dz} = \frac{V_0}{(1-a)} + \lambda \left\{ \frac{(\pi - \delta) - r}{1-a} - \eta \right\} = -\frac{d\lambda}{dt'}$$

where η_a represents the first derivative of η with respect to a. These conditions yield the following result for the debt ratio:

$$\dot{a} = \{ (1-a) \eta_a - \eta + r \} \frac{(\pi - \delta) - r - (1-a)^2 \eta_a}{2(1-a)\eta_a - (1-a)^2 \eta_{aa}}, \qquad (A.5)$$

where $\eta_{aa} = \partial^2 \eta / (\partial a)^2$.

Now consider optimization of v subject to the steady state assumption of a constant growth rate, or, in terms of the present model, of a constant debt ratio ($\dot{a} = 0$). From equation A.2 we then obtain:

$$v = \frac{V_0}{1-a} \left\{ \frac{(\pi - \delta) - ra}{1-a} - \eta \right\}^{-1}.$$

The first-order condition $dv/da = 0$ is satisfied if:

$$(1-a)\eta_a - \eta + r = 0.$$

Comparing this result with equation A.5 proves that this solution derived from the steady state proposition indeed satisfies the condition for a true dynamic optimum.

4

Growth of the Firm: Some Extensions

4.1 Introduction

The basic model described in the foregoing chapter will now
be elaborated with respect to three important points. First,
we shall relax the assumption of full equity rationing and
introduce the possibility of issuing new shares (section 4.2).
Secondly, we analyse the consequences of positive costs of
growth for corporate strategy and the conflict of interests
between managers and shareholders (section 4.3). Finally, in
section 4.4 the assumption of a free initial capital stock will
be dropped and the adjustment process starting from a given
initial size of the firm will be examined.

4.2 Market valuation and corporate strategy

So far we have concentrated on a relatively small firm which
has no access to the equity market at all. Introduction of the
equity market adds two important dimensions to our analysis. First, the possibility of issuing new equity introduces
an additional source of finance to the firm besides internal
savings and external debt. Secondly, the market valuation of
shares imposes a constraint on the discretionary power of
managers.

This second aspect is probably more important than the role
of the equity market as an additional source of finance. In
practice funds raised by floating shares make up only a very
minor part of total funds. In the post-war period non-financial
firms in the United States raised some 60 to 70 per cent of
their funds internally, 30 to 40 per cent by external debt, and only
1 to 6 per cent by new equity (Taggart 1986: 19). Looking at the
net financing of firms, i.e. gross financing less accumulation of

financial assets, the figures are even more revealing. In a recent survey Mayer (1988) reports that the average contribution of shares in the period 1970–85 ranges from – 4 per cent in the UK to 5 per cent in France. Retentions are by far the most important source of finance ranging from some 60 per cent in France and Japan to more than 100 per cent in the UK (see Table 4.1).

These figures suggest that selling new shares is not a normal way of funding investment. Mayer (1988: 1189) accordingly concludes that 'the issuance of stocks is much more related to the problem of power in the firm and, in this respect, is restricted to very special moments in the life of the firm'.

TABLE 4.1 *Net financing of private physical investment 1970–1985* (percentage of total finance)

	Retentions	Debt	Shares
France	62	32	5
Germany	73	26	1
Japan	65	31	4
U K	107	– 3	– 4
USA	90	13	– 3

Source: Mayer 1988: 1174.

Nevertheless the equity market plays an important role in corporate strategy, not so much as a source of finance, but rather because of the impact of market valuation on the discretionary power of managers. If the managerial strategy presses the market valuation too far down this may provoke a reaction by shareholders to reduce the power of the present management, or even to dismiss them. In addition, a low valuation makes the firm more susceptible to take-overs, as outsiders can make a capital gain by taking over control of the firm.

This section investigates the influence of market valuation on the strategy of a large corporate firm which has access to a well-developed equity market. Nevertheless the equity market is imperfect in the sense that there is only a limited demand for the firm's shares. This imperfection manifests itself in a falling demand curve for the firm's shares. This is in accordance with the empirical observation that share prices fall as more new equity is issued,[1] which is usually explained by the greater reliance on more pessimistic and risk-averse agents when the flotation of equity is increased (cf. Nickell 1978: 184).

Market valuation

The falling demand curve for shares can be represented by a rising rate of discount as the amount of equity issued increases. For simplicity, it is assumed that shareholders are fully aware of the mutual relationship between new equity raised and dividends paid out. Neglecting liquidity constraints and distorting taxation, the net amount of dividends and new equity raised can then be considered as a homogeneous variable (see Appendix 4.1). This difference between the gross pay-out of profits and new equity raised will in the following discussion be represented by the pay-out rate δ, which is now conceived as a *net* rate.

The functional relationship between the market rate of discount η_s and the net pay-out rate δ may—modifying equation 3.13 of the foregoing chapter—be written as:[2]

$$\eta_s = \xi_s + \tfrac{1}{2}\,\alpha_s\,\text{var}\,(\rho) + \sigma_s(\delta); \qquad \sigma_s' < 0;\; \sigma_s'' > 0; \qquad (4.1)$$

where the subscript s refers to shareholders. As in our basic model, $\text{var}\,(\rho)$ is again determined by the debt ratio and the probability distribution of π and r (eq. 3.8). Given this discount rate and a constant growth rate ρ the market valuation ratio q is:

$$q = \frac{1}{V_o} \int_0^\infty \delta K(0)\,\exp\{(\rho - \eta_s)\,t\}\mathrm{d}t, \qquad (4.2)$$

where V_o is the initial net worth. The convexity of the relation between the rate of discount and the net pay-out rate

---

[1] Empirical evidence for the falling demand curve of shares is given by e.g. Shleifer (1986).

[2] For simplicity we neglect the relation between the risk premium and the probability distribution of the market rate of return. According to the CAPM model only the non-diversifiable part of the variance of ρ is relevant to the risk premium. However, incorporation of this relation would not essentially change the subsequent analysis.

ensures that an interior solution can exist for the maximization of q, i.e. the optimum strategy from the point of view of shareholders (for a proof, see Appendix 4.2).

4.3 Managerial strategy

As we have mentioned the valuation of shares on the equity market imposes a significant restraint on the discretionary power of managers. The precise modelling of this restraint is not generally agreed on, but it is widely accepted that it arises from fear of dismissal by dissatisfied shareholders or take-over by new owners when the market value of shares is pressed too far down. An interesting approach is given by Odagiri (1981), who shows that in an uncertain environment the probability of take-over depends on its expected costs and benefits. As the costs will be fairly constant over time and the benefits vary directly with the divergence between the actual market value and the potential value, he argues that this divergence is the principal determinant of the risk of take-over.

In the following analysis we shall introduce this risk for managers by a hazard rate σ reflecting the chance of being dismissed. Following Odagiri this hazard rate is related to the difference between the actual market valuation q and the potential maximum valuation q_{max}. As the utility of managers after they have been dismissed is zero, the 'effective' future size of the firm from the point of view of the present management should be discounted by this hazard rate in addition to time preference and risk premium, thus:

$$\eta = \xi + \tfrac{1}{2} \alpha \, \text{var} \, (\rho) + \sigma(q_{max}, \, q);$$

$$\partial\sigma/\partial q < 0; \; \sigma(q = 0) = \infty; \qquad (4.3)$$

$$\sigma(q = q_{max}) = 0;$$

where q_{max} follows from the maximization of equation 4.2 above.

The discount rate of managers now incorporates two kinds of risk: the financial risk (var(ρ)) which is related to the firm

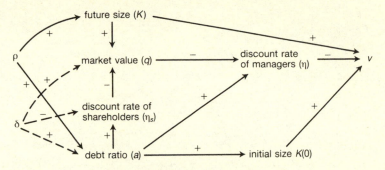

FIG. 4.1 Growth, pay-out, and valuation

as a whole, and the managerial risk (σ) which is specifically attached to the position of the managers. The σ function reflects the ownership structure of the firm. If shareholders have full power over the firm the (left-hand) derivative $\partial\sigma/\partial q$ would be infinite at $q = q_{max}$; that is, all managers will immediately be dismissed at the slightest discrepancy between q and its maximum. If shareholders have no influence at all, $\partial\sigma/\partial q$ would be zero for all (q_{max}, q).

Given this relation for η the optimization problem for the managers is to select a constant growth rate ρ, net pay-out rate δ, and technique of production l that maximizes:

$$v = \frac{1}{V_o} \int_0^\infty K(0) \exp\{(\rho - \eta)t\}\,\mathrm{d}t. \tag{4.4}$$

The basic considerations with respect to the choice of ρ and δ can be explained with reference to Fig. 4.1. For expository reasons the explanation again refers to the case with $(\pi - \delta) > r$ and $\rho > r$. Starting from a low growth rate close to r (where $a = -\infty$) it can be assessed that an increase in ρ initially has a beneficial influence on v because of its positive effect on the initial and future scale of the firm. Also the market valuation q rises at first, thereby diminishing the managerial risk (σ) and pushing v up even more.[3] However,

---

[3] If $(\pi - \delta) > r$ the relevant region for ρ starts at $\rho = r$. At $\rho \downarrow r$ the debt ratio tends to $-\infty$ so that the variance becomes equal to var(r). Provided that covar(π, r) < var(r) the rise in ρ also contributes to a higher q and v because of the declining financial risk var(ρ) as the debt ratio is raised.

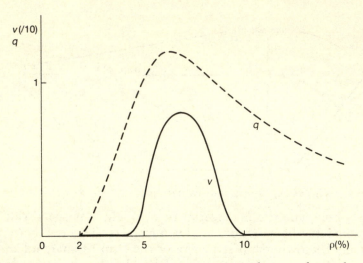

Note: This figure is based on a numerical example with $\sigma_s = v.\exp(-\omega\delta)$; $\sigma = \theta(\exp[\varphi\{q(\max) - q\}/q] - 1)$; $\delta = 0.05$; $\pi = 0.10$; $r = 0.02$; $\xi = 0.025$; $\xi_s = 0.02$; $\kappa = 0.01$; $\varphi = 20$; $\theta = 15$; $v = 0.1$; $\alpha = \alpha_s = 10$; $\text{var}(\pi) = 0.006$; $\text{var}(r) = 0.005$; $\text{covar}(\pi, r) = 0.002$. The σ_s and σ functions will be discussed below with reference to Table 4.3

FIG. 4.2 Growth and valuation

as ρ and thus the debt ratio are raised further, the negative effects of the increasing financial risk on the discount rates η and η_s become stronger, and will sooner or later outweigh the positive effects on the firm's size. Thereafter, further raising of ρ goes together with a fall in v. In the limit, if $\rho \to \infty$ and $a \to 1$ the discount rates of shareholders and managers tend to infinity, so that v and q fall to zero:

$$\lim_{\rho \to \infty} v = 0; \quad \lim_{\rho \to \infty} q = 0;$$

The resulting growth–valuation frontiers for v and q are shown in Fig. 4.2.

With regard to the net pay-out rate we find that the q ratio starts at zero at $\delta = 0$. As the risk of dismissal is then infinitely large, the valuation ratio of managers (v) starts at zero as well, thus:

$$q(\delta = 0) = 0; \quad v(\delta = 0) = 0$$

If δ is raised above zero the q ratio starts to rise, and thanks to the falling risk of dismissal v rises as well. Beyond some point, however, the negative effects of δ on the debt ratio, and thus on var (ρ), become dominating, so that q and v begin to fall again. Eventually, when δ approximates $\delta_o = (\pi - r)$ where the debt ratio becomes equal to unity, the financial risk (var (ρ)) becomes infinitely large so that q and v fall to zero again (see Fig. 4.3), thus:

$$\lim_{\delta \to \delta_o} q = 0; \quad \lim_{\delta \to \delta_o} v = 0; \quad \text{where } \delta_o = (\pi - r).$$

The convexity of these functions ensures that an interior solution exists to the maximization of v. Provided that the growth–stock paradox does not occur and that a finite maximum exists for q_{max}, the first-order conditions for v are:

$$\frac{\partial v}{\partial l} = \frac{\partial v}{\partial \pi} \frac{\partial \pi}{\partial l} = 0, \tag{4.5}$$

$$\frac{\partial v}{\partial a} = v^2 \left\{ \eta - r - (1-a)\frac{\partial \eta}{\partial a} \right\} = 0, \tag{4.6}$$

$$\frac{\partial v}{\partial \delta} = -v^2 \left\{ (1-a)\frac{\partial \eta}{\partial \delta} + 1 \right\} = 0. \tag{4.7}$$

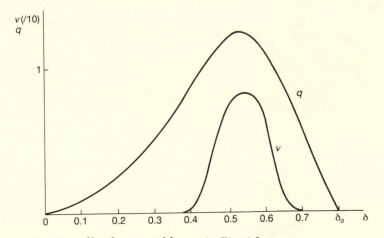

Note: $\rho = 0.06$; all other variables as in Fig. 4.2

FIG. 4.3 Pay-out and valuation

For convenience the conditions have now been written with respect to l, δ, and a. The growth rate is, of course, implied in the solution of these variables. The first condition determines the optimum technique of production (where $y' = W$). Both the other conditions determine the simultaneous solution for a and δ. As $v(q = 0) = 0$ and $v(a = 1) = 0$, the conditions (4.6) and (4.7) ensure that the managers always select a policy with positive net pay-out ($\delta > 0$) and a debt ratio less than unity ($a < 1$), and thus a strategy with finite growth rate ρ. Note that if the demand curve for the firm's shares does not fall (hence $\partial\eta/\partial\delta = 0$) the last condition (4.7) cannot be satisfied for any $v > 0$. The assumption of a limited supply of new equity is thus a necessary condition for an interior solution of the firm's strategy to exist in this model.

Conflicting strategies

The differences between managerial strategy and the strategy desired by shareholders can be established by evaluating the first-order conditions for v in the optimum for q. But if the conditions for v prove to be satisfied in the shareholders' optimum (l, a, $\delta | q = q_{max}$), this will of course represent an optimum for the managers too. If the conditions for v are not satisfied at $q = q_{max}$, the managers will select a different strategy. After some manipulation it can be found for the first derivatives of v evaluated in (l, a, $\delta | q = q_{max}$):

$$\frac{\partial v}{\partial l} = 0, \tag{4.8}$$

$$\frac{\partial v}{\partial a} = v^2 \left\{ \eta - \eta_s - (1 - a)\left(\frac{\alpha - \alpha_s}{\alpha_s}\right)\frac{\partial \eta_s}{\partial a} \right\}, \tag{4.9}$$

$$\frac{\partial v}{\partial \delta} = -v^2. \tag{4.10}$$

The derivation of these results is given in Appendix 4.3. The first equation shows that managers select the same technique of production as shareholders.[4] The first-order conditions for

---

[4] This conclusion is only valid if managers measure the size of the firm by its capital stock. If, however, managers maximize production rather than capital stock it is obvious that they will choose a more labour-intensive technique, with a higher production per unit of capital (see also s. 3.6).

a and δ are, however, generally not satisfied. Managers will therefore pursue a different strategy towards growth, debt, and pay-out from the q-maximizing strategy preferred by shareholders. Equation 4.10 implies that the partial derivative with respect to δ is always negative ($\partial v/\partial \delta < 0$) irrespective of the debt ratio a. For maximization of v managers will therefore always choose a lower pay-out than shareholders.

With regard to the debt ratio the outcome is less clear-cut. Equation 4.9 implies that managers select a higher debt ratio ($\partial v/\partial a > 0$) if they have a higher time preference than shareholders (hence $\eta > \eta_s$), or if they are less risk averse ($\alpha < \alpha_s$). However, if managers have a lower time preference and are more risk averse than shareholders, they will prefer a lower debt ratio than shareholders.

As the growth rate depends on both the debt ratio and the pay-out rate it cannot be unambiguously determined whether managers do desire a higher growth rate than shareholders. The positive effect of the lower pay-out rate may in principle be offset by a reduction in the debt ratio. However, as we have seen this is only possible in the case of a very conservative management, that is, if managers are more risk averse or have a lower time preference than shareholders. Given the enterprising nature of managers this possibility seems hardly likely. Therefore, it can be concluded with reasonable confidence that the management realizes a higher growth rate than that preferred by shareholders.

The differences between the corporate strategy (maximizing v) and the optimum strategy for shareholders (maximizing q) are summarized in Table 4.2. The size of the divergence depends largely on the ownership structure of the firm reflected by the σ function. Differences in strategy will be smaller if the chance of dismissal when $q < q(max)$ is greater. This is corroborated by the numerical results of Table 4.3. This table is based on the following explicit functions for σ_s and σ

$$\sigma_s = v.\exp(-\omega\delta), \qquad (4.11)$$

$$\sigma = \theta[-1 + \exp\{\varphi(q_{max} - q)/q\}]. \qquad (4.12)$$

TABLE 4.2 *Corporate strategy*

	Normal management $(\eta \geqslant \eta_s, \alpha \leqslant \alpha_s)$	Conservative management $(\eta < \eta_s, \alpha > \alpha_s)$
Choice of technique	$l_{v\max} = l_{q\max}$	$l_{v\max} = l_{q\max}$
Pay-out of profits	$\delta_{v\max} < \delta_{q\max}$	$\delta_{v\max} < \delta_{q\max}$
Debt ratio	$\alpha_{v\max} \geqslant \alpha_{q\max}$	$\alpha_{v\max} \lessgtr \alpha_{q\max}$
Growth rate	$\rho_{v\max} \geqslant \rho_{q\max}$	$\rho_{v\max} \lessgtr \rho_{q\max}$

Note: $v\max$ = corporate strategy; $q\max$ = optimum strategy for shareholders.

These functions satisfy the theoretical requirements of the implicit functions given above (eqs. 4.1 and 4.3). In the second equation the chance of dismissal varies with φ. If $\varphi = \infty$, the risk of dismissal is infinite for any $q < q_{\max}$. In this case shareholders effectively have full control over the firm and will thus enforce a strategy that maximizes q. In the numerical example presented in the table this entails a choice of $\rho = -0.4$ per cent and $\delta = 1.01$ yielding a maximum q of 1.40. If φ becomes smaller, the influence of shareholders weakens, which is reflected in a lower pay-out rate, higher growth rate, and higher debt ratio. In the extreme if $\varphi = 0$ the risk of dismissal is nil $(\sigma = 0)$ for any q. In this hypothetical case the management can freely lower the pay-out and raise the flotation of equity without worrying about the market valuation and the continuity of their jobs. In this case, obviously, no interior solution for δ and the growth rate can be found as managers can always find a policy where $\rho > \eta$, so that the optimization is inevitably subject to the growth–stock paradox.

TABLE 4.3 *Some numerical results for the corporate firm*

φ	v	q	$\rho(\%)$	δ	a
∞	5.70	1.40	-0.4	0.10	0.12
50	6.70	1.38	2.1	0.08	0.26
20	7.49	1.33	3.9	0.07	0.32
10	8.42	1.26	5.9	0.06	0.37

Note: $\pi = 0.10$ $r = 0.02$ $\xi = 0.025; \xi_s = 0.02;$ $\theta = 0.01;$ $v = 0.1; \omega = 15;$ $\alpha = \alpha_s = 10;$ $\text{var}(\pi) = 0.006;$ $\text{var}(r) = 0.005;$ $\text{covar}(\pi, r) = 0.002.$

4.4 Costs of growth

So far we have assumed that capital stock as well as employment can be adjusted instantaneously and without any cost. This enabled us to concentrate on the financial restraints on growth of the firm. The introduction of 'real' cost of growth in our model does not change the basic conclusion of the foregoing analysis, although it may—as we will see—affect the optimum for the growth rate and sharpen the conflict between managers and shareholders.

We shall not deal in detail here with the explanation of the real cost of growth. One may follow the conventional (neo-classical) approach which points to the adjustment cost related to changes in capital stock or employment. Alternatively, one can also think in terms of the negative growth–profitability frontier which is central in the—much richer, but less formalized—managerial theories of growth. As mentioned in section 3.2 there appear to exist basically two ways to explain this frontier: the internal approach, inspired by Penrose (1959), which emphasizes the organizational costs related to the expansion of the firm, and the external approach which follows Marris (1964) and concentrates on the product-market constraints and the 'demand shifting' effort necessary to maintain a certain growth of sales.

We shall however skip the modelling of underlying marketing-, organization-, and production-decisions and just posit a negative relation between profitability and the rate of growth:

$$\pi = \pi(\rho) ; \quad \pi' < 0 .^5 \tag{4.13}$$

The consequences of this function for the firm's strategy and the conflict between managers and shareholders will be discussed with reference to the basic model described in the foregoing chapter.

First, it can be established that the negative effect of growth on profitability leads to a lower optimum growth rate.[6] This

---

[5] As rapid shrinkage of the firm requires great organizational effort, just like fast expansion, it seems likely that the growth-profitability relation is positive for $\rho \ll 0$. For the moment, however, we shall neglect this possibility, and concentrate on the downward-sloping segment of the $\pi - \rho$ frontier.

[6] In comparison with the 'old' first derivative with respect to ρ (eq. 3.16), the first-order condition for optimum growth rate becomes: $dv/d\rho = dv/d\rho$ (old) + $\delta v/\delta \pi . \pi' = 0$. Since $\delta v/\delta \pi > 0$ and $\pi' < 0$ the marginal effect of

is not surprising as this negative $\pi - \rho$ relation reduces the marginal benefits (in terms of a higher valuation ratio) of a higher growth rate.

More interesting, however, is that the existence of cost of growth drives a wedge between the interests of managers and shareholders. This is the basic tenet of the managerial theories of the firm. In Chapter 3 it was established that if managers maximize the capital stock there is no essential conflict between managers and shareholders regarding the investment–risk trade-off, except due to differences in time preference or risk aversion. The introduction of a negative growth–profitability relation gives rise, however, to a more fundamental conflict of interests. Since in the steady state the relation between v and q is given by $v = q/\delta$ (see eqs. 4.2 and 4.4), the first-order condition for v can be written as:

$$\frac{dv}{d\rho} = \frac{1}{\delta}\left(\frac{dq}{\delta\rho} - v\delta\pi'\right).$$

(4.14)

This equation shows that in the shareholder's optimum $q = q_{max}$ where $dq/d\rho = 0$ the growth rate still has a positive effect on v (thus $dv/d\rho > 0$) because of $\pi' < 0$. Therefore it can be concluded that managers aim at a higher growth rate than shareholders:

$$\rho_{vmax} > \rho_{qmax} \quad \text{for any } \pi' < 0,$$

and consequently a lower profit rate and a higher debt ratio.

4.5 The adjustment process

So far we have concentrated on the optimum growth path under the restriction of a once and for all constant growth rate. This steady growth approach was warranted in the simple model where the capital stock could be varied instantaneously and without any cost. However, after the incorporation of costs of growth this approach is no longer warranted.

the growth rate on v is always negative at the old optimum, where of course $dv/d\rho$ (old) $= 0$. Therefore, it can be concluded that there is a finite optimum for the growth rate, which is lower as the slope of the $\pi - \rho$ frontier is steeper.

One cannot on the one hand assume that growth of capital and production requires organizational and marketing costs, and at the same time let the initial stock of capital be varied freely.[7]

For this reason we shall in this section drop the assumptions of a once and for all constant growth rate and a free initial stock of capital, and return to the general formulation of the optimization problem for the fully equity-rationed firm (eq. 3.9a in the foregoing chapter). After substitution for ρ this can, for a given pay-out rate, be written as:

$$\text{Maximize}_{\rho}\, v = \frac{1}{V_o}\int_0^{\infty} K\,(0)\,\exp$$

$$\left[\int_0^t \{\,\rho_\tau - \tfrac{1}{2}\alpha\,\text{var}(\rho)_\tau - \xi\}\,d\tau\right]dt. \quad (4.15)$$

Unfortunately the mathematical form of this equation is too complex to handle on the analytical level. But in order to be able to get an impression of the adjustment process we shall analyse the following simplified variant which is more familiar in control theory.

$$\text{Maximize}_{\rho}\int_0^{\infty}[\{\,\rho_t - \tfrac{1}{2}\,\alpha\,\text{var}(\rho)_t\}e^{-\xi t}]\,dt, \quad (4.16)$$

subject to:

$$\pi = \pi_o - \chi(\rho - \rho_o)^2, \quad \chi > 0, \quad (4.17)$$

and the budget constraint (eq. 3.5 in the foregoing chapter) which determines the change in the state variable, i.e. the debt ratio (a). The variance of the growth rate, var(ρ), is given by the known function of the debt ratio a (eq. 3.8). According to equation 4.16 managers maximize the certainty equivalent of the *growth* of the firm, rather than the discounted size. Since the initial size of the firm is given this alternative representation is not fundamentally different from the original model. The basic considerations regarding the time path of ρ are similar; the trade-off between growth and (future) risk is still the central relationship.[8] As will be argued below,

[7] This is not always recognized properly in models of corporate growth (cf. Marris 1971, Slater 1980, Odagiri 1981).

[8] Under the restriction of a given initial size and constant growth rate, both formulations also yield the same solution, namely the growth rate that maximizes the risk-disconnected growth rate, $\{\rho - \tfrac{1}{2}\alpha\,\text{var}(\rho)\}$.

most of the conclusions based on the simplified version are valid for the original model as well. However, as the timing of the growth–risk trade-off is different, the precise shape of the adjustment trajectory will be different.

Equation 4.17 represents a simple version of the growth–profitability frontier. All determinants of π other than ρ are included in the autonomous factor π_o. The quadratic shape of this function can be motivated by the observation that not only the rapid growth but also the rapid shrinkage of the firm requires large organizational or adjustment costs. According to equation 4.17 the costs of growth decline when $\rho < \rho_o$ and rise when $\rho > \rho_o$. The costs of growth are thus minimal at $\rho = \rho_o$; that is if the firm shrinks at the rate $-\rho_o$ (we assume $\rho_o \leqslant 0$).

On the basis of these functions the optimum time path can be established from the present value Hamiltonian (suppressing the time subscripts):

$$H^* = \rho - \tfrac{1}{2}\alpha \, \mathrm{var}(\rho) - \lambda[\{\pi_o - \delta - \chi(\rho - \rho_o)^2\}$$

$$- ra - (1 - a)\,\rho], \qquad (4.18)$$

subject to a given initial debt ratio $a(t = 0) = a_o$ and the transversality condition:

$$\lim_{t \to \infty} e^{-\xi t}\lambda(t) \cdot a(t) = 0.$$

The first-order conditions for the optimum are:

$$\frac{\mathrm{d}H^*}{\mathrm{d}\rho} = 0 \quad \text{and} \quad \frac{\mathrm{d}H^*}{\mathrm{d}a} = \xi\lambda - \dot{\lambda}; \qquad (4.19)$$

which gives our model:

$$1 + \lambda\{(1 - a) + 2\chi(1 - \delta')(\rho - \rho_o)\} = 0;$$

$$\tfrac{1}{2}\alpha\,\frac{\partial\mathrm{var}\,(\rho)}{\partial a} + \lambda\,(\rho - r) = \dot{\lambda} - \xi\lambda; \qquad (4.20)$$

where $\delta'(= \partial\delta/\partial\pi)$ stands for effect of profits on the pay-out. These conditions can be resolved into the following differential equation for ρ:

$$\dot{\rho} = \frac{1}{2\chi(1-\delta)} \left[r - \xi(1-a) - \{\pi_o - \delta - \chi(\rho - \rho_o)^2\} \right.$$

$$- 2\chi(1-\delta')(\rho - \rho_o)(\rho + \xi - r) + \alpha\{(1-a)$$

$$+ 2\chi(1-\delta')(\rho - \rho_o)\}^2 \cdot \{var(\pi) + a \cdot var(r)$$

$$\left. - (1+a)covar(\pi, r)\}(1-a)^{-3} \right]. \tag{4.21}$$

Together with the budget constraint (3.5) this equation determines the dynamics of the state variables ρ and a.

Debtor firm

Although this differential system cannot be solved explicitly it can be analysed qualitatively by means of the phase diagram (Fig. 4.4) which shows the $\dot{\rho} = 0$ and $\dot{a} = 0$ loci in the (ρ, a) plane. Because of the quadratic shape of the ρ–π relation more than one solution may exist, but there is only one optimum solution A($\rho = 4.9$ per cent, $a = 0.29$) characterized by the familiar saddle-point configuration. The dashed line shows the hypothetical adjustment trajectory towards this optimum.

The same figure also shows the $\dot{\rho} = 0$ and $\dot{a} = 0$ loci for a higher interest rate (8 per cent instead of 4 per cent) yielding a new optimum A′ at a lower growth rate and a smaller debt ratio ($\rho = 4.2$ per cent, $a = 0.12$). It can be seen from the figure that the impact effect of the increase in r on growth is greater than its ultimate effect. After the rise in r, the growth rate falls to a point B on the lower adjustment trajectory, whereafter it gradually rises again as the debt ratio tends to its new, lower steady state optimum.

The magnitude of the difference between the impact effect and the ultimate effect depends on the slope of the π–ρ frontier. If π is very sensitive to changes in ρ(χ large) it is very costly to vary ρ much along the adjustment trajectory. Thus the optimum trajectory will be flat. As a corollary the adjustment process will also take longer. As χ becomes smaller the initial drop in ρ becomes sharper, and the adjustment time shorter. If χ falls to zero the speed of adjustment becomes infinitely large.

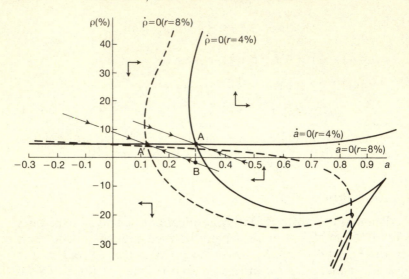

Note: $\pi_o = 0.10$; $\chi = 1$; $\rho_o = -0.04$; $\xi = 0.02$, and all other parameters as in Table 4.3

FIG. 4.4 The adjustment process

Creditor firm

In the above case both the impact effect and the ultimate effect of a higher interest rate on the growth rate are negative. As we have seen in Chapter 3 this is not necessarily so. When the firm is a net creditor ($a < 0$) and π is low in relation to r, the steady state effect of the rise in r may be reversed, thus yielding a *higher* growth rate.

This is illustrated in Fig. 4.5, which shows the adjustment trajectory when the interest rate rises further from 8 per cent to 12 per cent. The new steady state position at $r = 12$ per cent is now characterized by a higher growth rate and a lower debt ratio ($\rho = 5.3$ per cent, $a = -0.10$). This new equilibrium can, however, only be reached by temporarily reducing the growth rate in order to let the rate of indebtedness decrease. After the discrete reduction in the growth rate, it will gradually recover again as debt declines over time. Ultimately ρ will even rise above its original level. Hence, in this case the higher interest leads to a lower growth rate in the short term and a higher growth rate in the long term.

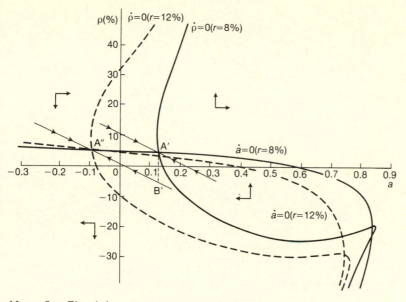

Note: See Fig. 4.4.

FIG. 4.5 A creditor firm

The impact and ultimate effects of the higher interest rate for the debtor and the creditor firm are summarized in Fig. 4.6. This figure shows the time paths of the capital stock, the growth rate, and the debt ratio after a permanent rise in the interest rate at time t_0. Fig. 4.6a refers to the 'normal' case with negative impact and ultimate effects and Fig. 4.6b to the 'perverse' case with negative impact effect and positive ultimate effect.

Fall in profitability

One of the characteristics which clearly emerges from Figs. 4.4–4.6 is the 'overshooting' of the adjustment process. Similar overshooting processes may occur after exogenous changes in the profitability of investment (π_o) or in the state of risk (indicated by the variability of the profit rate var(π) or the interest rate var(r)). As a final example we shall therefore consider a shift in profitability. Fig. 4.7 shows that a fall in

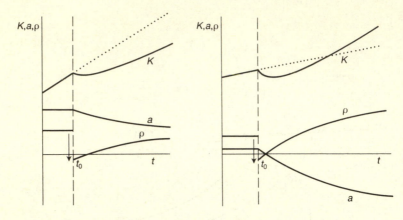

FIG. 4.6 A rise in interest rate: time-paths of K, ρ, and a

π_o from 10 per cent to 6 per cent eventually leads—after a similar overshooting process—to a lower steady state debt ratio ($a = 0.23$) and a lower growth rate ($\rho = 2.4$ per cent).

In addition this figure shows the trajectory when the fall in profitability is foreseen by entrepreneurs at an earlier moment. This may happen, for instance, if it is announced at time t_1 that wages, or taxes, are to be raised at $t_2 (> t_1)$. In this case the firm will already reduce its growth at the moment of the announcement (t_1).This is shown in the figure by the discrete fall to point C; then the growth rate gradually falls further until the actual fall in profit rate at t_2. From that moment onwards the growth rate starts rising again along the trajectory B–A. Thus, as soon as the future fall in profits becomes known, the growth is reduced immediately in order to achieve a better point of departure, i.e. a lower debt ratio, before profits actually fall. This is illustrated in Fig. 4.8.

These conclusions based on the simplified model will not really be different from the conclusions which can be drawn on the basis of the original version of the optimization problem. The ultimate effects on the growth rate found above correspond to the conclusions from the steady state analysis in the foregoing chapter, for the debtor firm as well as for the creditor firm. As to the impact effects it can be seen that their

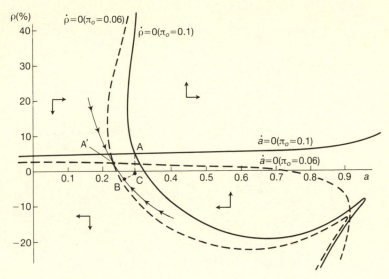

Note: See Fig 4.4

FIG. 4.7 A (foreseen) fall in profitability

direction must be the same for the original model as well;[9] an ultimate decrease in the debt ratio will always require a (temporary) reduction of the growth rate, and an ultimate rise in debt an increase in ρ.

The dynamics considered above arises from the fact that the firm's debt ratio is a state variable which can be adjusted only slowly. This follows from the assumptions of a given initial stock of capital and given initial net worth of the firm. In the above model the firm has been assumed to have no access to the equity market at all. This is, of course, relevant for many firms in reality. The analysis may, however, be generalized for the case of a big corporation which can raise funds by floating equity as well. It is evident that if the firm can raise

[9] This follows from the fact that the optimum must be characterized by a saddle-point configuration and that the $\dot{a}$ function is, of course, identical in both the formulations of the optimization problem. As can be seen from Figs. 4.6–4.8 above the adjustment trajectory must therefore always lie under the $\dot{a} = 0$ locus in the case of a reduction in a and above this locus in case of a rise in a.

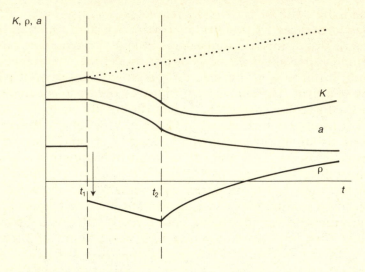

FIG. 4.8 A foreseen fall in π : time-paths of K, ρ, and a

equity freely without any limitation, there is no need for a delayed adjustment to the desired debt ratio. If, however, as we have argued in section 4.2, there is only a limited demand for the firm's shares, so that equity can only be raised at increasing costs, these costs will impose an effective constraint on the adjustment of the firm's financial position.[10] Then, the adjustment process will not be essentially different for a big corporation with access to the equity market from what it is for a small firm without access as was considered above.

4.6 Conclusion

Although the equity market has only a very limited role as a source of finance, it is nevertheless very important as the market valuation of shares acts to discipline the managers

[10] If the costs of raising equity are related to the flow of new ('outside', see s. 3.3) equity, these costs may put a similar restraint on the adjustment of the firm's net worth, as the adjustment costs of investment prevent discrete changes in capital stock. A motivation for the relation between costs and the flotation of shares can be found in Jensen and Meckling (1976), who assume that agency costs rise with the amount of outside finance.

from the point of view of shareholders. In this chapter this was formalized by the introduction of a hazard function for the risk of dismissal for managers linked to the market valuation of shares. On the basis of this model the simultaneous equilibrium was established for the growth and pay-out policy of a firm. The analysis corroborates the basic conclusion of the foregoing chapter that when the supply of equity capital is limited (i.e. absent as in Chapter 3, or subject to rising costs as in this chapter), the 'principle of increasing risk' provides an effective restraint on the firm's growth.

Introduction of the costs of growth did not significantly change the conclusions of the basic model. It sharpens, however, the conflict between management and shareholders, as the pursuit of rapid growth now directly affects the profit rate. This implies that managers generally aim at higher growth and lower profits than are desired by shareholders. All results with respect to differences in strategy between a managerial (v-maximizing) firm and a firm that maximizes market valuation (q) are summarized in Table 4.4. By way of reference the results of Seoka (1985) are also given. This summary shows that managers generally aim at a higher growth rate and lower pay-out rate than shareholders. Only in the case of 'conservative' managers with a higher risk aversion and lower time preference is the outcome for the growth rate and the debt ratio ambiguous. In the case of positive costs of growth, or if managers maximize production (or sales) rather than the capital stock, the firm's strategy will deviate from instant profit-maximizing. In that case the profit rate will thus be less than would be desired by shareholders.

If one allows for costs of growth one should also drop the assumption of a free initial size. Analysis of the adjustment process revealed that changes in profit rates and interest rates may lead to significant changes in investment, in the short term as well as the long term. In the presence of imperfect equity markets changes in profits and interest rates affect investment in two ways: through the availability of internal finance and through the change of the desired financial structure. The first, 'internal savings', effect is essentially a short-term effect, as it implies direct adjustment of investment to the flow of internal finance. The second effect may, however, produce quite persistent changes in investment. This is because the firm's balance sheet can only be adjusted slowly to the desired new structure. The combination of both effects means that the adjustment process is often characterized by overshooting; that is, the impact effect of an exogenous change proves to be stronger than the ultimate effect. For a creditor firm the impact and ultimate effects may even have different signs. This corroborates our observation in Chapter 3 that the interest effect on investment may be reversed for a creditor firm.

TABLE 4.4 *Differences between a v-maximizing firm and a q-maximizing firm* (+ indicating a positive difference)

	ρ	δ	a	$K(0)$	y	π
Small firm ($\pi' = 0$)						
Capital-maximizing	+	—[a]	0	0	0	0
Production-maximizing	+	—[a]	0	0	+	-
Small firm ($\pi' < 0$)	+	—[a]	+	+	±	-
Large firm ($\pi' = 0$)						
Normal management	+	-	+	+	0	0
Conservative management	±	-	±	±	0	0
Seoka (1985)	+	—[a]	—[a]	+	—[a]	-

[a] No result given.

This analysis of the adjustment process brings out that an aggregate shock, like for example a fall in profitability due to oil price increases, may lead to a long-term process of financial restructuring besides its (medium-term) impact effect on investment through its impact on the availability of finance. The consequences of such processes of financial adjustment to the macroeconomic dynamics of growth and debt are investigated in Chapters 6 and 7. However, at this stage it should be remembered that our analysis was restricted to an individual firm facing a smooth development of demand. So far, we have thus neglected the impact of aggregate demand on investment. The foregoing model of investment is therefore more suited for the long period than for shorter periods where fluctuations in aggregate demand are the dominant factor. Investment will then be guided by the aim to keep up with demand rather than being constrained by financial considerations. This will be considered in the next chapter before we turn to the long period in which financial constraints are assumed to be decisive to investment and growth.

Appendix 4.1 Equity and dividends

This appendix shows the equivalence of dividends and equity raised. Define J = number of shares, P_e = price of shares, d = dividend ratio, and $j = (dJ/dt)(1/J)$, then the market valuation of all outstanding shares is given by the present value of dividends on these shares:

$$P_e J = \int_0^\infty dK(0) \cdot \exp\{(\rho - j - \eta)t\}dt.$$

Under the usual assumptions this can be solved into:

$$P_e J = dK(0)/(\eta + j - \rho).$$

Since we have defined pay-out of profits net of equity raised $(\delta K = dK - jP_e J)$, we find for the total value of shares $P_e J = \delta K(0)/(\eta - \rho)$. This latter result shows that the market valuation $P_e J$ depends on net pay-out only, and is thus independent of the division of net returns $\delta K(0)$ in dividends $dK(0)$ and new equity raised $jP_e J$.

Appendix 4.2 Shareholders' optimum

The optimum strategy from the point of view of shareholders is the strategy which maximizes the q ratio. Absent the growth–stock paradox q can be written as:

$$q = \frac{\delta}{\delta + (1 - a)\eta - (\pi - ar)} . \tag{A.1}$$

Given the relation for the discount rate (eq. 4.3) the first order conditions for l, a, and δ are:

$$\frac{\partial q}{\partial l} = \frac{\partial q}{\partial \pi}\frac{\partial \pi}{\partial l} = 0; \tag{A.2}$$

$$\frac{\partial q}{\partial a} = \frac{q^2}{\delta}\left\{\eta_s - r - (1 - a)\frac{\partial \eta_s}{\partial a}\right\} = 0; \tag{A.3}$$

$$\frac{\partial q}{\partial \delta} = \frac{q^2}{\delta^2}\{(1 - a)\eta_s - (\pi - ar) - (1 - a)\delta\sigma_s'\} = 0. \tag{A.4}$$

The solution for ρ is implied by the simultaneous optimum for δ and a. The first condition (A.2) determines the optimum technique of production. The other conditions yield the optimum debt ratio and pay-out rate. If $\sigma_s' = 0$ the discount rate is independent of δ, so that A.3 determines the optimum of the debt ratio (a) independently of δ (see also n. 17 in Chapter 3). However, in this case (or if $\sigma_s'' = 0$) the last condition A.4 cannot be fulfilled for any finite δ; hence $\sigma_s'' > 0$ is a necessary condition for an interior solution to exist for the optimum pay-out rate.

Appendix 4.3 Managerial strategy

The difference between the strategy of the firm and the desired strategy by shareholders can be established by comparing the first-order conditions for v and those found for q in Appendix 4.2. The optimality conditions for v are:

$$\frac{\partial v}{\partial l} = \frac{\partial v}{\partial \pi} \frac{\partial \pi}{\partial l} = 0;$$

$$\frac{\partial v}{\partial a} = v^2 \left\{ \eta - r - (1-a) \frac{\partial \eta}{\partial a} \right\} = 0;$$

$$\frac{\partial v}{\partial \delta} = -v^2 \left\{ (1-a) \frac{\partial \eta}{\partial \delta} + 1 \right\} = 0.$$

These conditions shall now be evaluated in the optimum for q. First, notice that in this optimum:

$$\frac{\partial \eta}{\partial \delta} = \frac{\partial q}{\partial \delta} \sigma' = 0 \text{ and } \frac{\partial \eta}{\partial a} = \frac{\alpha}{\alpha_s} \frac{\partial \eta_s}{\partial a}.$$

After substitution of the results for the maximum of q found in Appendix 4.1, the partial derivatives of v become:

$$\frac{\partial v}{\partial l} = 0;$$

$$\frac{\partial v}{\partial a} = v^2 \left\{ \eta - \eta_s - (1-a) \left(\frac{\alpha - \alpha_s}{\alpha_s} \right) \frac{\partial \eta_s}{\partial a} \right\};$$

$$\frac{\partial v}{\partial \delta} = -v^2.$$

These results are discussed in the text (section 4.2).

5

The Keynesian Corridor

5.1 Introduction

According to Leijonhufvud (1981) the dynamics of the economy is characterized by a 'corridor': within certain bounds around the equilibrium the system will 'home in' in the way presumed in pre-Keynesian economics, but outside this corridor the system is dominated by Keynesian destabilizing forces. The system is thus capable of handling small shocks, but in the case of a large displacement stability may break down. In technical terms the corridor implies that the system exhibits local stability and global instability.

The basic source of the corridor is—according to Leijonhufvud—a non-linearity in aggregate demand due to a qualitative change associated with large displacements. This can be explained, for example, by the occurrence of bankruptcies (this idea can already be found in Fisher (1931), see Howitt (1978), or liquidity constraints (cf. van de Klundert and van Schaik 1990).

In this chapter it will be shown that this corridor is an important feature of the medium-period dynamics. Following Malinvaud (1977) we assume that the medium period is characterized by a rigid technique of production and sluggish prices and expectations. Disequilibrium between aggregate demand and supply is therefore a basic feature of the medium-period. In this chapter we shall also allow for monetary forces. It is precisely the antagonism between the basically destabilizing multiplier-accelerator mechanism and the generally stabilizing feedback of the monetary sector which will prove to give rise to corridor dynamics.

Leijonhufvud has only given a qualitative description of the corridor. In this chapter we shall develop a simple non-linear medium-period model which will enable us to give a formal analysis of the corridor in terms of an unstable limit cycle. The analysis of this and the next chapters develops the macroeconomic analysis of Chapter 2 and the microeconomic analysis of corporate growth in Chapters 3 and 4. In contrast with the 'steady state' analysis in Chapter 2, which assumes an exogenous rate of growth and a constant interest and profit rate, the present analysis focuses on the underlying dynamics that should ensure steady state growth. Therefore we shall develop a model which incorporates a dynamic conception of investment behaviour, a monetary explanation of the interest rate, and a more sophisticated representation of fiscal policy. As the medium period is characterized by disequilibrium between aggregate demand and supply, investment is assumed to be guided by volume signals rather than price signals. For the moment we shall thus neglect the impact of financial factors stressed in the foregoing chapters, but these become relevant again in the long-term analysis in Chapters 6 and 7.

We start with a discussion of static aspects of the model (section 5.2). Because of the prominent role of the government budget constraint in our analysis, the representation of fiscal policy will be discussed at some length in section 5.3. Next, in sections 5.4–5.6 the medium-period model is elaborated and analysed with respect to its static and dynamic properties. Finally, section 5.7 gives an assessment of the impact of the policy regime on the stability of the system.

5.2 The basic model

The basic structure of the medium-period model as well as the long-period models to be considered in the next chapters is the following:

1. The economy is divided into three sectors: workers, the corporate sector, and the government. Workers receive labour income (wages and unemployment benefits) as well as interest income on their holdings of government debt and corporate debt. The corporate sector encompasses all firms and their owners; this sector receives the profits after payment of debt service to the workers. In order to avoid the complications connected with the valuation of shares and capital goods (see

section 2.3) it is assumed that workers do not possess shares; all shares are owned by the conglomerate of the entrepreneurs, (top) managers, and the large shareholders who control the corporate sector.[1] The third sector in this model is the government which receives income from taxes on the income of workers and the corporate sector and seigniorage, and spends it on exhaustive expenditure (consumption) and debt service.

2. Workers have a lower propensity to save from their income than members of the 'corporate class'. For both classes, consumption also depends on the interest rate and the amount of wealth.

3. Unlike the traditional 'Ricardian' model considered in Chapter 2, the rate of interest is not simply derived from the profit rate but determined—in a Keynesian fashion—by portfolio equilibrium. The portfolio consists of money and bonds only. Government debt and private debt are perfect substitutes. For simplicity, all money is assumed to be held by workers; firms are supposed to be able to hold all their liquidities in the form of interest-bearing assets.

In the medium period it is further assumed that prices are sluggish in the sense that the level of prices is fixed at every instant, but that the rate of change of prices (the inflation rate) may vary. The model is characterized by disequilibrium between aggregate demand and supply. With respect to investment it is therefore assumed that the decisive determinant of investment is the aim to adjust capacity to the expected demand for goods. For simplicity the impact of financial variables on investment is neglected.

In order to keep the model within manageable proportions we assume the technique of production and the share of

---

[1] This division between workers and the corporate sector reconciles Kaldor's argument, that differential saving arises from the corporate structure of the modern economy, with Pasinetti's argument that workers also accumulate wealth. The basic problem with Kaldor's approach concerned the 'vanishing' of retained earnings (see s. 2.3). By taking shareholders and firms together we avoid this problem. Retained earnings are fully taken into account now, but because of the higher propensity to save of the 'corporate class', the impact of retained earnings on consumption is only small. This modelling is to be preferred to letting retained earnings vanish completely (cf. Chiang 1973, Darity 1981, Kuipers 1981).

wages (w/y) to be fixed in the medium period. For the moment we shall also neglect the accumulation of corporate and public debt. This can be motivated by the fact that public and corporate debt are slow variables in relation to the medium-term dynamics of aggregate demand and supply. The analysis of the accumulation of public and corporate debt is postponed till the long-period analysis in the next chapters. This does not mean, however, that the distribution of wealth is neglected in the present analysis; on the contrary, it will be seen below that the size of public and corporate debt is an important determinant of the stability of the system in the medium period.

The model uses the following symbols:

a debt of firms (net of holdings of government bonds)
b government debt
C_j total consumption of class j
g government expenditure
h utilization rate
i net investment ($\equiv$ growth rate of capital stock)
m (base) money supply
m_d (base) money demand
p inflation rate
r real interest rate
ρ growth rate of production capacity
T_j taxes of class j
w sum of wages
y production
y_c production capacity
y_j disposable income of class j
z_j wealth of class

where $j = 1$ for workers and $j = 2$ for the corporate class. All stock and flow variables are written as ratios to capital stock. Expectation variables are indicated by the subscript e. The basic equations of the model can be written as follows:

Income relations

$$y_1 = w + r(a + b) - pm - T_1; \tag{5.1}$$

$$y_2 = y - w - ar - T_2 ; \tag{5.2}$$

$$T_1 = \tau_0 w + \tau_1\{r(a + b) - pm\}; \quad 0 \leqslant \tau_0,\ \tau_1 \leqslant 1; \tag{5.3}$$

$$T_2 = \tau_2(y - w - ar); \quad 0 \leqslant \tau_2 \leqslant 1; \tag{5.4}$$

$$h = y/y_c. \tag{5.5}$$

Expenditure relations

$$y = C_1 + C_2 + i + g\ ; \tag{5.6}$$

$$C_j = C_j(y_j, (1 - \tau_j)r, z_j)\ ;$$
$$0 < \partial C_j/\partial y_j < 1;\ \partial C_j/\partial r < 0;\ \partial C_j/\partial z_i > 0\ j = 1, 2; \tag{5.7}$$

$$i^* = i^*(\rho_e^d, h - 1)\ ;$$
$$\partial i^*/\partial \rho_e^d > 0,\ \partial i^*/\partial h > 0;\ i^*(h = 1) = \rho_e^d;$$
$$i^*(h = 0) = -\infty. \tag{5.8}$$

Money and prices

$$p = p(h - 1, p_0);$$
$$\partial p/\partial h > 0;\ p(h = 1) = p_0; \tag{5.9}$$

$$m_d = m_d(y, r + p, z_1);$$
$$\partial m_d/\partial y > 0;\ \partial m_d/\partial (r + p) < 0;\ \partial m_d/\partial z_1 > 0; \tag{5.10}$$

$$m_d = m; \tag{5.11}$$

$$z_1 = m + a + b; \tag{5.12}$$

$$z_2 = 1 - a. \tag{5.13}$$

Some equations need comment. Equations 5.1 and 5.2 define disposable income for both classes including interest payments net of inflation losses. Taxes are levied with fixed rates on wages income (tax rate τ_0), property income of workers τ_1, and net income of the corporate class τ_2 (eqs. 5.3 and 5.4).[2] Consumption of each class depends on disposable income, wealth, and the interest rate after taxes (eq. 5.7). Note that consumption depends in two (possibly opposite) ways on the rate of interest: positively through the amount of interest

---

[2] By attaching tax rates to real interest income, we implicitly assume that inflation losses on nominal assets are taxed at the same rate as nominal interest income. Although this is generally not true in practice, it seems a reasonable simplification in the context of the present analysis. Moreover, there is some evidence that positive and negative biases in the tax system more or less offset one another (cf. Tanzi 1984).

income, and negatively through the substitution from consumption towards savings.[3]

Equation 5.8 relates the desired rate of investment i^* to the expected growth of demand (ρ_e^d) [4] and the utilization rate.[5] This second factor serves as a kind of error correction term ensuring that the system always centres at full capacity utilization ($h = 1$). If capacity is fully utilized ($h = 1$) investment is such that capacity grows at the same rate as expected demand. In case of overcapacity ($h < 1$) firms will slow down capacity growth relative to expected demand growth ($i^* < \rho_e^d$) and vice versa in case of a too low capacity. If, in the limit, utilization falls to zero ($h = 0$) desired investment tends to $-\infty$. This is obvious because at zero demand for their products firms want to close down all existing capacity. These observations concern desired investment. Following Harrod actual investment is assumed to adjust only gradually to the desired level. This will be elaborated when dealing with the dynamics. Equation 5.9 relates inflation of the utilization rate h. As in the medium period the rate of unemployment (not explicitly modelled here) varies with the utilization rate, this equation may also be considered as a Phillips curve relation. At normal capacity utilization ($h = 1$) inflation is equal to core inflation p_o. The next two equations define portfolio equilibrium with a conventional money demand function (5.10) and the equilibrium condition (5.11). Finally, equations 5.12 and 5.13 define the wealth of both classes.

In this model the actual rate of investment (i) and real money supply (m) are the essential predetermined state variables which will be explained later when discussing the dy-

---

[3] By relating savings to the real interest rate it is assumed that there is no 'inflation illusion' or other inflationary distortions, for example arising from the tax system or liquidity constraints (due to the 'front-loading' effect of higher nominal rates).

[4] $\rho_e^d = \{(dY/dt)(1/Y)\}_e$, where Y stands for real production or demand in absolute terms.

[5] It is beyond the scope of this book to give a robust microeconomic motivation of investment behaviour in the presence of demand disequilibrium. Instead we have adopted this *ad hoc* relation between investment and demand growth as a short cut. This does not mean that this function has no microeconomic content. See e.g. Kuipers (1981) and van Ewijk (1986) for a discussion of the microeconomic foundation of this proposition.

namics. Technique of production (and thus y_c) as well as the debt variables a and b are assumed to be constant. Throughout the following we shall concentrate on the case of positive net liabilities of the government ($m + b > 0$). The determination of government expenditure g will be explained in the next section.

5.3 Fiscal policy regime

Government behaviour is in reality hampered by bureaucracy as well as political and institutional constraints. It seems therefore appropriate, at least for the present analysis, to conceive budgetary policy as rule-guided rather than to derive it from optimizing discretionary policy. Budgetary policy will thus be represented by certain well-defined regimes formulated in terms of the instruments (expenditure and tax rates) (cf. Blinder and Solow 1973, Tobin and Buiter 1976, Christ 1979) or in terms of specific targets such as the budget deficit (cf. Domar 1957) or the size of public debt (cf. Barro 1979). These regimes have to be distinguished from more dynamic ('feedback') rules for fiscal policy relating taxes or expenditure to the evolution of macroeconomic variables such as unemployment or the ratio of public debt to national income. These rules have been put forward in some theoretical studies (cf. Buiter 1986, van de Klundert and van der Ploeg 1987) and are intended to describe actual government behaviour rather than behaviour prescribed by a certain regime. Moreover, these rules are often used to impose stability of public debt, and are thus less interesting from the present point of view.

In order to examine the consequences of different fiscal policy regimes for the medium-term dynamics, we shall adopt a general representation of fiscal policy that encompasses each of the following regimes which are well known in the literature:

1. fixed expenditure (Blinder and Solow 1973);
2. fixed sum of expenditure and nominal interest payments (Christ 1979);
3. fixed sum of expenditure and interest payments net of taxes (Tobin and Buiter 1976);

4. fixed budget deficit (Domar 1957: ch. II);
5. constant debt ratio (Barro 1979).

In terms of the model developed above these regimes (named after the authors mentioned) may be written as:

1. Blinder and Solow	g	$= \text{constant};$
2. Christ	$g + (r + p)b$	$= \text{constant};$
3. Tobin and Buiter	$g + (1 - \tau_1)(r + p)b$	$= \text{constant};$
4. Domar	$g - T + (r + p)b$	$= \text{constant};$
5. Barro	$g - T + (r + p)b$	$= (\rho + p)(b + m);$

where $T = T_1 + T_2$ denotes total tax receipts. In the regimes (1) to (3) the tax rates are assumed to be fixed as well. Note that $(r + p)$ is the nominal interest rate and $(\rho + p)$ the nominal growth rate of production capacity. We have followed the authors in their interpretation of the government deficit. There exist, however, some intricate difficulties with respect to the measurement of the budget deficit. Some of them are discussed in Appendix 5.1

The first regime is the standard textbook case with exogenous tax rates and government expenditure. As total outlays consist of interest payments in addition to expenditure the budget deficit in this regime varies with debt service. Therefore, Tobin and Buiter (1976) suggested that the sum of expenditure and interest payments might be a better measure of the stance of fiscal policy than expenditure alone. This approach is followed by Christ, but he uses the sum of expenditure and *gross* interest payments while Tobin and Buiter take interest payments net of taxes levied on interest income. It may be noted that both regimes imply some form of internal crowding-out as government expenditure has to be reduced automatically when interest outlays grow.

The last two regimes imply some form of internal crowding-out too as they require government expenditure or taxes to be adjusted in order to realize the target for the budget deficit (regime 4) or debt (regime 5). The case of a constant budget deficit was originally investigated by Domar, who found on the basis of a partial analysis that a positive nominal growth rate $(\rho + p)$ was sufficient for stability of the accumulation of public debt. Note that the 'classical' balanced budget regime can in fact be regarded as a special—zero deficit—case of the Domar regime. According to the final regime, the government adopts a target directly for the size of public debt (as a ratio to capital stock or production capacity). As the outstanding stock of liabilities $(m + b)$ is continuously 'eroded' by real growth (ρ) and inflation (p), the budget should in this regime show a deficit $(= g - T + (r + p)b)$ equal to this sum of real and inflationary erosion $(= (\rho + p)(m + b))$. Although this regime is not strictly advocated by Barro (1979), it is nevertheless called after him because it was the (long-term) starting-point of his famous tax-smoothing rule. Although this rule is more sophisticated and has been developed for a stochastic environment our representation captures some of its basic idea since the debt target is related to production capacity rather than actual production. This means that debt does not have to accommodate all temporary changes in production.

In order to incorporate these regimes into our model we shall adopt the following general formulation of fiscal policy:

$$g = g_0 + \gamma_1 T - \gamma_2 (r + p)b + \gamma_3 p(m + b) + \gamma_4 \rho(m + b);$$

$$0 \leqslant \gamma_1 , \gamma_2 , \gamma_3 , \gamma_4 \leqslant 1. \tag{5.14}$$

This equation relates government expenditure to tax receipts (with coefficient γ_1,) nominal interest outlays (γ_2), inflationary erosion of liabilities (γ_3), and the 'real' erosion due to income growth (γ_4). By choosing proper γ this fiscal policy function can represent all regimes discussed above and, of course, many kinds of hybrid regimes as well. The above summing-up of regimes can be reduced to the parameter settings shown in Table 5.1.

TABLE 5.1 *Budgetary regimes*

Regime	g_0	γ_1	γ_2	γ_3	γ_4
1. Blinder and Solow	g_0	0	0	0	0
2. Christ	g_0	0	1	0	0
3. Tobin and Buiter	g_0	0	$1 - \tau_1$	0	0
4. Domar	g_0	1	1	0	0
5. Barro	0	1	1	1	1

5.4 Static solution

In order to allow for an explicit solution of the model we shall adopt a linear consumption function:

$$C_j = c_j y_j - c_{jr}(1 - \tau_j)r + c_{jz}z_j + c_{jo};$$
$$0 < c_j < 1; \; c_{jr}, \; c_{jz} > 0 \text{ for } j = 1, 2; \qquad (5.7')$$

and the following explicit for money demand:

$$m_d = \mu y/(r + p - r_o). \qquad (5.10')$$

As the debt ratios a and b are constant in the medium period these variables have been omitted in this money demand function. In portfolio equilibrium ($m_d = m$) this equation implies for the interest rate:

$$r = \eta(y/m) + r_o - p, \qquad (5.15)$$

which result has the attractive properties that $\lim_{m \to 0} r = \infty$ and $\lim_{m \to \infty} r = r_o$. The first characteristic implies that the interest rate can in principle be pushed up infinitely by monetary contraction, and the second represents the liquidity trap.

Next consider the following explicit functions for investment and inflation:

$$i^* = \rho_e^d + \vartheta_1(1 - 1/h); \qquad (5.8')$$

$$p = \varphi(h - 1) + p_o. \qquad (5.9')$$

Both functions satisfy the theoretical requirements stated earlier with respect to the implicit functions. With respect to the dynamics it is important to note that whereas inflation has a linear relation to the utilization rate, investment is linked to the inverse of h. This concurs with the Keynesian idea that there is an asymmetry in the dynamics between high and low states of the economy in the sense that for low utilization rates investment falls more rapidly than inflation ($i^* \to -\infty$ but $p \to p_o - \varphi$ for $h \downarrow 0$) while at high utilization rates inflation rises faster than investment. Further, note that the equations for investment and prices together yield a consistent medium-term equilibrium at $h = 1$ characterized by $p = p_o$.

As a first step in the static solution of the model substitute for c and g in the aggregate demand equation. Noticing that a fixed production technique implies that the growth rate of production capacity (ρ) equals the growth of capital stock (i), one obtains the following solution for production:

$$y = \frac{\varepsilon_0 + (\varepsilon_1 - \varepsilon_2)r - \varepsilon_3 pm - (\gamma_2 - \gamma_3)pb + \{1 + \gamma_4(m + b)\}\rho}{1 - \varepsilon_4}, \quad (5.16)$$

where:

$$\varepsilon_0 = c_{1o} + c_{2o} + g_o + c_{1z}(a + b) + c_{2z}(1 - a);$$

$$\varepsilon_1 = c_1(1 - \tau_1)\, b + \{c_1(1 - \tau_1) - c_2(1 - \tau_2)\}a - \gamma_2 b$$
$$\quad + \gamma_1\{\tau_1 b + (\tau_1 - \tau_2)\, a\};$$

$$\varepsilon_2 = c_{1r}(1 - \tau_1) + c_{2r}(1 - \tau_2)\ (> 0);$$

$$\varepsilon_3 = c_1(1 - \tau_1) - \gamma_1\tau_1 + \gamma_3;$$

$$\varepsilon_4 = c_1(1 - \tau_0)(w/y) + c_2(1 - \tau_2)(1 - w/y)$$
$$\quad + \gamma_1\{\tau_0(w/y) + \tau_2(1 - w/y)\}.$$

This equation states that aggregate demand, and thereby production, is positively associated with autonomous expenditure ε_0 and the growth rate ρ. The impact of the interest rate is divided into the distribution effect ε_1 and the substitution effect $- \varepsilon_2$. The substitution effect is unambiguously negative, but the distribution effect (i.e. the sign of ε_1) is uncertain: it depends on the distribution of wealth among the three sectors of the economy and on their respective reactions to the changes in interest income. As normally $a > 0$, a higher interest rate leads to a redistribution of income in favour of workers, which generally causes aggregate consumption to rise. Further, if $b > 0$, the higher interest rate also leads to a redistribution of income from the government to workers. The impact of this income shift on aggregate expenditure depends on the budgetary regime: if government expenditure and taxes are autonomous ($\gamma_2 = 0$), as in the Blinder–Solow regime, aggregate expenditure will rise as workers spend more. However, if $\gamma_2 > 0$ as in all other regimes, the higher consumption of workers may be offset by lower expenditure by the government; hence aggregate expenditure may fall.

Note that if $\varepsilon_1 > 0$ the overall impact of the interest rate is uncertain. If the distributive effects are positive and strong in comparison with the 'substitution' effect ($\varepsilon_1 - \varepsilon_2 > 0$) a higher interest rate might well lead to a larger aggregate demand. From the above aggregate demand function (5.16) it can be established that such a reverse interest effect is more likely if:

1. the debts of the government and the corporate sector are larger;
2. the marginal propensity to consume of workers is higher;
3. the government responds less to changes in debt service.

In analogy with the discussion on the (reverse) Pigou effect (cf. Tobin 1980), one might call this positive interest effect a 'reverse Keynes effect'.

The impact of the rate of inflation (p) on demand is ambiguous too. Inflation leads to a redistribution between the government and the workers through the erosion of real balances. Just as in the case of the interest rate, the overall effect of inflation on demand (dy/dp) depends on these sectors' reactions to the changes in income. If the workers react strongly to the shift in income then the government overall demand will fall (e.g. in the Blinder–Solow regime), and vice versa if the government's reaction is stronger (as in the Barro regime). Because in this model inflation also affects the real interest rate (through the Tobin–Mundell effect and—if $\gamma_2 \neq \gamma_3$— through inflationary biases in the government budget) it will affect demand along this route as well.

As the utilization rate is the central variable in the dynamics of this model (as we will see below) the static part of this model is solved with respect to this variable. Substitution for p and r (eqs. 5.9' and 5.15) in equation 5.16 yields the following result for h in terms of the state variable ρ and m:

$$h = m\frac{\{1 + \gamma_4(m + b)\}\rho + \{c_{1z} - \varepsilon_3(\varphi - p_o)\}m + h_1}{h_2 m + h_3 + \varepsilon_3 \varphi m^2}, \qquad (5.17)$$

where:

$$h_1 = \varepsilon_0 + (\varepsilon_1 - \varepsilon_2)(r_o - p_o + \varphi) + (\gamma_2 - \gamma_3)(\varphi - p_o)b;$$

$$h_2 = (1 - \varepsilon_4)y_c + (\varepsilon_1 - \varepsilon_2)\varphi + (\gamma_2 - \gamma_3)b\varphi;$$

$$h_3 = -(\varepsilon_1 - \varepsilon_2)\mu y_c.$$

This function is too complex to elaborate for all possible outcomes. In order to delimit our analysis to economically sensible results and to reduce it to manageable proportions we shall adopt the following assumptions: First, the utilization rate should, of course, be non-negative ($h > 0$). Secondly, we shall assume $h_1 > 0$ and $h_2 > 0$. This seems reasonable as it implies that aggregate demand should be positive at zero investment (even if $c_{1z} = 0$), and that income has a positive impact on demand. Further, we shall—for the moment—restrict our analysis to the case with a normal interest effect, thus $\varepsilon_1 - \varepsilon_2 < 0$, and therefore $h_3 > 0$. This restriction will be relaxed in section 5.6. Finally, in order to ease our argument we shall neglect the impact of inflationary tax (pm) on aggregate expenditure ($\varepsilon_3 = 0$). Note that given these assumptions both investment and money supply have an unambiguously positive impact on the utilization rate, thus $dh/d\rho > 0$ and $dh/dm > 0$.

5.5 Dynamics

The dynamics of the model is determined by the following differential equations for the growth rate of production capacity and for the stock of money:

$$\dot{\rho} = \vartheta_2(\rho^* - \rho); \tag{5.18}$$

$$\dot{m} = m(v - \rho - p). \tag{5.19}$$

The first equation represents the Harrodian idea that capacity growth only gradually adjusts to the rate which is desirable from the point of view of expected demand growth. The desired growth rate ρ^* is given by the equation for desired investment (5.8′) above. The growth of money supply simply follows from time differentiation of nominal money stock, where v denotes the exogenous growth of nominal money supply in absolute terms.[6]

After substitution for ρ^* and p (eqs. 5.8′ and 5.9′) we obtain the differential equations:

$$\dot{\rho} = \vartheta_2(\rho_e^d - \rho) + \vartheta_2\vartheta_1(1 - 1/h); \tag{5.18′}$$

---

[6] Denote nominal money stock (in absolute terms) by M, capital stock by K and the price level by P, then $m = M/PK$ and time differentiation of m yields $dm/dt = m\{(dM/dt)(1/M) - (dK/dt)(1/K) - (dP/dt)(1/P)\}$, and hence $dm/dt = m(v - \rho - p)$.

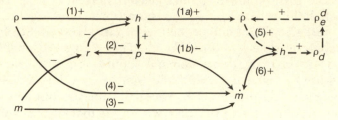

FIG. 5.1 Causal links between money and growth

$$\dot{m} = m\{v - \rho - p_o - \varphi(h - 1)\}; \qquad (5.19')$$

where h is the known function of the state variables ρ and m (5.17). First, notice that the steady state solution of the system ($\dot{m} = \dot{\rho} = 0$) is characterized by full capacity utilization ($h = 1$) and core inflation ($p = p_o$). The equilibrium rate of growth is then determined by the real growth of money, $\rho = v - p_o$. As to the dynamics, Fig. 5.1 illustrates the essential causative links (the scheme is made up for the case with a normal interest effect on demand).

The fundamental destabilizing causation arises from the positive linkage of $\dot{\rho}$ to ρ through the utilization rate (linkage 1a in the scheme). This is the accelerator-like causation from higher investment to larger demand and thereby to a further stimulation of investment. In the present model the effect of utilization h on demand is magnified by the induced rise in inflation p and the consequential fall in the real interest rate r (linkage 2). The monetary sector seems to have a principally stabilizing influence on the system, on the one hand through the negative linkage of $\dot{m}$ to m (3), but more importantly, through the negative feedback of a higher growth rate ρ and higher inflation p on the growth of money stock $\dot{m}$ (linkages 4 and 1b).

The dashed lines give the additional effects arising from the impact of $\dot{\rho}$ on the growth of (expected) demand, and thereby on investment again. On the one hand this may reinforce the destabilizing impact of investment through the positive feedback of higher investment growth on demand growth (linkage 5); on the other hand it also exerts a stabilizing influence as it makes the impact of money on investment stronger (linkage 6).

As a first approximation of the dynamics we shall concentrate on the role of the utilization rate, and thus neglect for the moment the influence of expected demand growth on investment (linkage 5 in the scheme). Therefore equation 5.18′ is reduced to the simple equation:

$$\dot{\rho} = \vartheta(1 - 1/h). \tag{5.18''}$$

A simple Harrodian model

If we follow Harrod and neglect any feedback from the monetary sector, this model can be shown to exhibit the well-known knife-edge dynamics. Therefore let the interest rate and the inflation rate be fixed, and neglect the impact of the real money stock on demand, then production becomes a simple linear function of income and investment:

$$y = \frac{1}{1 - \varepsilon_4} \left[y_o + \{1 + \gamma_4(m + b)\}\rho \right], \tag{5.16'}$$

where y_o now comprises all constant factors. The growth of production ρ_d is equal to the sum of capacity growth ρ and the relative change in the utilization rate:

$$\rho_d = \rho + \dot{h}/h. \tag{5.20}$$

Finally, assuming naïve expectations with respect to demand growth ($\rho_e^d = \rho_d$) and neglecting the budgetary response to real erosion ($\gamma_4 = 0$) we obtain from (5.18″) after some manipulation:

$$\dot{\rho} = \vartheta \frac{\rho + y_o - (1 - \varepsilon_4) y_c}{\rho + y_o}. \tag{5.21}$$

This result entails an unambiguously positive relation between $\dot{\rho}$ and ρ. This means that every rise in growth causes an even larger rise in growth. This is the well-known knife-edge characteristic of the warranted rate of growth in the Harrodian model.[7]

This model hinges, however, on the strong assumptions. In particular, it totally neglects the role of money which may be

---

[7] The warranted growth rate is given by $\rho = (1 - \varepsilon_4)y_c - y_o$ where $\dot{\rho} = 0$. Remembering that ρ is equal to the growth rate of production and that y_c is the reciprocal of the capital coefficient the similarity between this result and Harrod's is obvious.

expected to have a dampening impact on the disequilibrium dynamics. Therefore we shall now consider a more sophisticated model which takes account of the feedback from the monetary sector.

Monetary feedback

The dynamics of the full system with monetary feedback given by equations 5.18″ and 5.19′ above can be discussed with reference to the phase diagram Fig 5.2 which draws the loci for $\dot{\rho} = 0$ and $\dot{m} = 0$ in the (ρ, m) plane. As we are interested in the global dynamics rather than the dynamics close to the equilibrium the (ρ, m) plane is projected on an infinite horizon (cf. Jordan and Smith 1987). As money cannot be negative $(m \geq 0)$ only the positive hemisphere needs to be considered.

Since $h_1, h_2, h_3 > 0$ and $\varepsilon_3 = 0$ we obtain the following characteristics for the $\dot{\rho} = 0$ and $\dot{m} = 0$ loci:

$$\dot{\rho} = 0 \text{ if } \rho = \frac{-c_{1z}m - h_1 + h_2 + h_3/m}{1 + \gamma_4(m + b)} \; ; \tag{5.22}$$

$$\dot{m} = 0 \text{ if } \rho = \frac{\xi h_3 - (\varphi h_1 - \xi h_2) m - \varphi c_{1z}m^2}{h_3 + (h_2 + h_3 + \varphi\gamma_4 b) m + \varphi\gamma_4 m^2} \; ; \tag{5.23}$$

where $\xi = v - p_o + \varphi$. The $\dot{\rho} = 0$ locus proves to be monotonically decreasing in the (ρ, m) plane starting from the upper left corner in the phase diagram $(\rho = \infty, m = 0)$ and reaching the $m = \infty$ horizon at $\rho = -c_{1z}/\gamma_4$ in case of the Barro regime $(\gamma_4 > 0)$ or at $\rho = -\infty$ for the other regimes $(\gamma_4 = 0)$. In the limit the slope of the locus becomes:

$$\lim_{m \to \infty} d\rho/dm = 0, \qquad \text{if } \gamma_4 > 0 \text{ (Barro regime)};$$

$$\lim_{m \to \infty} d\rho/dm = -c_{1z}, \qquad \text{if } \gamma_4 = 0 \text{ (other regimes)}.$$

In the figure the $\dot{\rho} = 0$ locus for the Barro regime would therefore reach the horizon at the m-axis as it becomes parallel to this axis at infinity. For all other regimes (where $\gamma_4 = 0$) the locus reaches the horizon below the m-axis. This latter case is actually shown in the figure.

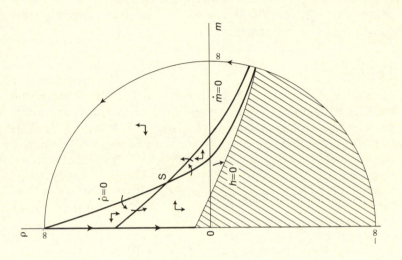

FIG. 5.2 Phase diagram ($\gamma_4 = 0$)

The $\dot{m} = 0$ locus is monotonically decreasing too, except when $\varphi h_1 - \xi h_2 < 0$. In that latter case, which occurs if prices are very sluggish (φ low), it may have an upward-sloping segment for low m. The $\dot{m} = 0$ locus has a finite starting-point for $m = 0$ and tends to $\rho = -c_{1z}/\gamma_4$ if $m \to \infty$ for the Barro regime ($\gamma_4 > 0$). As for the $\dot{\rho} = 0$ locus the slope in the limit tends to zero then, so that it reaches the horizon at the m-axis. For the other regimes (with $\gamma_4 = 0$) the growth rate falls to $-\infty$ at the horizon. The slope in this case becomes:

$$\lim_{m \to \infty} d\rho/dm = -\varphi c_{1z}/(h_2 + \varphi), \quad \text{if } \gamma_4 = 0.$$

Note that this slope is less negative than for the $\dot{\rho} = 0$ condition. This implies that it reaches the horizon at a point above the point where the $\dot{\rho} = 0$ locus meets the horizon, but of course under the m-axis (see the figure).

Given these characteristics of the two loci, and given the fact that the equilibrium condition $h = 1$ always yields one negative and one positive solution for m,[8] it can be concluded that the two loci always cross once in the positive hemisphere. That is, there will always exist a unique steady state solution of the system.

Dynamics

Now consider the dynamics of the system. First notice that there is yet another condition to be taken account of, namely the condition of a non-negative utilization rate ($h \geqslant 0$). This requires (eq. 5.17):

$$\{1 + \gamma_4(m + b)\} \rho + c_{1z}m + h_1 > 0.$$

It can easily be seen that this lower boundary has a negative slope in the (ρ, m) plane too. In the limit, when $m \to \infty$, the slope becomes equal to 0 for $\gamma_4 > 0$ or $-c_{1z}$ if $\gamma_4 = 0$. This implies that this locus reaches the horizon in the same point as the $\dot{\rho} = 0$ locus. Further, it can be established that the $\dot{\rho} = 0$ locus lies above this boundary for any $m > 0$. The economic significance of this lower boundary is that if ρ becomes too low it will depress aggregate demand so much ($h \to 0$) that firms want to close down all existing capacity. Consequentially, the economy will slide into an acute depression with the desired rate of investment falling to $-\infty$, thereby further reducing aggregate demand, etc. In mathematical terms this $h = 0$ boundary is thus a sink which absorbs all phase paths that come too close to it.

On the basis of these global results we can make several inferences. Intersection S of these loci is an equilibrium point which may or may not be stable. If it is stable it can, however, only be *locally* stable; there always exists some area around the $h = 0$ locus from where the system can never return to S. Thus the equilibrium S is at best stable within a certain zone.

---

[8] For $h = 1$ the following quadratic expression for m is obtained: $(c_{1z} + \gamma_4\rho)m^2 + \{h_1 - h_2 + (1 + \gamma_4b)\rho\}m - h_3 = 0$. Excluding a negative steady state growth rate (hence $\rho \geqslant 0$) this equation always yields one positive and one negative solution for m in case of a normal interest effect on expenditure ($h_3 > 0$).

This means that after small shocks the system will return to S, but that large disturbances may push the system beyond the critical 'stable' zone, so that the system gets unbalanced for ever. As it can further be shown that the point (∞, 0) does not represent a stable solution it can be concluded that the system cannot move upward for ever (see Appendix 5.2). This implies that any path outside the stable zone around S must sooner or later come into the attraction zone of the $h = 0$ locus.

In comparison with the simple Harrodian model these re-sults make clear that the introduction of monetary feedback has a stabilizing impact on the Harrodian model; a stable equilibrium (the warranted rate of growth) may now exist, but only within certain boundaries. Although the monetary feedback appears to provide a sufficient check in an upward direction, there still always exists some zone along the $h = 0$ boundary where the system gets unstable; starting from a point in this zone the system will fall into a cumulative process of declining demand and falling investment. These global dynamics correspond remarkably well to Leijonhuf-vud's (1981) description on the 'corridor' characteristic which in his view is typical of Keynesian dynamics.

Hopf bifurcation

So far we have taken for granted that the solution S can be locally stable. We shall now look somewhat more closely at the stability of equilibrium point S. Therefore consider the linearization of the differential equations 5.18″ and 5.19′ evaluated in the steady state (m_s, ρ_s):

$$\begin{bmatrix} \dot{m} \\ \dot{\rho} \end{bmatrix} = \begin{bmatrix} -m\varphi dh/dm & -m(1+ \varphi dh/d\rho) \\ \vartheta dh/dm & \vartheta dh/d\rho \end{bmatrix} \begin{bmatrix} m - m_s \\ \rho - \rho_s \end{bmatrix} \qquad (5.24)$$

From this system we obtain the following (Routh–Hurwitz) conditions for stability:

$$\mathrm{Tr}(J) = \vartheta dh/d\rho - m\varphi dh/dm < 0;$$

$$\mathrm{Det}(J) = m\vartheta dh/dm > 0; \qquad (5.25)$$

where $\mathrm{Tr}(J)$ and $\mathrm{Det}(J)$ denote the trace and the determinant of the (Jacobian) matrix of partial derivatives in equation 5.24. Since we have already established that $\mathrm{d}h/\mathrm{d}m > 0$ it can be seen that the first condition $\mathrm{Tr}(J) < 0$ is decisive to stability. Unfortunately this condition yields no neat algebraic solution. None the less, it is evident that the reaction speed of investment ϑ is a crucial determinant of the stability of S. This is not really surprising, as this 'acceleration' factor is known to be the principal factor in the instability of Keynesian business cycle models. This result is straightforward as h, and thus the equilibrium solution, is independent of ϑ. From the first condition we can therefore derive the critical value of this parameter beyond which the system becomes unstable. Denoting this critical value (or bifurcation point) by $\vartheta_{\max}$ we find:

$$\vartheta_{\max} = \varphi m \, \frac{\mathrm{d}h/\mathrm{d}m}{\mathrm{d}h/\mathrm{d}\rho} . \tag{5.26}$$

As long as ϑ does not exceed $\vartheta_{\max}$ the equilibrium is (locally) stable, but for any $\vartheta > \vartheta_{\max}$ it is unstable. In other words, whenever prices show some flexibility ($\varphi > 0$) the equilibrium may be stable if ϑ is sufficiently low; that is, if investment does not react too strongly to deviations in the utilization rate.

Further characteristics of equilibrium point S can be established from Fig. 5.3. This figure shows the Routh–Hurwitz conditions in relation to ϑ. This figure brings out that S is a stable node for low values of ϑ; as ϑ becomes larger (but still $< \vartheta_{\max}$) the equilibrium becomes a stable spiral. If ϑ rises above $\vartheta_{\max}$ the solution S becomes an unstable spiral and eventually an unstable node. The critical case with $\vartheta = \vartheta_{\max}$ may represent a centre or spiral. If it is a spiral—as it is presumably in our model—the system is characterized by a 'Hopf bifurcation'. In that case a limit cycle may be generated around the equilibrium point S when ϑ is moved away from its critical value. The radius of this limit cycle varies with ϑ. Because of the complexity of the system we shall not pursue a full analytical characterization of this critical point, but instead proceed with some numerical simulations for plausible parameters of the model.

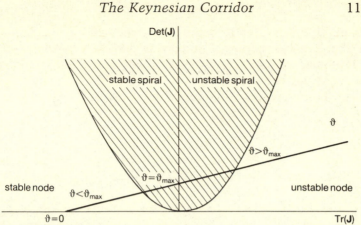

FIG. 5.3 Characteristics of equilibrium S

Unstable limit cycle

The above inferences regarding the characteristics of S are corroborated by Fig. 5.4 which shows the simulation of the adjustment trajectories from a given starting-point (0.05, 0.5) for different values of ϑ (0.01; 0.1; 0.2). For the parameters on which these simulations are based the equilibrium S is characterized by: [9]

$$\rho = 5\%, m = 0.18, r = 3.9\%, h = 1, p = 2\%.$$

As in this case the critical value is given by $\vartheta_{max} = 0.151$ the phase paths for $\vartheta = 0.01$ and $\vartheta = 0.1$ are stable (a node and a spiral respectively) while the phase path for $\vartheta = 0.2$ produces an unstable process, which eventually collapses on to the $h = 0$ boundary.

Further this numerical example can be shown to produce an unstable limit cycle around S when $\vartheta < \vartheta_{max}$. This cycle is unstable because whenever the system starts from a point inside this cycle it will eventually tend towards the equilibrium point S, but when it starts outside the cycle the trajectory will recede from the cycle for ever. The size of this cycle varies with ϑ. This implies that the system becomes more stable. i.e. the limit cycle becomes wider, as the reaction speed of investment is less. This is illustrated by Fig 5.5, which shows the limit cycles for three different values of ϑ

[9] In the next chapter we shall give a motivation for these parameter values.

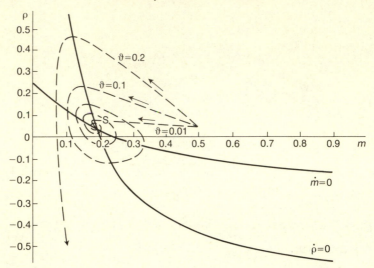

Note: This figure is based on the following numerical values: $r_0 = 0.02$; $p_0 = 0.02$; $g/y_c = 0.22$; $\tau_0 = \tau_1 = \tau_2 = 0.2$; $b/y_c = 0.5$; $a = 0.5$; $c_1 = 0.9$; $c_2 = 0.6$; $c_{1r} = -1$; $c_{2r} = -1$; $c_{1z} = 0.05$; $c_{2z} = 0.05$; $c_{1o} = 0.055$; $c_{2o} = -0.01$; $\mu = 0.1$; $\varphi = 0.2$; $\nu = 0.07$; $w = 0.3$; $y_c = 0.38$; $\gamma_1, \gamma_2, \gamma_3, \gamma_4, = 0$ The simulations are based on an approximation of the differential system by the Runge–Kutta method (cf. Cohen 1973).

FIG. 5.4 Adjustment trajectories for ϑ

close to ϑ_{max} (0.140; 0.145; 0.150). For $\vartheta > \vartheta_{max}$ the limit cycle vanishes completely; in that case S thus becomes unstable globally as well as locally. In terms of bifurcation theory these characteristics corroborate the existence of a subcritical Hopf bifurcation (Gabisch and Lorenz 1989). It is evident that for ϑ close to the critical value, although the equilibrium S is still stable locally, the system can hardly be considered to be stable as even a small displacement from S is sufficient to push the system beyond the limit cycle and lead it away from S for ever.

5.6 Some extensions

So far we have assumed a normal interest effect on demand ($\varepsilon_1 - \varepsilon_2 < 0$) and neglected the role of expectations on demand growth. These restrictions will be relaxed in this section.

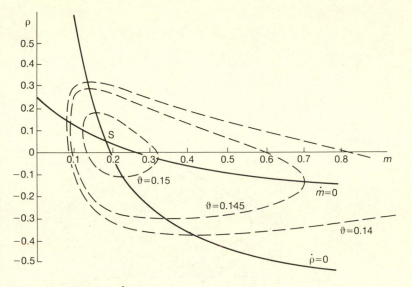

Note: See Fig. 5.4 above

FIG.5.5 Limit cycles for $\vartheta = 0.14;\ 0.145;\ 0.15$

Reverse interest effect

Fig. 5.6 gives a phase diagram for the case with a reverse interest effect $\varepsilon_1 - \varepsilon_2 > 0$. As the interest effect becomes dominant for low m (when the interest rate is high) the $\dot{\rho} = 0$ locus approximates the y-axis now at $-\infty$. This is because the positive effect of the high interest rate on consumption must be compensated by the negative effect of a low utilization rate on consumption and investment. For a high m the impact of money on the interest rate becomes very small (the liquidity trap) so that the wealth effect of money ($c_{1z} > 0$) becomes dominant, ensuring a positive association between money and demand again. As a result the $\dot{\rho} = 0$ locus will slope downward again for a large m; eventually its shape will become similar to that of the locus in the original case with a normal interest effect.

Because of this hump-shaped $\dot{\rho} = 0$ locus it can be seen that the system has either two solutions or no solution at all in the positive hemisphere. Fig. 5.6 illustrates the case with two

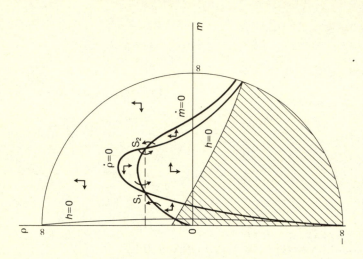

FIG. 5.6 Reverse interest effect

solutions (S1 and S2). Both solutions, of course, entail the same equilibrium for the growth rate ($\rho = v - p_0$), but different solutions for the stock of money. The figure brings out that only one of these solutions may be stable (S2); the other, lower, solution (S1) is evidently a saddle-point, and thus unstable. Therefore we can conclude that if S2 is locally stable again, some zone must exist around this solution beyond which the system is unstable. If S2 is not stable, there is no stable finite solution at all.

In case of a reversed interest effect $h_3 < 0$ the denominator of equation 5.17 for the utilization rate is no longer unambiguously positive. One should therefore also take account of the condition of a positive denominator, which implies that there is a lower boundary for money stock ($m > - h_3/h_2$). If the system

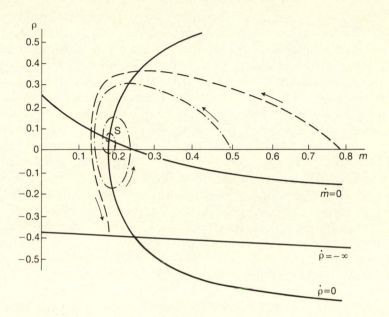

FIG. 5.7 Demand expectations ($\vartheta_2 = 0.5$)

approaches this boundary the utilization rate becomes infinitely high ($h \to \infty$), and because at a high h prices adjust faster than investment it can be seen that $\dot{\rho}/\dot{m} \to 0$. This means that the economy comes into an upward spiral of ever increasing demand and inflation. Hence we can conclude, that, in contrast with the case of a normal interest effect, the system may be unstable in an upward as well as a downward direction.

Demand expectations

So far we have neglected the impact of demand expectations on investment. Fig. 5.7 gives the phase diagram for the same numerical example on the basis of the more general investment function (5.8′) with partial adjustment of investment to expected demand growth ($\vartheta_2 = 0.5$). For simplicity it is

assumed that entrepreneurs have naïve expectations with respect to demand growth ($\rho_e^d = \rho_d$). Although the steady state
position is not changed (because $\rho_e^d = \rho_d = \rho$ in equilibrium),
this figure brings out some remarkable changes with regard
to the dynamics outside the equilibrium position. In the first
place $\dot{\rho} = 0$ locus is no longer a monotonically decreasing
curve. Instead it bends forward in the region above the
$\dot{m} = 0$ locus. This is due to the positive impact of $\dot{m}$ on
demand growth and thereby on desired investment. A second
remarkable difference is the appearance of a new lower
boundary where $\dot{\rho} \rightarrow -\infty$. This boundary arises from the condition that the secondary effect of demand growth on $\dot{\rho}$ should
not exceed the primary effect. If the system approaches this
boundary it slips into a process of ever falling demand, deteriorating expectations on demand, and declining investment.
This new lower boundary can be shown to be more restrictive
than the $h = 0$ condition; that is, it lies above the $h = 0$ locus
for all $m > 0$ (see Appendix 5.3).

Apart from these differences, the dynamics exhibit basically
the same characteristics. At the given parameter values the
equilibrium is stable, so that there exists a critical zone
around this equilibrium. The figure shows two trajectories,
one starting within the critical zone at ($\rho = 0$; $m = 0.5$) and the
other starting outside it at ($\rho = 0$; $m = 0.8$).

5.7 Fiscal policy and stability

In order to assess the impact of various (policy) variables on
the stability of the system Table 5.2 gives the partial effects
of these variables on ϑ_{max} (eq. 5.26). As we have established
above, this parameter has a clear-cut impact on stability
while it does not change the equilibrium position. If a variable has a positive effect on this critical value, ϑ_{max}, it can be
concluded to have a stabilizing impact on the system. A
negative effect corresponds to a destabilizing impact. The
higher ϑ_{max} is, the smaller is the chance that the actual ϑ
exceeds this critical value and that the system is unstable.
Further, we have seen that the radius of the limit cycle, i.e.

the width of the corridor, which emerges for $\vartheta > \vartheta_{max}$ increases with the gap between ϑ and ϑ_{max}. In the table all effects are given in relation to the reference case given in Fig. 5.5 above.

TABLE 5.2 *Partial effects on ϑ_{max}*

g_0	0.076
γ_1	-0.004
γ_2	0.021
γ_3	-0.0002
γ_4	-0.028
τ_0	-0.055
τ_1	-0.039
τ_2	-0.145
μ	0.015
v	0.198
φ	0.754
a	-0.025
c_1	-0.008
c_2	0.055
c_{1r}	-0.083
c_{2r}	-0.083
c_{1z}	-0.164
c_{2z}	-0.099
c_{10}	0.199
c_{20}	0.199
r_0	-0.266
p_0	0.073
w	0.015
b	-0.025

Note: All effects are measured with reference to the steady state given in Fig. 5.5 above. The effect of the γ coefficients has been corrected for the impact effect on government expenditure. One should be careful to compare the absolute effects because an equal change in each variable may produce quite different impacts in absolute amounts.

A general conclusion that emerges from these results is that all factors raising autonomous expenditure improve the stability of the system. Further, these results corroborate our earlier inference that the system becomes more stable as the monetary feedback is stronger; the sensitivity of the interest rate to money and income (μ) as well as the interest effects on consumption (c_{1r}, c_{2r}) and the degree of price flexibility (φ) have significant positive effects on ϑ_{max}. In addition, the system becomes more stable as money growth (v) is faster, core inflation (p_o) higher, and the autonomous interest rate (r_o) lower. Also a larger corporate debt tends to destabilize the system; this is because the distribution effect arising from corporate debt weakens the negative feedback of the interest rate on expenditure.

With regard to fiscal policy these results indicate that the system becomes more stable as autonomous government expenditure is higher and taxes are lower. The Christ regime, with $\gamma_2 = 1$ and the other γ coefficients equal to zero, clearly emerges as the best policy regime to choose for the medium period. This conclusion proves to be robust for different parameter sets in the neighbourhood of our reference set. This is not really surprising as the $\gamma_1, \gamma_3,$ and γ_4 parameters relate expenditure to procyclical variables (tax receipts, inflation erosion, and real erosion of liabilities) whereas γ_2 attaches expenditure to nominal interest outlays, which vary countercyclically.

This is corroborated by Table 5.3 which gives ϑ_{max} for each of the regimes considered. This table brings out that the Christ regime performs best, closely followed by the Tobin–Buiter regime. The Barro regime, aiming at a constant debt ratio, is apparently the most procyclical; it yields the lowest ϑ_{max}.

TABLE 5.3 *Stability of budgetary regimes (more stable as ϑ_{max} is higher)*

Blinder–Solow	0.151
Christ	0.172
Tobin–Buiter	0.168
Domar	0.149
Barro	0.127

Note: See Table 5.2 above.

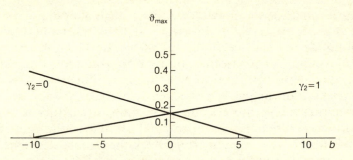

FIG. 5.8 Public debt and stability

Finally, consider the impact of public debt on the system's stability. It is obvious that this impact is closely connected with the policy regime, in particular with the reaction coefficient with respect to interest outlays (γ_2). As a larger government debt entails a larger interest income of the private sector, it makes consumption more procyclical (because the interest rate is a procyclical variable). Therefore, if γ_2 is small, an increase in debt has a destabilizing impact on the system. However, when γ_2 is high, the procyclical behaviour of consumption will be compensated by a counter-cyclical movement of government expenditure. In that case an increase in debt may even be stabilizing from a medium-period perspective. This is illustrated in Fig. 5.8 which gives ϑ_{max} in relation to government debt for $\gamma_2 = 0$ (as in the Blinder–Solow regime) and $\gamma_2 = 1$ (as in most other regimes). If $\gamma_2 = 0$, the maximum ϑ decreases as b goes up. At $b = 6.1$ it even becomes zero, which implies that for any debt above this critical value no steady state is feasible whatever the adjustment speed of investment ϑ. If $\gamma_2 = 1$ the maximum for ϑ proves to rise with b. In this case b should not be too low ($b > -10$) for a stable solution to be feasible.

5.8 Conclusion

The medium-period dynamics explored in this chapter are governed by the antagonism between the basically unstable multiplier-accelerator mechanism and the stabilizing feed-back of the monetary sector. On the basis of a simple non-linear model it was shown that this antagonism may give rise to a 'corridor' as was put forward by Leijonhufvud (1981). In formal terms the 'corridor' manifests ifself as an unstable limit cycle. Starting from a point within this cycle the system recedes to its equilibrium position, but whenever it is dis-placed out of the cycle it will never return.

Another interesting feature of the global dynamics is that it exhibits a fundamental asymmetry. Whereas the monetary feedback provides an effective check on upward movements, it cannot prevent the system from falling into a downward trap of insufficient demand and falling investment. At first sight this concurs with the well-known, but less well-founded, Keynesian idea that the economy is more stable for upward shocks than in case of downward disturbances. But our analysis shows that not the direction of the displacement is conclusive but rather its size; also an upward shock may destabilize the system and eventually cause a depression.

The idea of corridor stability has interesting implications for the role of economic policy. It suggests that as long as shocks are not too large and the economy remains within the corridor, the medium-period dynamics is basically self-correcting, so that there is no need for active policy (fine tuning). However, in the event of large displacements discre-tionary policy is necessary to bring the economy back into the stable zone.

From a policy point of view it is important to note that the width of the corridor can be influenced by fiscal and mon-etary policy. It is evident that the risk of instability is smaller as the corridor becomes wider. Our analysis, which concen-trates on fiscal rather than monetary policy, brings out that a proper choice of the policy regime may significantly con-tribute to the system's stability. In general, stability is im-proved as fiscal policy is more responsive to changes in debt service (γ_2 high), and less to change in tax receipts, and the inflationary and real erosion of government liabilities. There-fore the regimes with target for debt (Barro) and—to a lesser degree—expenditure (Blinder–Solow) prove to be less stable than other regimes. The Christ regime with a target for total outlays (expenditure and interest payments) emerges as the most stable regime.

The impact of public debt on the system's dynamics depends on the fiscal policy regime. If the regime entails a low responsiveness to changes in debt service the system becomes less stable as debt is larger. Beyond some critical value the system proves to be unstable however low the accelerator factor of investment, and however high the flexibility of prices. This indicates that, although public debt is a slow variable in comparison to the demand variables that dominate medium-period dynamics, it may have an important impact in the long period. Gradual growth of public debt may sooner or later affect the stability of the system, and turn it from a (locally) stable system into an unstable system; that is, it may give rise to a 'catastrophe'.

In the next chapter we shall examine the dynamics of growth and asset accumulation from a long-term point of view. In contrast with the present chapter, the analysis will then concentrate on the dynamics of income distribution and the accumulation of public and corporate debt.

Appendix 5.1 Measurement of the government budget deficit

In our discussion of the alternative budgetary regimes in section 5.3 we followed the authors in their interpretation of the government budget constraint. There exist, however, significant conceptual difficulties with respect to the measurement of the budget deficit, especially with respect to the measurement of the real burden of debt. In its conventional definition the deficit on a cash basis is given by:

$$\text{deficit} = g - (T_1 + T_2) + (r + p)b.$$

If we define government income as the sum of taxes and inflation tax, hence $y_g = T_1 + T_2 + pm$, it can be seen that this deficit is not equal to the excess of expenditure g over income y_g, nor to the change in government liabilities ($\dot{m} + \dot{b}$):

$$g - y_g = \text{deficit} - pm;$$

$$(\dot{b} + \dot{m}) = \text{deficit} - (\rho + p)(b + m).$$

The difference between the deficit and $(g - y_g)$ consists of the inflation tax on money. The difference from the change in the ratio of government liabilities $(\dot{m} + \dot{b})$ given by the government budget constraint (GBC) consists of the sum of inflationary erosion and the 'real' erosion of liabilities.

These results indicate that for a proper account of the burden of debt one should take nominal interest outlays net of devaluation of outstanding liabilities through inflation. In much IS/LM modelling of the GBC this problem is avoided as the price level is assumed to be fixed anyway (cf. Tobin and Buiter 1976 and Christ 1978, 1979). In a more complex analysis one cannot, however, neglect this problem.

Nevertheless, from a practical point of view, when modelling actual government behaviour it may be doubted whether the real or the nominal burden of debt offers a more relevant measure of the burden of debt. Politicians often seem to be more impressed by the nominal interest payments than by the less apparent benefits of devaluation of current liabilities (public debt and base money) through inflation. This is further stimulated by the conventional 'book-keeping' methods used for accounting and budgeting. Especially in times of fiscal restraint the use of cash accounting methods, sometimes even in the form of explicit cash limits (cf. Rau 1985), favours a nominal bias in the budgetary regime.

Besides changes in the value of money, changes in the market value of public debt may also affect the real burden of debt. When the general level of interest rates falls or adverse shifts occur in portfolio preferences towards public debt, the market value of outstanding public debt goes up, thereby raising the true burden for the government. This leads to very intricate difficulties with respect to the discount rates and time-horizons of the public and the government.[10] In the present analysis we neglect these difficulties by assuming that all government debt has a fixed nominal value and a variable interest rate. Since it is further assumed that public debt and private sector debt are perfect substitutes, we may neglect portfolio shifts as well; there is only one homogeneous sort of debt and one interest rate.

Appendix 5.2 Stability of the point $(\infty, 0)$

In order to know if any unstable path sooner or later tends to the lower boundary at $h = 0$, or if it can also move upwards for ever, we

---

[10] See Buiter (1983) and Tanzi, Blejer, and Teijeiro (1987) for comprehensive accounts of these problems.

have to establish whether the point $(\infty, 0)$ is stable or not. This can be investigated by expressing the model in polar coordinates around the origin which gives the following equation for the radius v:

$$v . \dot{v} = \rho\vartheta(1 - 1/h) + m^2\{v - \rho - p_o - \varphi(h - 1)\}.$$

After substitution for h and looking at the largest terms only it can be seen that for a sufficiently large radius v (and thus large m and ρ) the sign of $\dot{v}$ is determined by the sign of the term $-\varphi\gamma_4 m^3\rho/h_3$ (or $-\varphi m^2(\rho + h_1 m)/h_3$ if $\gamma_4 = 0$). Since $h_1, h_3 > 0$ this implies that there exists a finite circle around the origin where the sign of $\dot{v}$ is negative for any positive ρ and m ; that is, at a sufficiently wide circle around the origin every path in the first quadrant crosses this circle bending towards the origin.

Appendix 5.3 Demand expectations

This appendix establishes the position of the lower boundary in the model with demand expectations (section 5.6). Since:

$$\rho_d = \rho + \dot{h}/h = \rho + (dh/d\rho) (1/h)\dot{\rho} + (dh/dm)(1/h)\dot{m},$$

we find from (5.18') that:

$$\dot{\rho} = \vartheta_2\{(dh/d\rho)(1/h)\dot{\rho} + (dh/dm)(1/h)\dot{m}\} + \vartheta_1\vartheta_2(1 - 1/h).$$

Now requiring that the secondary effect $\vartheta_2(dh/d\rho) (1/h) < 1$ we obtain the condition:

$$\rho > \vartheta_2 - (h_1 m + h_2)/\{1 + \gamma_4(m + b)\},$$

whereas the condition for $h > 0$ was

$$\rho > - (h_1 m + h_2)/\{1 + \gamma_4(m + b)\}.$$

For any $\vartheta_2 > 0$ this boundary thus lies above the $h = 0$ locus for all $m > 0$.

6

Long-Period Dynamics of Growth and Debt

6.1 Introduction

Despite these critical results with respect to medium-period stability, income–expenditure equilibrium with full capacity utilization is taken as the starting-point of the long-period analysis. This is necessary to concentrate on the dynamics of growth and asset accumulation, in particular the role of the government budget constraint in the long-term dynamics of the economy. As in the foregoing chapter we shall assess the stability of the system for different regimes of fiscal policy.

Since the seminal papers of Christ (1968) and Blinder and Solow (1973) many studies have been published on the dynamics of growing public debt and interest payments. One of the main conclusions common to most of these studies is the basically unstable nature of public debt when the deficit is financed by issuing interest-bearing debt. The essential destabilizing element in this process is the interest payment on outstanding debt which has to be financed too, thereby further increasing the debt and so on. For the process to be stable it is required that other factors sufficiently neutralize this destabilizing tendency. In most models this is accomplished only if the income and wealth effects of the growing public debt on private expenditure and thereby on national income are so strong that the resulting increase in tax revenue exceeds the rise in interest payments. Since the income effect of interest paid on public debt will never be sufficient to produce a one-for-one increase in tax receipts, stability in these models proves to hinge on the strength of the wealth effect of the growing public debt.

A common feature of the studies mentioned above is their focus on the short- or medium-term dynamics of the government budget. In most cases they are restricted to a basically stationary IS/LM framework, in which autonomous expenditure, labour supply, and often even the capital stock[1] are taken as fixed. Although there may often be good reasons to avoid the 'complex issues of disequilibrium growth theory' (Rau 1985: 214), we believe that for assessment of the stability of public debt it is indispensable to take account of the interrelationship between the accumulation of public debt and the real growth of the economy. Confining the analysis to the (arbitrary) zero growth situation is in our view too restrictive; it obscures the basic factor determining stability, namely the growth rate of income. It is well known that if growth is sufficiently high any economy can 'grow out' of its debt without great difficulties. But little is known on how high the growth has to be and what are the interrelationships between growth and debt.

In this chapter we shall develop a long-period model of disequilibrium growth. The analysis starts from the basic model given in the foregoing chapter. Section 6.2 completes this model for the long period and introduces a macroeconomic investment function based on the microeconomic analysis of the growth of the corporate firm in Chapters 3 and 4. Section 6.3 analyses the long-term dynamics of public debt and income distribution for a reduced (two-dimensional) model concentrating on the accumulation of public debt and income distribution, while section 6.4 discusses the fully dynamic model including the interaction between investment and corporate debt.

6.2 The long-period model

The set-up of the long-period model follows that of the medium-period model considered in the foregoing chapter. The same relations are adopted for income, wealth, and consumption (eqs. 5.1–5.4, 5.6–5.7, and 5.10–5.13); budgetary policy is modelled similarly (eq. 5.14). The main differences concern the assumption of full capacity utilization adopted in this

---

[1] Cf. Blinder and Solow (1973) in their first model, Turnovsky (1976), Christ (1978, 1979), Calvo (1985), Rau (1985).

chapter and the incorporation of the dynamics implied by the budget constraints of the government sector and the corporate sector.

As our discussion of the medium-period dynamics has raised serious doubts with regard to the 'automatic' equilibrium-restoring mechanisms, we shall assume that medium-term equilibrium is achieved by discretionary monetary policy which ensures that money supply is always sufficient to generate full capacity utilization.[2]

The long-period model may then be completed as follows. In the absence of demand problems the behaviour of firms will be modelled in line with the microeconomic analysis of Chapters 3 and 4, thus concentrating on the financial constraints. In the present macroeconomic model shareholders and managers are, however, lumped together in the corporate class. This class owns all capital stock and reinvests its savings in the corporate sector in the form of equity. For convenience, workers are supposed to own no shares; they invest their savings in public or corporate debt (with a variable interest rate). This implies that in the present model internal savings of the corporate sector are equal to total sector income less consumption ($y_2 - C_2$). The budget constraint for the corporate sector (hereafter abbreviated as CBC) is therefore similar to that of the fully equity-rationed firm, except that the pay-out of profits is now replaced by consumption of capitalists (C_2) thus:

$$\dot{a} = -y_2 + i + C_2 - i.a, \qquad (6.1)$$

where y_2 represents disposable corporate income, defined as $y_2 = y - w - ar - T_2$ (eq. 5.2). For simplicity we shall neglect the choice of technique so that production as a ratio to capital stock (y) can be treated as given. This reduces the firm's decision to the simultaneous investment-financing decision. Given the above budget constraint the desired amount of

[2] As an alternative, fiscal policy can also be assumed to take care of income–expenditure. In that case government expenditure, or taxes, should always be such that the budget deficit precisely offsets the excess of savings over investment by the private sector at the prevailing rate of interest. In fact, this case is identical to the balanced current-account regime to be considered in the next chapter, and will therefore be left out of consideration here.

investment can be split up into two components, one representing the rate of investment consistent with the given debt ratio ($\dot{a} = 0$), and the other following from the desired change in the debt ratio when the desired debt ratio (a^*) deviates from the actual ratio (a), thus:

$$i^* = \frac{1}{1-a}\{(y_2 - C_2) + \Omega(a^* - a)\}; \quad \Omega > 0; \; a, a^* < 1. \quad (6.2)$$

One may notice the similarity between this function and Kalecki's function based on his 'principle of increasing risk' (see section 3.2) which also included an internal savings component and a 'shift' variable representing changes in the marginal rate of return schedule. As regards the desired debt ratio our analysis of the growth of the firm yielded the following determinants:

1. the profit rate and the interest rate;
2. the state of risk (the variance of net returns);
3. the time preference and risk aversion of shareholders;
4. the preferences towards growth and risk of managers;
5. the discretionary power of managers *vis-à-vis* shareholders.

The factors (2)–(5) may be assumed to be exogenous to the problems considered in this chapter, and will therefore be captured in the parameter ζ. In that case the desired rate of indebtedness can be written as a function of π, r, and this parameter ζ:

$$a^* = a^*(\pi, r, \zeta); \quad a^* < 1. \quad (6.3)$$

Note that the first (internal savings) term in the investment function (6.2) implies that the interest rate may have a *positive* influence on internal savings, and thereby on investment as well, when the firm is a net creditor. However, besides this income effect the interest rate also has a substitution effect on investment as it will probably change the desired debt ratio a^* in the second term. Also the profit rate has a direct impact on investment through internal savings and an indirect effect via the desired debt ratio. Whether this indirect effect is positive or negative is ambiguous. It may be noted that in the basic model considered in Chapter 3 the impact happened to be just zero. This was, however, a quite specific model. In our numerical exercises below we assume a positive impact of the profit rate on a^*, which supposes that a higher profit rate induces entrepreneurs to accept a larger indebtedness.

For the purpose of our analysis the dynamics of prices and wages may be conceived in the following simple fashion. As monetary policy ensures full capacity utilization we assume that inflation is given by core inflation p_o (as in Chapter 5 at $h = 1$), thus:

$$p = p_o. \qquad (6.4)$$

As inflation is kept in check by monetary policy changes in money wages cannot be (fully) passed on in prices. Changes in wages are therefore not neutral and do affect the real wages. In this it is therefore natural to assume that the evolution of real wages depends on labour-market disequilibrium, in a general form:

$$\dot{w} = f(\dot{u}, u - u_0); \qquad f(0, 0) = 0; f_1, f_2 \leqslant 0; \qquad (6.5)$$

where u = unemployment rate; u_0 is the unemployment rate compatible with a constant income distribution.[3]

As mentioned, the interest rate is manipulated by monetary policy in order to ensure demand equilibrium. This is achieved by open-market policy. Although the total amount of government liabilities $(m + b)$ is given at any moment, it is assumed that the monetary authority (i.e. the government) can instantaneously vary the mix of money and debt. The sum of money and debt $(m + b)$ only changes as a result of the government budget deficit.[4] This is a consistent modell-

---

[3] This rate is neither the natural rate of unemployment nor the Keynesian equivalent, the NAIRU (Non Acceleration Inflation Rate of Unemployment), but the unemployment rate which is compatible with a constant distribution of income, i.e. constant shares of wages and profits, or, in 'new speak' economics, the 'CIDRU' (Constant Income Distribution Rate of Unemployment).

[4] As monetary policy must maintain equilibrium between demand and supply, the mix of debt and money is an endogenous variable in the present model unlike in most (medium-term) analyses of the government budget constraint which generally assume a specific rule for the money-debt mix.

ing of the relation between the government budget constraint and monetary policy within the context of our analysis.

Now the static part of the model is completed. For momentary equilibrium the stocks of corporate debt (a) and government liabilities ($m + b$) as well as the unemployment rate (u) and wages (w) are given. Given these four state variables monetary policy manipulates the money supply and the interest rate in such a manner that aggregate demand equals the given production capacity.

The dynamics of the state variables is determined by the budget constraint for the corporate sector (eq. 6.1) and labour-market disequilibrium (eq. 6.5). In addition we have to take account of the government constraint (GBC) and the evolution of the rate of unemployment. Let z represent total government liabilities ($= m + b$), so that the GBC reduces to:

$$\dot{z} = g - T_1 - T_2 + rb - pm - \rho z, \tag{6.6}$$

stating that the change in government liabilities is determined by the excess of spending on consumption g and interest payments rb over tax receipts $T_1 + T_2$, inflationary taxes on money pm, and the 'real' erosion of liabilities through growth of production ρz. The change in unemployment $\dot{u}$ is found by differentiation of u with respect to time:

$$\dot{u} = (1 - u)(n - \rho); \quad 0 < u < 1; \tag{6.7}$$

where n stands for the growth of labour supply (in efficiency units) and ρ for the growth rate of production, which is equal to the growth of capital stock (i) because of the fixed technique of production. Together these equations yield a four-dimensional dynamic system. It needs little argument that this is hardly tractable at the analytical level. Therefore, before presenting some numerical experiments for this model, we shall as a first approximation consider a reduced, two-dimensional, version of it.

6.3 A reduced model

The dimensionality of the model can be reduced without changing the essence of it by concentrating on the dynamics of the two crucial state variables: income distribution (represented by the profit rate π) and government liabilities (z). For the moment we assume therefore that firms hold on to a given level of corporate debt (a = constant). Further, the unemployment rate can be eliminated as a state variable by choosing a simpler version of the labour-market dynamics, namely:

$$\dot{\pi} = \vartheta_\pi(n - \rho); \quad \vartheta_\pi > 0. \tag{6.5a}$$

According to this function the profit rate falls when the labour market tightens, and rises when unemployment increases. This equation implies that in equilibrium the rate of unemployment is constant. At what level this is achieved is not determined by the model; it is fully state dependent. In economic terms this may be interpreted as a case of 'full hysteresis'. There is no mechanism in the model that restores unemployment to some natural or NAIRU rate.

This function for $\dot{\pi}$ together with the GBC (eq. 6.6) determines the dynamics of this reduced model. In order to allow for an explicit solution we adopt a linear modelling of the consumption function (see equation 5.20 in the foregoing chapter), and the following explicit functions for the interest rate and the desired rate of indebtedness a^*. These functions are modelled in such a manner that they satisfy the theoretical requirements, not only near equilibrium but also for extreme positions. This is necessary because we are interested not only in the (local) dynamics near the equilibrium solution but also in the global dynamics when the economy moves further away from its equilibrium. For the interest rate we adopt the function:[5]

$$r = r_o + \mu_1 \exp(\mu_2 y/m + \mu_3 b) - p; \quad r_o, \mu_1, \mu_2, \mu_3 > 0 \tag{6.8}$$

which has the important features that the interest rate can be pushed up infinitely by reducing money supply (subject to $dm + db = 0$). However, as the nominal interest rate cannot become negative the interest rate will fall into a liquidity trap ($r \downarrow r_o - p$) if m becomes very large (and b very low). Further, it can be seen that the interest rate rises with the size of

---

[5] This equation for the interest rate follows from the demand for money function: $m_d = \mu_2 y/[\log\{(r + p - r_o)/\mu_1\} - \mu_3 b]$. This function implies that money demand increases if the interest rate falls and public debt rises.

public debt within the limit $r \to \infty$ if $b \to \infty$ and $r \to r_o - p$ if $b \to -\infty$. For the desired debt ratio a^* we choose:

$$a^* = 1 - \{\zeta(1 + \varepsilon_1\pi - \varepsilon_2 r)\}^{-1}; \quad \zeta, \varepsilon_1, \varepsilon_2 > 0;$$

$$1 + \varepsilon_1\pi - \varepsilon_2 r > 0. \tag{6.3a}$$

This equation states that a^* is positively related to the profit rate π and the 'state of risk' parameter ζ, and negatively to the interest rate r. Entrepreneurs are thus supposed to accept a larger indebtedness as the profit rate is higher and the interest rate lower. Equation 6.3a has the plausible characteristics that in the limit firms will speed up investment to infinity (so that $a \to 1$) if the profit rate becomes infinite. On the other hand, if the profit rate falls to some critical minimum value $\pi_0 = (\varepsilon_2 r - 1)/\varepsilon_1$ entrepreneurs decide to invest all their wealth in financial assets (government bonds) and close down productive capacity. Hence $\lim_{\pi \to \infty} a^* = 1$ and $\lim_{\pi \downarrow \pi_0} a^* = -\infty$.

Despite these simplifications the model is, unfortunately, still too complex to handle on an analytical level. Therefore, we shall proceed with some numerical exercises for a plausible set of parameters. Before turning to these numerical simulations, we make a brief digression on the numerical values of the parameters, and some of the ensuing properties of the model.

6.4 A digression on the numerical parameter values

The analysis which follows is based on this reference set of parameters:

$$r_0 = 0.02; \; p_o = 0.02; \; g/y = 0.22; \; \tau_o = \tau_1 = \tau_2 = 0.2; \; c_1 = 0.9;$$

$$c_2 = 0.6; \; c_{1r} = -1; \; c_{2r} = 0; \; c_{1z} = 0.05; \; c_{2z} = 0;$$

$$c_{1o} = -0.016; \; c_{2o} = 0; \; \zeta = 1; \; \varepsilon_1 = \varepsilon_2 = 12; \; \mu_1 = 0.0001;$$

$$\mu_2 = \mu_3 = 1; \; a = 0.5; \; y = 0.38.$$

The basic characteristics of the long-period model with these parameters can be established from the partial effects given in Table 6.1, where aggregate savings (S) are defined including government savings (thus $S = y - C_1 - C_2 - g$). This table refers to the Blinder–Solow regime (all γ zero). These results are in line with general empirical evidence.[6] As we have already observed in the foregoing chapter the effect of the interest rate on savings is very sensitive to the budgetary regime, especially to the reaction coefficient with respect to interest outlays (γ_2). Moreover, it varies with the size of public debt (and thus interest income of the private sector). This is corroborated by Table 6.2 which gives the interest effect for a Domar or Barro regime ($\gamma_1, \gamma_2 = 1$) besides a Blinder–Solow regime ($\gamma_1, \gamma_2 = 0$) for range of public debt ratios.

TABLE 6.1 *Some sensitivities*

Wealth effect on aggregate savings	$dS/dz = -0.05$
Profit effect on aggregate savings	$dS/d\pi = 0.24$
Interest effect on aggregate savings	$dS/dr = 0.52$
Interest effect on growth	$d\rho/dr = -1.1$
Profit effect on growth	$d\rho/d\pi = 1.3$
Money elasticity of interest rate	$dr/(dm/m) = -3.8$
Debt elasticity of interest rate	$dr/(db/b) = 0.15$

Note: These effects have been evaluated at the steady state solution to be discussed below: $\pi = 0.11$; $b/y = 0.58$; $m/y = 0.17$; $n = 0.05$; $r = 0.04$.

TABLE 6.2 *Interest effect on aggregate savings (in points)*

Public debt (b)	-1	0	1	2	4
$\gamma_1, \gamma_2 = 0$	1.4	0.7	-0.04	-0.76	-2.2
$\gamma_1, \gamma_2 = 1$	0.6	0.7	0.76	0.84	1.0

In case of a Blinder–Solow regime ($\gamma_1, \gamma_2 = 0$) the interest effect on savings proves to fall as debt grows. For a large debt (in the present example $b \geqslant 1$) the interest effect even becomes negative; a higher interest rate then leads to an increase in consumption rather than a decrease. This reverse interest effect is due to the distribution effect which becomes

---

[6] Following Modigliani (e.g. Modigliani 1971), the wealth effect on consumption is remarkably often found to be -0.05. The result for the money elasticity of the interest rate implies a semi-interest-elasticity of money demand of -0.25 which is in accordance with empirical evidence (cf. Judd and Scadding 1982).

stronger as the flow of interest payments from the government to the private sector is larger. For the Domar or Barro regime (γ_2, $\gamma_1 = 1$) the interest effect turns out to be practically constant, only increasing slightly as b goes up. In this case the distribution effect is much weaker: the positive effect of higher interest payments on private consumption is now offset by the simultaneous reduction of government expenditure.

The non-loglinear modelling of portfolio equilibrium (eq. 6.5) implies a variable elasticity of the interest rate with respect to money and debt. The numerical results in Table 6.3 indicate that the impact of public debt on the interest rate becomes stronger as the size of debt increases. This is in accordance with the empirical notion that the influence on the interest rate becomes significant only for a large debt. As a corollary the impact of money on the interest rate also becomes stronger as debt is larger in relation to the money supply.[7]

TABLE 6.3 *Semi-elasticities of the interest rate*

Public debt (b)	-1	0	1	2	4
$dr/(dm/m)$	-2.2	-3.5	-4.6	-5.2	-5.5
$dr/(db/b)$	-0.4	0.001	0.8	1.9	4.0

6.5 Dynamics of the reduced model

The dynamics of the system is determined by the differential equations for z and π (eqs. 6.6 and 6.5a). In order to assess the global dynamics the (cross) relations between z and π should be established. First, consider the determination of $\dot{z}$ by z and π. After substitution for tax receipts (T_1 and T_2) the GBC (6.6) can be written as:

$$\dot{z} = g + (1 - \tau_1)rz - \tau_1 y.$$

$$- (\tau_2 - \tau_1)(\pi - ra) - (1 - \tau_1)(r + p)m - \rho z \quad (6.6a)$$

The impact of the size of government liabilities z on its rate of change $\dot{z}$ can be decomposed into the following four types

---

[7] For negative debt the elasticity is, of course, negative.

of effects[8] (all effects are discussed for a deficit position and a given stock of money m):

1. Scale effect: the impact of a given budget deficit on the growth rate of z is smaller as the initial size of z is larger (the term $-\rho z$ in equation 6.6a);
2. Budgetary effect: a larger z increases debt service and thereby the budget deficit. This effect is mitigated by higher tax receipts on the interest income of workers and by the adjustment of government expenditure in reaction to the higher interest payments (if $\gamma_2 > 0$). The overall effect of a change in z on the budget is, after substitution for g, equal to $\{1 - \gamma_2 - (1 - \gamma_1)\tau_1\}r - (\gamma_2 - \gamma_3)p + \gamma_4\rho$.
3. Income and wealth effects: a rise in z leads to an increase of private consumption through the increase in wealth and (interest) income. Both effects push up the interest rate and thus lead to a higher deficit and a larger $\dot{z}$.
4. Portfolio effect: at a given stock of money the larger z leads to a higher interest rate and thus to a larger $\dot{z}$.

The two first effects can be regarded as the direct effects of z on the government's budget; the other effects affect the budget more indirectly through their influence on the interest rate. Since these indirect effects always lead to a larger $\dot{z}$, it can be concluded that the direct effects should at least be negative if the overall effect is to be negative. Therefore:

$$- (1 - \gamma_4)\rho + \{1 - \gamma_2 - (1 - \gamma_1)\,\tau_1\}r - (\gamma_2 - \gamma_3)p < 0 \qquad (6.9)$$

is a necessary—but not sufficient—condition for $\partial \dot{z}/\partial z < 0$. For the conventional Blinder–Solow regime (all γ zero) this condition yields the requirement that the growth rate should exceed the real interest rate after taxes ($\rho - (1 - \tau_1)r > 0$). For other regimes this condition is considerably relaxed as these

---

[8] Rau (1985) distinguishes between transfer, wealth, money-market, and Friedman effects. His transfer effect corresponds to our income effect, his wealth effect to our wealth effect, and his money market effect is what we prefer to call the portfolio effect. His Friedman effect (called after Benjamin Friedman) refers to the positive effect of increasing debt on share prices and thus on investment; this effect, which arises from imperfect substitution between debt and equity, is neglected in the present analysis as we have consolidated the corporate sector with its owners and shareholders.

entail a negative feedback of debt service on government expenditure ($\gamma_2 > 0$).

The overall effect of z on its rate of change is thus ambiguous. However, as the interest rate rises with the volume of government liabilities it can be established that the overall impact of z on $\dot{z}$ will be positive (and thus destabilizing) at high levels of z, thus:

$$\partial \dot{z}/\partial z > 0 \quad \text{for a large } z.$$

For low levels of z it may be positive or negative. All effects have been discussed with respect to the deficit situation ($z, b > 0$). It is obvious that when the government is a net creditor the conclusions will be quite different, particularly because the scale and income effects change direction. When $b < 0$ a higher interest rate *improves* the position of the government so that $\dot{z}$ decreases, etc. As this case is of little relevance from a practical point of view we shall leave it as it is, and concentrate on the conventional debtor case.

Next consider the influence of the profit rate on the GBC. If we neglect the consequences of possible differential taxing of profits and wages (therefore let $\tau_2 = \tau_1$) it can be established that the overall effect of the profit rate π on $\dot{z}$ depends on several opposite effects given in Fig. 6.1.

First, a higher profit rate leads to a higher growth rate (ρ) and thereby to a smaller change in the liability ratio z (linkage 1 in the scheme); this negative 'real erosion' effect is larger in absolute terms as z is larger. This effect is, however,

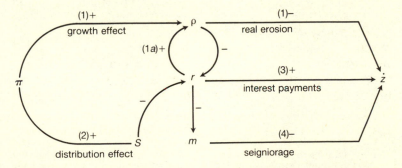

FIG. 6.1 Profit rate and the government budget deficit

weakened by the rise in the interest rate associated with the increase in investment (linkage 1*a*). Secondly, a higher π increases savings (distribution effect) and thereby lowers the interest rate; this reduces the burden of interest payments and pushes the growth rate up, both factors leading to a lower growth of *z* (linkage 2). Note that the effect of the lower interest rate is reinforced by the corresponding rise in money stock, and thus fall in debt, which raises seigniorage and reduces debt service (linkage 4).

The overall outcome is ambiguous, but it is again possible to say something on how these effects relate to the size of *z*. As the real erosion effect of the higher growth rate (linkage 1) becomes stronger as *z* increases while the other effects are independent of *z*, it can be concluded that the real erosion effect becomes dominant for a sufficiently large *z*, so that the overall effect of π on the growth of *z* becomes negative. Hence there will exist a critical size of liabilities z_0 for which

$$\partial \dot{z}/\partial \pi < 0 \text{ for } z > z_0.$$

This result together with the effect of *z* on $\dot{z}$ established above implies that the $\dot{z} = 0$ locus has a positive slope in the (z, π) plane when *z* is large. In this segment the positive (destabilizing) effect of larger liabilities on its pace of growth must be offset by a higher π which has a negative (stabilizing) impact on $\dot{z}$. This is corroborated by the phase diagram (Fig. 6.2) which is based on the parameter set given above. In this numerical example the critical size of liabilities z_0 where $\partial \dot{z}/\partial \pi = 0$ is found to be negative.[9] This gives rise to an asymptote in the figure close to the π-axis (for expository reasons not drawn in the figure). As we wish to concentrate on the debtor case we shall not bother about the region to the left of the asymptote ($z < z_0$). In the relevant region the $\dot{z} = 0$ locus can be seen to fall for low *z* when the scale effect is dominant (hence $\partial \dot{z}/\partial z > 0$), and to rise beyond some *z* when the interest rate becomes high ($\partial \dot{z}/\partial z > 0$).

---

[9] This is due to the apparently strong distribution effect of π which implies that at $z = 0$ higher profits raise savings more than investment, so that the interest falls. Therefore $\partial \dot{z}/\partial \pi < 0$ at $z = 0$, and thus a critical $z_0 < 0$.

The figure also draws the $\dot{\pi} = 0$ locus. This has a positive slope because the higher interest rate associated with larger public debt must be compensated by a higher profit rate in order to maintain growth equilibrium. The intersection between these two loci (the solid lines) determines the steady state which is characterized by:

$$n = 0.05; \pi = 0.11; b/y = 0.58; m/y = 0.17; r = 0.04.$$

(For convenience public debt and money stock are given in relation to national income.)

Fig. 6.2 gives the phase diagram for a Domar regime ($\gamma_1, \gamma_2, \gamma_3 = 1$).[10] In the given range this model yields only one solution, which can be seen to be stable within a fairly wide area. The figure also exhibits a lower boundary for the profit rate at $\pi = -0.09$. This arises from the bottom in the interest rate function (liquidity trap); if π approaches this boundary the interest rate can no longer fall sufficiently to avoid total disinvestment of production capacity ($\rho = -\infty$). In the shaded area at low $z (\ll 0)$ no momentary equilibrium can be found because of inconsistency between saving and investment for any possible monetary policy. In this region private income has become so low and government income so high (as a result of the large interest payments by the private sector *to* the government) that savings exceed investment even at the lowest possible interest rate.

In the figure a second locus for $\dot{\pi} = 0$ is also shown (the dashed line) corresponding to a higher natural rate of growth, $n = 0.10$. The latter locus lies, of course, above the first as a higher growth rate requires a higher profit rate. Note that the $\dot{z} = 0$ locus is independent of n. The figure brings out that a higher natural growth rate yields a higher steady state profit rate and lower liability ratio. A higher growth rate thus generally relieves the burden of debt. With respect to the stability it can be made up from the phase diagram that the system is basically stable within a fairly wide range around the steady state solution.

---

[10] Throughout the following analysis we assume that the government has no inflation illusion and treats inflationary effects on debt and money stock on the same footing as nominal interest payments, hence $\gamma_3 = \gamma_2$.

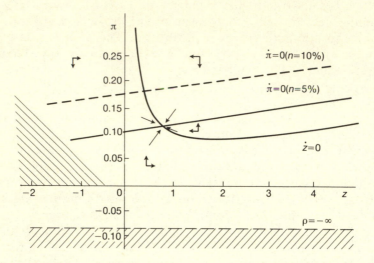

Note: This figure is based on the reference set of parameters given in section 6.4

FIG. 6.2 Dynamics for a Domar regime ($\gamma_1, \gamma_2, \gamma_3 = 1; \gamma_4 = 0$)

Blinder–Solow regime

This general stability may change drastically for other budgetary regimes. Fig. 6.3 presents the results for the Blinder–Solow regime with fixed government expenditure ($\gamma_1, \gamma_2 = 0$) in Fig. 6.3*a*, and for an intermediate regime ($\gamma_1 = \gamma_2 = 0.5$) in Fig. 6.3*b*. Comparison of these figures brings out that, although neither the steady state nor its local stability changes, the system is considerably less stable when the fiscal response to interest payments (γ_2) is low. Especially for initial positions with high debt and low profits there is a great risk of a cumulative process of growing debt and interest payments. This difference between the Domar regime and the Blinder–Solow regime arises from the automatic 'crowding-out' of government consumption if interest payments increase which is implied by the Domar regime, and the Christ and Barro regimes as well. In the Blinder–Solow regime the amount of government expenditure is exogenous, so that a rise in interest payments (after taxes) leads to a one-for-one

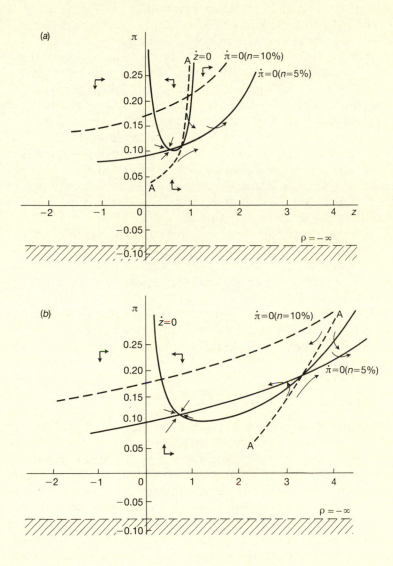

Note: See Fig. 6.2

FIG. 6.3 The Blinder–Solow regime ($\gamma_1 = 0$, $\gamma_2 = 0$) and an intermediate regime ($\gamma_1 = 0$, $\gamma_2 = 0.5$)

increase in the budget deficit, and therefore to a further growth of debt and interest payments.

The figure for the Blinder–Solow regime further reveals that there may exist a second restpoint at a higher debt ratio. This solution is, however, characterized by a saddle-point configuration, and is thus unstable. Therefore, whenever the system starts from a too-high debt ratio it will follow a path with ever-rising debt. In order to reach the stable steady state equilibrium it must start from a point left of the dashed A–A curve, thus at a sufficiently low initial level of debt. But whenever it starts at a point at the right of this separatrix it falls into an unstable spiral of ever-rising z and π. It is evident that this process in the event must lead to a breakdown of the model as π cannot rise infinitely (contrary to what is implied by the linear function for $\dot{\pi}$ (eq. 6.5a)).

Note that the two solutions practically coincide for the Blinder–Solow regime ($\gamma_1, \gamma_2 = 0$) if the natural growth rate is 5 per cent. In this case the system is thus particularly unstable in the event of downward disturbances in π and for upward disturbances in z. A significant fall in π or rise in z will lead the system away from the equilibrium for ever. The stability of this system is essentially asymmetrical; the system can handle upward disturbances much better than downward shocks.

Catastrophe manifold

What is the impact on stability if the natural rate of growth rises to a higher level? As in earlier exercises the growth rate proves to have a significant stabilizing influence. Although the basic asymmetrical instability remains, the region within which the system is stable is considerably larger for $n = 10$ per cent than for $n = 5$ per cent. This indicates that the dynamics is very sensitive to the height of the natural rate of growth. If the growth rate falls below 5 per cent the steady state solution even disappears altogether. Therefore there exists some critical minimum for the growth rate below which the system changes from a system with one (potentially) stable solution into a totally unstable system without any solution at all.

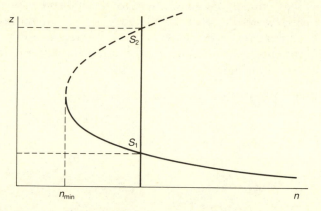

FIG. 6.4 Catastrophe manifold

In formal terms this critical growth rate represents the bifurcation point of the catastrophe manifold of this system.[11] This is shown in Fig. 6.4. In fact, this figure depicts the equilibrium points for z in relation to n. As we have seen above, the equilibrium points on the upper branch are unstable and those on the lower branch stable. For $n < n_{min}$ no equilibrium exists.

As before we can use this critical value of n to assess the impact of different variables and regimes on the stability of the system. The results for a selection of the variables of the model are presented in Table 6.4. A variable is stabilizing if it reduces the critical growth rate and destabilizing if it raises the rate required for a stable equilibrium.

As might be expected higher propensities to save and a lower autonomous part of the real interest rate $(r_o - p_o)$ lead to a more stable system. This is because these factors lead to a lower real interest rate, and therefore mitigate the cumulative debt–interest spiral. As in Chapter 2, the wealth effects on consumption turn out to reduce the system's stability, in contrast with most IS/LM based models where, as already

---

[11] This is a catastrophe manifold for a 'fold catastrophe' which—as we have seen in Ch. 2—produces a rather smooth catastrophe, unlike, for example, the more typical 'cusp catastrophe' which produces a sort of jump of the system.

mentioned, strong wealth effects are essential for stability. In the present model, however, where production capacity is fully utilized, the wealth effects imply that an increase in public debt causes an increase in private expenditure, thereby raising the interest rate and thus producing a larger deficit in the government budget.

TABLE 6.4 *Partial effects on* n_{min}

g_0	2.770
γ_1	0.026
γ_2	-0.073
γ_3	0.011
γ_4	0.048
τ_0	-1.302
τ_1	-0.089
τ_2	0.283
r_0	0.009
p_0	-0.134
c_1	0.156
c_2	0.015
c_{1r}	-0.026
c_{2r}	-0.013
c_{1z}	0.678
c_{2z}	0.203
c_{10}	0.565
c_{20}	0.385

Note: all effects are measured with reference to the intermediate regime given in Fig. 6.3. The effects of the γ coefficients have been corrected for their impact effect on government expenditure. One should be careful to compare the absolute effects because an equal change in each variable may entail quite different impacts in absolute terms.

With regard to the fiscal policy instruments we find that stability can be improved by raising taxes on wages and interest income of workers. A rise in taxes on profits, however, worsens the system's stability. This is obviously due to the negative impact on the growth rate. Also autonomous government expenditure proves to have a strong destabilizing impact as it raises the primary deficit and thereby the steady state size of debt. As to the budgetary regime it can be seen that the reaction coefficient with respect to interest payments (γ_2) has a stabilizing effect, while the other fiscal reaction coefficients tend to reduce the system's stability. The stabilizing impact of the internal crowding-out when interest payments rise ($\gamma_2 > 1$) corroborates our conclusion with regard to the differences between Figs. 6.2 and 6.3 for the Blinder–Solow and the Domar regimes above. Although the magnitude of these effects may change, the pattern of signs of the effects proves to be robust for other numerical simulations in the neighbourhood of the reference model.

All these partial effects have been measured with reference to an intermediate regime with partial adjustment of government expenditure to changes in interest payments ($\gamma_2 = 0.5$). Another way of looking at the determinants of stability is to compare the alternative budgetary regimes. This is done in Table 6.5 which gives the minimum growth rates for each of the regimes considered. These results corroborate our inferences above: a strong budgetary reaction to changes in interest payments as in the Christ regime and, to a lesser degree, in the Tobin–Buiter regime improves the stability of the system. The Blinder–Solow regime is the least stable. The Barro regime is stable for any growth rate, which is hardly surprising as it presupposes that the government aims at a constant debt.

TABLE 6.5 *Minimum growth rate (%) for alternative policy regimes*

Blinder–Solow	4.8
Christ	-1.2
Tobin–Buiter	0.9
Domar	0.3
Barro	stable for any n

Note: See Table 6.4 above

6.6 Long cycles

We now return to the full model. In addition to the dynamics of income distribution and government liabilities this model takes account of the dynamics of unemployment and corporate debt as well. For generality we also incorporate the possibility of slow adjustment of investment and government expenditure. Then choosing suitable explicit functions the full dynamic system is determined by the following differential equations:

$$\dot{a} = -y_2 + \rho + C_2 - \rho a; \tag{6.1'}$$

$$\dot{z} = g - (T_1 + T_2) + rb - pm - \rho z; \tag{6.6}$$

$$\dot{u} = (1 - u)(n - \rho); \qquad 0 < u < 1; \tag{6.7}$$

$$\dot{\pi} = \left\{ \vartheta_{\pi 1} \dot{u} + \vartheta_{\pi 2}(u - u_o) \right\} / u; \quad \vartheta_{\pi 1}, \vartheta_{\pi 2} \geqslant 0; u_o > 0; \tag{6.5b}$$

$$\ddot{a}^* + \vartheta_{a1} \dot{a}^* = \vartheta_{a2}(a^{**} - a^*); \qquad \vartheta_{a2} > 0; \tag{6.10}$$

$$\dot{g} = \vartheta_g(g^* - g); \qquad \vartheta_g > 0; \tag{6.11}$$

$$\dot{\rho} = \vartheta_\rho(\rho^* - \rho); \qquad \vartheta_\rho > 0; \tag{6.12}$$

where $\ddot{a}$ is the second-order time derivative of a ($= d^2a/dt^2$) and a^{**}, g^*, and ρ^* are given now by the equations for desired a^*, g, and ρ (eqs. 6.8, 5.11, and 6.3) above. The first two equations restate the budget constraints for the corporate sector and the government. The third equation again gives the time derivative of the unemployment rate. Equation 6.5b relates the change in income distribution to the evolution of the unemployment rate. For $\vartheta_{\pi 1} = 0$ and $\vartheta_{\pi 2} > 0$ this function is akin to the relation Goodwin (1972) uses in his famous model of the Marxian business cycle. The modelling of this relation is such that $\dot{\pi}$ tends to infinity when u becomes zero. This is in accordance with Goodwin's 'ideal function' (1972: 444), although at variance with the linear approximation function he uses in his actual model. We prefer the non-linear 'ideal' function; moreover, it has the convenient implication that it precludes the occurrence of absolute labour shortage ($u < 0$).

The change in the desired debt ratio a^* is now modelled by a second-order differential equation. This is in accordance with the view that norms on proper debt ratios change only very slowly (eq. 6.10). If $\vartheta_{a1} = 0$ this function implies a second-order adjustment, i.e. the rate of change in a^* is conceived as a state variable which can only change gradually over time. The last two equations are partial adjustment functions for g and ρ.

At the given parameter values of the reduced model considered above, the fully dynamic model yields basically the same steady state solution, namely $m/y = 0.17$; $b/y = 0.77$; $\pi = 11.0$ per cent; $r = 4.8$ per cent. The minor differences arise from the fact that the desired debt ratio is endogenous now with a steady state value of 0.43 instead of the arbitrarily chosen rate of 0.50 in the reduced model above. In order to gain some insight into this complex model we shall discuss some numerical simulations of it. All simulations are made with reference to the Christ regime as this regime ensures the dynamics will be stable. It needs, however, little imagination to understand that other regimes, especially the Blinder–Solow regime, may produce trajectories that lead away from steady state equilibrium for ever (these unstable trajectories are in fact very similar to the unstable trajectory shown in Fig. 2.5 above).

A real cycle

By way of reference, first consider a simulation of a 'real' Goodwin-like cycle (with $\vartheta_{\pi 2} > 0$) where the interaction between the labour market and income distribution is the basic cyclical mechanism.[12] In order to isolate this cycle from the financial dynamics to be considered below desired debt is assumed to be exogenous (ϑ_{a1}, $\vartheta_{a2} = 0$). Fig. 6.5 shows the evolution of public and corporate debt (Fig. 6.5*a*) and profit, growth, and interest rate (Fig. 6.5*b*) after a combined shock at $t = 5$. This shock represents on a very abstract level the rupture in economic growth of the 1970s which was caused by:

1. a fall in profits, as a result of oil price rises;

---

[12] See van der Ploeg (1983) for a sophisticated analysis of the Goodwin cycle in a continuous time model.

2. a structural decline in the natural rate of growth, through the slow-down of productivity growth and population growth;
3. an adverse shift in business confidence leading to more prudential financial policies, as a reaction to the growing uncertainty.

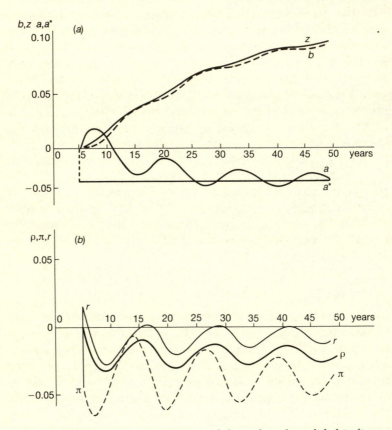

Note: In addition to the parameters of the reduced model this figure is based on: $\Omega = 0.1$; $\vartheta_p = 0.5$; $\vartheta_g = 0.3$; $\vartheta_{\pi 1} = 0.05$; $\vartheta_{\pi 2} = 0.01$; $\vartheta_{\alpha 1} = 0$; $\vartheta_{\alpha 2} = 0$. As to the policy regime it is assumed that $\gamma_2 = 1$ and all other γ are zero (the Christ regime). The simulation is based on a numerical approximation of the differential system by the Runge–Kutta method (see e.g. Cohen 1973).

FIG. 6.5 A real cycle (deviations from initial equilibrium)

This combined economic shock caused a structural slow-down of investment and economic growth. In our model this shock is represented by a discrete fall in π by 4 points, a permanent decline in n from 5 per cent to 3 per cent, and a once and for all fall in ζ by 20 per cent. This latter shift in 'state of risk' implies a discrete fall in the desired debt ratio a^{**} from 0.43 to 0.28.

Fig. 6.5 shows the evolution of each variable as (absolute) deviation from its initial steady state value. It can be seen that the negative shock gives rise to a (dampened) cyclical movement, eventually leading to a larger government debt and smaller corporate debt, and a lower growth rate and profit rate. The differences between the new steady state and the initial equilibrium are summarized in Table 6.6.

TABLE 6.6 *Steady state effects of the combined shock*

	Initial Equilibrium	New steady state
ρ (%)	5.0	3.0
π (%)	11.0	7.7
r (%)	4.8	3.3
a	0.43	0.28
m/y	0.17	0.19
b/y	0.77	1.32

The adjustment process towards the new steady state can be explained as follows. After the shock at $t = 5$ growth declines because of the fall in profits and the adverse shift in 'animal spirits'. As a result unemployment starts to grow and wages to fall; after some time profitability therefore recovers leading to a new expansion of investment and employment. Sooner or later this expansion will be checked by the tightening of the labour market as a result of which wages start to rise again and profits to fall. This is the basic cyclical mechanism of Goodwin's Marxian cycle. Unlike the original Goodwin model, the present model takes account of a cyclical movement of the interest rate too, which obviously has a dampening influence on the cycle.

As regards corporate debt it can be seen that the fall in profits at $t = 5$ initially leads to a rise of corporate debt, because investment does not adjust instantaneously to the lower internal savings. Thereafter, as investment falls and profits recover, corporate debt declines and tends cyclically to its new (lower) steady state level. At the same time public debt grows to a higher structural level, corresponding to the lower natural rate of growth.

Regarding the duration of these processes one may notice that this cycle refers to the long 'Kuznetz' cycle, or even the Kondratieff cycle, rather than the conventional (short) business cycle. The Kuznetz cycle, or 'long swing', is generally thought to have a length of 10–15 years whereas the conventional (American) business cycle has a length of only some 5 years. The (non-existing)[13] Kondratieff wave even has an alleged duration of some 40–60 years.

A financial cycle

As an alternative to this 'real' explanation of the business cycle, our model also offers a 'financial' explanation, i.e. a cycle arising from corporate policies with regard to finance and investment. In order to concentrate on the financial dynamics now let $\vartheta_{\pi 2} = 0$, thus eliminating the 'Goodwin' propagation mechanism.

First, note that the ultimate effects of the combined shock are practically the same for the financial cycle as for the real cycle given above. The new steady state is now found at $n = 3$ per cent, $\pi = 8.1$ per cent, $r = 2.9$ per cent, $a = 0.22$, $m/y = 0.19$, and $b/y = 1.34$. Only the result for the debt ratio (a) is significantly different; this is obvious as for the real cycle a^* was assumed to be fixed.

The adjustment process is shown in Fig. 6.6. Just as in the real cycle above, corporate debt rises initially after the shock, as investment adjusts slowly to the lower internal savings. Only after some time, when investment is cut down sufficiently, does the rise in the debt ratio (a) turn into a decline. In the meantime the desired debt ratio a^* has fallen consider-

---

[13] This emerges from most of the empirical research on the Kondratieff cycle (see e.g. van Ewijk 1982*a*). Nevertheless, some investigations seem to yield more favourable results with respect to the existence of this long wave, see e.g. Metz (1984), Reijnders (1988).

ably due to the negative shock to the economy. Thereafter, while investment and actual corporate debt are still falling, desired debt starts to increase again thanks to the lower interest rate and the higher profit rate (due to the growing unemployment). Consequently, when corporate financial policy is relaxed, investment and growth will recover too. When the growth rate rises again above the (lower) natural growth

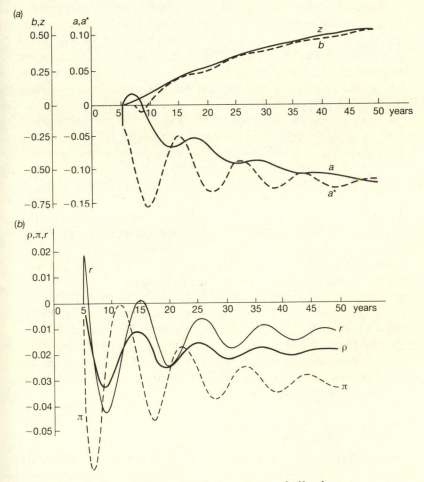

Note: $\vartheta_{\pi 1} = 0$; $\vartheta_{\pi 2} = 0.02$; $\vartheta_{a1} = 0.5$; $\vartheta_{a2} = 0.1$; and all other parameters as in Fig. 6.5

FIG. 6.6 A financial cycle (deviations from initial equilibrium)

the labour market starts tightening again. This leads to a fall in the profit rate, thereby pressing down the desired debt ratio again, inducing more restrictive corporate financial policies and thereby lower investment, etc.

This interaction gives rise to a clear cyclical pattern in the actual and the desired corporate debt ratios. The financial cycle may thus be interpreted as a succession of waves in the readiness to take risks and incur debts, or, in Schumpeterian terms, by waves in business optimism and pessimism. Eventually the debt ratio will tend to a lower long-term level corresponding to the structural fall in growth and the increase in uncertainty. As can be seen in the figure this process causes the growth rate to oscillate towards its new (lower) steady state value of 3 per cent. The interest rate moves more or less parallel; the profit rate appears to lead by a couple of years.

Now consider the evolution of government liabilities. As a result of the slow-down in economic growth, government liabilities begin to grow, initially largely in the form of money (due to the expansionary monetary policy necessary to maintain sufficient demand), but later mainly in the form of debt. Eventually z tends to a new steady level of 1.54. This higher government debt is the natural consequence of the slow-down in growth.[14]

The appearance of this 'financial' cycle is not really different from the real cycle above. There is, however, a qualitative difference as regards the causation of the cycle: in the real cycle the principal propagation mechanism arises from labour-market disequilibrium and income distribution, while the financial cycle is governed by the discrepancy between the actual and the desired corporate debt. Of course, no model is exclusively valid: both models clarify a certain aspect of the true dynamic system.

Steady state effects

What influence do the policy instruments have on the steady state? Table 6.7 gives the partial derivatives of main econ-

---

[14] For other regimes, or other parameters sets, the system may, of course, be unstable. Then, government liabilities keep growing for ever.

omic variables with respect to government expenditure and taxes. These results refer again to the above model with a stable Christ regime ($\gamma_1 = 0$; $\gamma_2 = 1$). The change in each of the instruments is normalized to a budgetary impulse of 1 per cent of national income y. As might be expected the rise in government expenditure leads to a higher interest rate and larger public debt. In order to maintain growth at its natural rate the profit rate must rise as well. Because of the higher interest rate the corporate debt ratio declines a little.

TABLE 6.7 *Steady state effects of a stimulus of 1 per cent of national income for different fiscal instruments*

Instrument	Change in				
	b	m	a	π^{a}	r^{a}
g_0	0.152	-0.002	-0.009	0.28	0.56
τ_0	0.151	-0.001	-0.009	0.31	0.53
τ_1	0.176	0.001	-0.001	0.05	0.08
τ_2	0.153	-0.001	-0.020	-0.08	0.04

[a] Effects in percentage points

Note that the ultimate increase in government expenditure is less than the initial increase. This is because the larger debt service leads to some internal crowding-out of expenditure (because $\gamma_2 = 1$). Furthermore, the final increase of government expenditure occurs at the expense of private consumption. This is accomplished by the higher interest rate and the shift in income distribution in favour of profits. In this model with a fixed technology and a given rate of growth there is no long-term crowding-out of investment. There will, of course, be some crowding-out in the short run through the higher interest rate, but eventually this negative effect on investment will be offset by a higher profit rate. It is obvious that in case of an endogenous technique of production the higher profit rate will lead to a decline in the desired capital–output ratio, and thus to some crowding-out of investment too. This effect will not, however, qualitatively change our results above.

The steady state effects of a reduction in taxes on wages (τ_0) are practically identical to those of the rise in g_0. A reduction in tax on the interest income of workers (τ_1) has smaller effects on the profit rate and the interest rate, but gives rise to a sharper increase in public debt. Obviously, the reduction in τ_1 not only raises the budget deficit directly, but also weakens the mitigating feedback of rising interest payments on tax receipts, and thereby on the growth of public debt. In contrast with the other cases, a reduction in taxes on net corporate returns (τ_2) leads to a fall in the profit rate. This is because fewer profits (before taxes) are necessary to keep up growth when taxes are lower. The steady state effects on public debt, the money stock, and the interest rate are basically similar to those of the other fiscal policy instruments.

6.7 Conclusion

In this chapter we have investigated the dynamics of growth and asset accumulation from a long-term point of view. With regard to income–expenditure equilibrium it was assumed that the monetary authorities have sufficient time to find the right policy to maintain full utilization of capacity. Therefore demand dynamics is shifted into the background in this chapter; instead we have concentrated on the interaction between asset accumulation and income distribution as the principal mover of economic development. For a plausible numerical model it was established that the stability directly depends on the natural rate of growth; the lower this growth rate the less stable is the system. Beyond some minimum growth rate (the bifurcation point of the catastrophe manifold) the system loses its stable solution altogether. Just as in the medium period the dynamics is essentially asymmetrical; long-period equilibrium is clearly more stable in an upward than in a downward direction.

The fiscal policy regime proves to have a great impact on the system's stability, especially the budgetary reaction to changes in nominal interest payments (γ_2). The rigid Blinder–Solow regime with $\gamma_2 = 0$ emerges as the least stable regime, and the Barro regime, which adopts a target for a constant debt ratio, as the most stable. Table 6.8 gives a comparison of the ranking of the regimes for the medium period and the long period. These rankings bring out that, although the Barro regime seems best from a long-term point of view, it performs worst in the medium period. The Blinder–Solow regime is the least stable from a long-term point of view and, after the Barro regime, the least stable in the medium period as well. A more attractive regime seems to be the Christ regime which performs best in the medium period and, after the Barro regime, best in the long period as well, closely followed by the Tobin–Buiter regime. Each of these regimes implies automatic reduction of government expenditure when interest payments increase. In the medium term this 'internal' crowding-out of government expenditure produces an anti-cyclical movement of expenditure; in the long term it mitigates the cumulative spiral of increasing debt and interest payments (see Table 6.8).

TABLE 6.8 *Stability of budgetary regimes*

	Medium period	Long period
Stable	Christ	Barro
	Tobin–Buiter	Christ
	Blinder–Solow	Domar
	Domar	Tobin–Buiter
Unstable	Barro	Blinder–Solow

Note that whether a regime leads to a stable system or not depends on the model as a whole, and especially on the natural rate of growth. Therefore, any structural change in the economy may turn a stable system into an unstable one. Furthermore, it is important to note that large disturbances, especially downward shocks, may lead to a displacement of the system from a 'stable' region, from where it will always return to its steady state, into an 'unstable' region, from where it recedes further and further from steady state equilibrium. These observations lead to the conclusion that there is no automatic rule or regime for fiscal policy which guarantees stability under all circumstances. Rules need to be reconsidered regularly.

7

The Stability of Public Debt in an Open and Growing Economy[1]

7.1 Introduction

In this chapter we shall generalize the foregoing analysis for the open economy. It will be shown that the dynamics of growth and asset accumulation is essentially different from that of the closed economy. In order to bring out these differences as clearly as possible, we shall concentrate on the extreme case of a small open economy which is a price-taker on the international commodity and financial markets.

The basic ingredients of the present analysis are the following: First, as mentioned, we focus on the open economy. The government budget constraint (GBC) is treated in the conventional way, allowing for bond financing as well as for money financing. The modelling of the balance of payments constraint (hereafter abbreviated as BPC) is akin to that of the small open-economy models of Domar (1957) and Hamada (1966), but with two important modifications. First, in order to bring out the specific role of saving from interest income the present analysis assumes a 'Kaldor' differential savings function. Secondly, the domestic interest rate is not determined by the international interest rate alone, but is dependent on the net international creditor or debtor position as well. Finally, the present analysis incorporates a 'conflict' model for the dynamics of income distribution.

The chapter is organized as follows. After some preliminary considerations on the determination of growth and income distribution in an open economy in section 7.2, we shall

---

[1] This chapter is largely based on the article 'Interest payments and the stability of the government budget deficit in an open and growing economy', in *De Economist* (van Ewijk 1986).

develop the 'static' part of the model describing the instanta-
neous equilibrium relationships which are required to hold
continuously (section 7.3). Then sections 7.4–7.6 analyse the
dynamics of the model which arises from the GBC, the BPC,
and the interaction between growth and income distribution.
Section 7.7 deals with the characteristics of the steady state
equilibrium. Finally, section 7.8 examines the consequences
when it is assumed that the government adopts a target for
the balance of payments on current account instead of some
fixed budgetary target.

7.2 Growth and distribution in the open economy

Before developing the open-economy model we first have to
discuss some problems which arise when the post-Keynesian
model, which is typically designed for the closed economy,[2]
is applied to the open economy. One of the basic theorems of
post-Keynesian theory, as we have discussed it in Chapter 2,
is that income distribution is solved from the side of demand
for output. Assuming a differential propensity to save from
wages and profits, it is argued that discrepancies between
aggregate demand and supply are solved by shifts in income
distribution. This adjustment in income distribution is
achieved by changes in the price level while nominal wages
are relatively rigid.

In this theory the nominal wage rate plays only a minor role.
Apart from the special situation in which the economy is
driven towards the inflation barrier (see Chapter 2) nominal
wages function primarily as the numeraire, fixing the general
level of prices. In an open economy this 'neutrality' view of
nominal wages is no longer warranted. In the presence of
international competition on the commodity markets a
change in nominal wages affects the competitive position of
domestic firms *vis-à-vis* foreign competitors. As a consequence changes in money wages cannot simply be passed on
in prices without affecting the competitive strength of do-

---

[2] Some contributions on particular aspects of the international theory of
growth and distribution have been made by Kregel (1975), Steedman (1979),
Steedman and Metcalfe (1979), and Pasinetti (1981).

mestic firms. In this environment money wages may therefore have a decisive influence on real wages and the profit
rate.

This has important consequences for the standard post-
Keynesian model. International competition on goods markets impedes the possibility of restoring equilibrium between
aggregate demand and supply through the redistribution of
income. In the extreme case of full arbitrage on the goods
markets (law of one price) there is no room for this redistribution mechanism at all: the profit margin and real wages are
completely determined by domestic nominal wages and the
international price level at the given exchange rate. The well-
known post-Keynesian causation from investment to prices
and income distribution breaks down in this case.[3] In principle the effect of a change in money wages might be offset
by an equivalent change in the exchange rate. This, however,
requires the monetary authorities to accommodate passively
any change in the domestic price level. As this is not very
plausible, we shall leave this possibility out of consideration.
This does not necessarily imply that the exchange rate must
be fixed. It may vary, but it is independent of (changes in) the
domestic level of wages.

Now imagine a rise in aggregate demand, caused, for
example, by an increase in investment. In the case of a substantial price elasticity of the foreign supply of goods, the rise
in demand leads to an increase in imports—when domestic
capacity is fully utilized—rather than a rise in domestic
prices. Hence, the link between demand and income distribution is now replaced by a link between demand and the balance of trade. Thus in the long period[4] discrepancies between

---

[3] Robinson (1962: 70) mentions that foreign competition may raise problems with respect to the distribution mechanism, but gives it no further
consideration. Kregel (1975:ch.12) pays more attention to this subject, rec-
ognizing that foreign competition 'may limit the ability of domestic producers to set the prices they desire', but fails to give a clear account of the
long-term implications of the openness of the economy for the determination of income distribution.

[4] Kalecki (1934), however, analyses a similar relationship between the
balance of trade and demand, and therefore profits but with a different view
on the causal direction. In his fixed-price short-term model the balance of
payment on current account provides an additional (external) source

ex ante savings and investment are not resolved by redistribution of income as in the closed economy, but are reflected in the balance of payments on current account.

The post-Keynesian position on these matters is not very clear. For the long term it is generally recognized that foreign prices exert a significant influence on domestic prices; however, opinions on the strength of this influence appear to diverge. 'Ricardian' post-Keynesian authors such as Steedman and Metcalfe (1979) and Pasinetti (1981) tend to accept that prices are fully determined by international prices. More 'Keynesian' post-Keynesians, as for example Kregel, hold on to the proposition that, although foreign prices may indeed have some influence, domestic factors still have a significant impact.

International equalization of profit rates

Now consider the determination of the profit rate. As we have seen, post-Keynesian theory explains the profit rate in a closed economy by the savings propensities and the rate of growth. It needs little argumentation to see that in the presence of international capital mobility this explanation can no longer be sustained. On the contrary, it may be expected that competition on international financial markets produces a tendency towards the international equalization of profit rates.

Overviewing post-Keynesian theory it appears that, although most authors recognize the tendency towards equal profit rates, it is generally treated in a rather ambivalent manner. For example, Steedman (1979) recognizes that capital mobility would imply equalization of profit rates, but subsequently excludes this possibility by postulating strict immobility of capital. Steedman and Metcalfe (1979) do allow the money rate of interest to be determined internationally, but relate the profit rate exclusively to domestic factors; the interest rate only functions as a minimum below which the profit rate cannot fall. Pasinetti (1981) is also ambiguous on

of demand besides investment and government expenditure. In the long period, however, when capacity is fully utilized, the causation runs from demand to the balance of trade.

this point; while he explains sectoral profit rates in a traditional post-Keynesian fashion by the (sectoral) rates of expansion, he nevertheless assumes profit rates to be equal internationally too. However, this is not explained by international capital mobility, but follows from Pasinetti's assumption 'for simplicity' that growth rates for each sector are equal in every country (Pasinetti 1981: 246).[5]

In the model to be developed in this chapter we shall adopt the Ricardian position and assume complete price arbitrage on commodity markets. With respect to the equalization of profit rates we shall develop a more dynamic view which allows for international differences in real interest rates and profit rates. Our model thus assumes full international mobility of capital but no perfect substitution.

7.3 The model

In order for us to be able to concentrate on the basic 'laws' governing the accumulation of financial assets the real side of the economy is represented by an elementary model of steady growth. It is assumed that capacity is always fully utilized, that technical change is purely labour augmenting, and that the capital–output ratio is constant. Hence the growth rates of production (ρ) and employment (in efficiency units) are equal to the growth rate of capital stock (i). The discrepancy between this rate and the (exogenous) growth rate of labour supply (the 'natural' rate of growth) determines the evolution of unemployment. Further, we shall adopt the small open-economy framework, which implies that the economy is a full price-taker on both the international, financial, and the commodity markets.

---

[5] A third problem with respect to the post-Keynesian theory for the open economy concerns the determination of relative prices. If one follows Sraffa and assumes that relative prices are determined by income distribution and fixed technical coefficients, international competition on goods markets will lead to full specialization of production in each country. In macroeconomic models this is often neglected by adopting a one-sector model (cf. Steedman and Metcalfe 1979). Pasinetti solves this problem by introducing decreasing returns to scale on the sector level. In the following analysis we shall avoid this problem by assuming homogeneity of goods.

In order to reduce the dimensionality of the model in this chapter we shall not distinguish between the corporate sector and workers, but adopt a Kaldorian consumption function which distinguishes between wages and property income. If it is taken into account that the property income of the private sector consists of profits from domestic production as well as real interest income received on financial wealth, the income identities of the model can be written as follows (all stocks and flows are again expressed in ratios to capital stock):

$$y = w + \pi; \tag{7.1}$$

$$y_2 = \pi + rb + re - pm. \tag{7.2}$$

The first equation divides domestic production (y) between wages (w) and profits (π). The second one defines private property income (y_2) as the sum of profits and real interest income over government debt (b) and the net external position (e), less inflationary tax (pm). The expenditure relations are straightforward. In order to bring out the specific role of spending from property income the consumption function distinguishes between the propensity to consume from disposable wage income c_1 and from disposable property income c_2. This simple Kaldorian function is modified by including a wealth effect (c_z) and an interest effect (c_r) on consumption as well:[6]

$$c = c\{(1 - \tau_1)w, (1 - \tau_2)y_2, r, z\}; \qquad c_1, c_2, c_z \geqslant 0; \ c_r \leqslant 0;$$

where τ_1 and τ_2 indicate the tax rates on wages and on property income, and $z = 1 + e + b + m$ denotes private wealth (as a ratio to capital stock). The first-order derivatives of c with respect to net wage income and net property income are written as c_1 and c_2. c_z and c_r stand for the derivatives to z and r respectively. With regard to taxes no distinction is made between the different components of property income. This implies that inflationary losses on nominal assets are taxed at the same rate as nominal interest income. Although this

[6] It has been assumed that consumers are not ultra-rational in the sense put forward by Barro (1974) and others, that they fully capitalize the effect of current issues of public debt on future taxes (see, for a critique of this so-called 'Ricardian doctrine', Tobin 1980).

is not wholly realistic, it does not seem an unreasonable simplification at the present level of abstraction.

In a price-taking economy the rate of investment should be explained in terms of (expected) profitability and financial factors, as discussed in Chapters 3 and 4. Note that because of the constant technique of production the growth of production in this model is again equal to the investment–capital ratio ($\rho = i$). As we further neglect the distribution of wealth within the private sector (and therefore debt of firms as well) the determination of investment and growth can be written as:

$$\rho = \rho(\pi,\, r,\, \tau_2,\, \zeta); \qquad \rho_\pi,\, \rho_\zeta > 0;\; \rho_r,\, \rho_\tau < 0; \qquad (7.4)$$

where the parameter ζ again captures the state of risk and all determinants of the conflict between managers and shareholders.

As regards the budgetary regime we shall for the moment follow Blinder and Solow (1973) and take government expenditure (g) and tax rates ($\tau_1,\, \tau_2$) to be fixed. Later we shall consider other regimes as well.

Then with given c, $i(=\rho)$, and g it can be established that the balance of trade (f) must be equal to the gap between domestic production (y) and aggregate expenditure,

$$f = y - g - c - \rho. \qquad (7.5)$$

This equilibrium will be ensured by the fact that in a small open economy with perfect competition on international markets, domestic producers are able to sell all goods produced at capacity level at the prevailing international prices.

The financial sector

So much for the real part of the model. For the financial sector straightforward relations will be chosen. The small open-economy assumption entails that prices always satisfy purchasing-power parity. The nominal interest rate (R) is assumed to be equal to the international interest rate (R_f) plus the (expected = actual) rate of depreciation $(d\Theta/dt)(1/\Theta)$ plus a factor (σ) measuring the risk premium on domestic assets for international portfolio-holders. In this model we assume that this risk premium is related negatively to the foreign creditor position (e), or equivalently, positively to the volume of foreign debt. All other factors determining σ are assumed to be constant in the present analysis. If it is finally assumed that demand for money (M) is a simple homogeneously linear function of domestic production (Py), the financial relations can be modelled as:

$$P = \Theta.P_f;$$

$$R = R_f + (d\Theta/dt)(1/\Theta) + \sigma(e); \qquad \sigma' < 0;$$

$$M = \mu Py; \qquad \mu = \text{constant};$$

where P = price level, Θ = exchange rate, and the subscript f denotes foreign variables. It is well known that these equations reduce to the following relations for the real interest rate r and money growth:

$$r = r_f + \sigma(e); \qquad \sigma' < 0; \tag{7.6}$$

$$(dM/dt)(1/M) = p + \rho. \tag{7.7}$$

The real interest rate is thus determined by the international interest rate r_f and the risk premium σ related to the net foreign position e. The second equation represents the familiar conclusion in these kinds of models that inflation is a purely monetary phenomenon. As to the regime of monetary policy the government can choose for either fixing the growth of money stock or adopting a fixed target for the rate of inflation (and thereby depreciation) and adjusting money growth to that target. The difference between those regimes may be important when the growth rate of production varies. In what follows it will be assumed that the government chooses the latter option, so that monetary policy is adequately represented by the target for the rate of inflation.

Now the static part of the model is completed. Its structure is very simple. It consists of 7 independent equations, 7 endogenous variables (w, y_2, r, c, ρ, f, $(dM/dt)(1/M)$), 4 policy variables (g, τ_2, τ_1, p), and 3 state variables (e, b, π) which are historically given and will be explained in the next section.

7.4. The dynamics

The dynamics of the model arises from the GBC and the BPC and the interaction between growth and income distribution. With respect to this latter process, it will be assumed that the rate of profit is determined by a conflict model of income distribution, the common outcome of which is that the rate of change in π depends in one way or another on the evolution of the unemployment rate. Since the change in the unemployment rate in turn depends on the difference between the actual and the natural growth rate, in our model this relationship may, as in the foregoing chapter (eq. 6.5*a*), be captured in the following linear expression:

$$\dot{\pi} = \vartheta_\pi(n - \rho); \quad v_\pi > 0; \tag{7.8}$$

where n = growth of labour supply (natural rate of growth) and ρ the growth rate of production and employment.

The evolution of the financial stocks e and b depends on the GBC and BPC. If one takes into account that the ratios of money and debt are continuously being reduced by the rate of inflation and the growth rate of production, these budget constraints are given by:

$$\dot{e} = y - g - c - i + (r + p)e - (\rho + p)e; \tag{7.9}$$

$$\dot{b} + \dot{m} = g + (r + p)b - \tau_1(y - \pi) -$$
$$\tau_2(\pi + rb + re - pm) - (\rho + p)(b + m); \tag{7.10}$$

where $r + p$ = nominal interest rate. According to the first equation the change in the foreign lending position depends on the balance of payments on current account ($= f + (r + p)e$) less the reduction in e through nominal production growth $(\rho + p)$.[7] The second equation states that the change in public debt and money stock is equal to government outlays (including interest payments) less tax revenue and less the reduction in b and m through nominal production growth. Since the ratio of money to national product is

---

[7] It has been assumed that the net stock of foreign reserves is nil, so that the balance of payments on current account must be fully financed by interest-bearing debt.

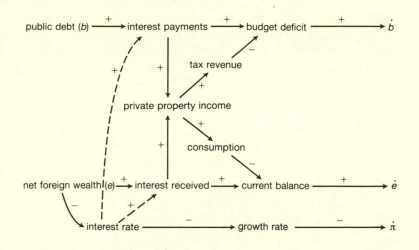

FIG. 7.1 Dynamics of public debt and foreign wealth

assumed to be constant (hence $\dot{m} = 0$) the fundamental causal relationships resulting from the GBC and the BPC can be illustrated by Fig. 7.1.

This figure, in which for expository reasons the effects of π have been disregarded, shows that greater public debt leads to greater interest payments to the private sector and thus on the one hand to a larger budget deficit and on the other hand to larger private property income. This larger property income increases tax receipts, thus mitigating the increase in the government's budget deficit, and consumption, thereby worsening the balance of payments on current account. This is one line in the scheme. The other runs from the net foreign position (e) to interest received from abroad and thus to the current account and via property income to tax revenue and the budget deficit. In addition e influences the system through its impact on the interest rate and thus on interest payments and the growth rate.

The impact of the profit rate on $\dot{b}$ and $\dot{e}$ —not shown in the scheme—is a rather complex one. In the first place a higher π leads to a higher growth rate and thus to a reduction in the absolute magnitude of $\dot{b}$ and $\dot{e}$. On the other hand a higher growth rate induces larger investments and therefore a decline of the trade balance. Finally, a change in π will change income distribution and thus tax revenue and consumption. Under the plausible assumptions that $\tau_2 \geqslant \tau_1$ and $c_2 < c_1$ a higher profit implies higher tax revenue (thereby reducing b) and lower consumption (thereby increasing $\dot{e}$).

Local stability

Whether or not this system is (locally) stable around its steady state solution (e_s, b_s, π_s) can be established from the linearized system based on equations 7.8, 7.9, and 7.10.

$$
\begin{bmatrix} \dot{e} \\ \dot{b} \\ \dot{\pi} \end{bmatrix} = \begin{bmatrix} \varepsilon_1 - n & -h_2 & -\varepsilon_5 \\ -\varepsilon_3 & \varepsilon_4 - n & -\varepsilon_6 \\ -\vartheta_\pi \rho_r \sigma' & 0 & -\vartheta_\pi \rho_\pi \end{bmatrix} \begin{bmatrix} e - e_s \\ b - b_s \\ \pi - \pi_s \end{bmatrix}, \qquad (7.11)
$$

where $\varepsilon_1 = r - c_2(1 - \tau_2)r - c_z$

$$- \sigma'\{c_r + c_2(1 - \tau_2)(b + e) - \rho_r(1 + e) - e\},$$

$$\varepsilon_2 = c_2(1 - \tau_2)r + c_z,$$

$$\varepsilon_3 = \tau_2 r + \sigma'\{\tau_2(b + e) + \rho_2(b + m) - b\},$$

$$\varepsilon_4 = (1 - \tau_2)r,$$

$$\varepsilon_5 = \rho_\pi(1 + e) - \{c_1(1 - \tau_1) - c_2(1 - \tau_2)\},$$

$$\varepsilon_6 = \rho_\pi(b + m) + (\tau_2 - \tau_1).$$

This system is stable if the real parts of the characteristic roots of the state matrix (subsequently denoted as the J-matrix) are negative, or by the modified Routh–Hurwitz conditions if:

  I. $\text{Tr}(J) < 0$; $\qquad\qquad\qquad\qquad\qquad\qquad\qquad\qquad$ (7.12)

  II. $\text{Det}(J) > 0$;

  III. $\text{Det} \begin{bmatrix} 2n - \varepsilon_1 - \varepsilon_4 & \varepsilon_6 & -\varepsilon_5 \\ 0 & n - \varepsilon_1 + \vartheta_\pi \rho_\pi & \varepsilon_2 \\ -\vartheta_\pi \rho_r \sigma' & \varepsilon_3 & n - \varepsilon_4 + \vartheta_\pi \rho_\pi \end{bmatrix} > 0.$

These conditions are difficult to deal with on an analytical level. Therefore we will start with a somewhat simpler specific case in which the real interest rate is independent of the net foreign debt, $\sigma' = 0$. In this manner we will be able to trace some of the basic determinants of stability. Thereafter we will return to the general model and check whether the characteristics found for the specific case are also valid if the assumption $\sigma' = 0$ is dropped.

7.5 A special case: exogenous interest rate

When $\sigma' = 0$ the real interest rate is simply given by the international interest rate and is thus exogenous to the present model. This considerably simplifies the solution of the conditions for stability. From equations 7.11 and 7.12 it can be found that the Routh–Hurwitz conditions now reduce to:

$$\text{I. } 2n - \varepsilon_1 - \varepsilon_4 + \vartheta_\pi \rho_\pi > 0; \tag{7.13a}$$

$$\text{II. } \vartheta_\pi \rho_\pi \{(n - \varepsilon_1)(n - \varepsilon_4) - \varepsilon_2 \varepsilon_3\} > 0;$$

$$\text{III. } (2n - \varepsilon_1 - \varepsilon_4)\{(n - \varepsilon_1)(n - \varepsilon_4) - \varepsilon_2 \varepsilon_3$$

$$+ \vartheta_\pi \rho_\pi (2n - \varepsilon_1 - \varepsilon_4 - \vartheta_\pi \rho_\pi)\} > 0.$$

If both conditions (I) and (II) are satisfied, it can easily be seen that the third condition can only be fulfilled if $\vartheta_\pi \rho_\pi > 0$ and $(2n - \varepsilon_1 - \varepsilon_4) > 0$. This implies that the above conditions reduce to:

$$\text{I. } 2n - \varepsilon_1 - \varepsilon_4 > 0; \tag{7.13b}$$

$$\text{II. } (n - \varepsilon_1)(n - \varepsilon_4) - \varepsilon_2 \varepsilon_3 > 0;$$

$$\text{III. } \vartheta_\pi \rho_\pi > 0.$$

This result is interesting for it implies a kind of dichotomy in the stability conditions. That is, these conditions would also have been found if the dynamics of growth and income distribution on the one hand and the accumulation of financial assets on the other hand were considered separately. Condition (III) is conclusive for the stability of income distribution and growth, and given a certain growth rate the conditions (I) and (II) determine the stability b and e.

Conditions (I) and (II) can be reduced by substituting for the ε coefficients;

$$n - r > 0; \tag{7.14}$$

$$n - (1 - c_2)(1 - \tau_2)r + c_z > 0.$$

Since $0 \leqslant c_2 \leqslant 1$, $0 \leqslant \tau_2 \leqslant 1$, and $c_z \geqslant 0$ it can easily be seen that the first condition is conclusive to stability for any $r \geqslant 0$. This is a very simple and clear-cut result. Since the interest rate is given internationally it means that the domestic growth rate n is the principal determinant of stability. Slowly growing economies will therefore be much more liable to unstable asset accumulation than similar economies with rapid growth. In a stationary economy ($n = 0$) instability proves even to be inevitable, unless the real interest rate is negative. This confirms the pessimistic view on stability emerging from studies based on stationary IS/LM models, as mentioned in Chapter 6. In our model this proves even to be true irrespective of the wealth elasticity of consumption c_z.

In addition to this main point we should make two other observations. First, the stability of the system is independent of the rate of inflation, and thus of the rate of depreciation. This implies that monetary policy cannot—in the long run— alter the stability of debt accumulation. This contrasts with the conclusion of Blinder and Solow and many others that the model will be less unstable as the degree of money financing is greater. In the present model even tax policy is ineffective with respect to stability or instability. This does not mean, however, that the monetary and fiscal policy are not important at all. Below we shall see that they may have some impact on stability when other policy regimes are chosen. Furthermore these policy instruments will be shown to have an important impact on the steady state values of b and e (section 7.4).

Secondly, it must be pointed out that for other fiscal policy regimes less stringent conditions for stability are found. So far we have followed Blinder and Solow in taking government expenditure (g) as the relevant exogenous policy variable. As we have discussed in Chapter 5, several alternative regimes have been put forward in the literature, namely:

- fixed expenditure including interest payments net of taxes (Tobin–Buiter);
- fixed expenditure including gross interest payments (Christ);
- fixed budget deficit (Domar);
- fixed debt ratio (Barro).

The results for these policy regimes are presented in Table 7.1. Since p cannot be less than $-r$ (otherwise the nominal interest rate would be negative) the conditions for each alternative regime prove to be less stringent than in the original case with fixed g. This is obviously due to the fact that these regimes imply that g declines endogenously as interest payments rise. It should however be noted that this automatic 'crowding-out' is bounded by the condition that government expenditure should not become negative.

TABLE 7.1 *Conditions for stability under alternative policy regimes*[a]

Regimes	Conditions	
1. Blinder–Solow fixed g	$n - r > 0$;	$n - (1 - c_2)(1 - \tau_2)r$ $+ c_z > 0$
2. Tobin–Buiter fixed $g' = g + (1 - \tau_2)(r + p)b$	$n - r$ $+ (1 - \tau_2)(r + p) > 0$;	$n - (1 - c_2)(1 - \tau_2)r$ $+ c_z > 0$
3. Christ fixed $g'' = g + (r + p)b$	$n + p > 0$;	$n - (1 - c_2)(1 - \tau_2)r$ $+ c_z > 0$
4. Domar fixed deficit	$n + p > 0$;	$n - (1 - c_2)(1 - \tau_2)r$ $+ c_z > 0$
5. Barro fixed b		$n - (1 - c_2)(1 - \tau_2)r$ $+ c_z > 0$

[a] In all regimes it is assumed that the target is achieved by adjusting g. A proof of these results is given in Appendix 7.1.

These results show that under each regime the condition $n - (1 - c_2)(1 - \tau_2)r + c_z > 0$ is a necessary, though not always a sufficient, condition for stability. It is evident that whenever this condition is conclusive, the government has a powerful instrument for ensuring the system's stability, namely the tax rate on property income τ_2. The conditions in the first column turn out to be different for each regime. For the Domar, Tobin–Buiter, and Christ regimes, they imply that monetary policy may contribute to stability by ensuring that the inflation rate is not too low ($p > -n$ in regimes (3) and (4), and $p > (\tau_2 r - n)/(1 - \tau_2)$ in (2)). Thus unlike the reference regime these alternative regimes leave considerable room for fiscal and monetary policy to influence the stability of the system.

Another interesting feature of the alternative regimes is that the system may be stable even in the absence of real growth. Provided that $p > 0$ (in regimes (3) and (4)) or $p > \tau_2 r/(1 - \tau_2)$ (in regime (2)) the evolution of debt will be stable if the wealth elasticity of consumption is sufficiently large; that is, if $c_z > (1 - c_2)(1 - \tau_2)r$. This corroborates the basic conclusion of the stationary IS/LM models that a positive wealth effect is an essential prerequisite for stability of public debt, but is, of course, in contrast with the conclusions of the previous chapter.

7.6 The general case

Returning to the general case it can first be shown that the conclusion on the decisive role of the growth rate and the interest rate is also valid when $\sigma' < 0$. Solving the Routh–Hurwitz conditions (7.12) it is found that:

I. $2n - \varepsilon_1 - \varepsilon_4 + \vartheta_\pi \rho_\pi > 0$;

II. $\vartheta_\pi \rho_\pi \{(n - \varepsilon_1)(n - \varepsilon_4) - \varepsilon_2 \varepsilon_3\} + \vartheta_\pi \rho_r \sigma' \{\varepsilon_2 \varepsilon_6 - (n - \varepsilon_4)\varepsilon_5\} > 0$;

III. $(2n - \varepsilon_1 - \varepsilon_4)(n - \varepsilon_1)\{(n - \varepsilon_4) - \varepsilon_2 \varepsilon_3$

$\quad + \vartheta_\pi \rho_\pi (2n - \varepsilon_1 - \varepsilon_4 + \vartheta_\pi \rho_\pi)\}$

$\quad - \vartheta_\pi \rho_r \sigma' \{\varepsilon_2 \varepsilon_6 + (n - \varepsilon_1)\varepsilon_5 + \vartheta_\pi \rho_\pi \varepsilon_5\} > 0$.

Provided that $\vartheta_\pi \rho_\pi > 0$ it can be seen that condition (I) is a positive linear function of n, condition (II) a positive quadratic function of n, and condition (III) a cubic function of n with a positive first term. This implies that the system will

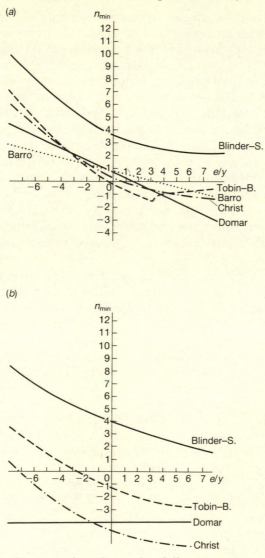

Note: This figure is based on the following parameter values: $y = 0.5$; $c_2 = 0.2$; $c_1 = 0.9$; $\tau_1 = 0.3$; $\tau_2 = 0.4$; $c_r = -0.2$; $\sigma' = -0.01$; $\rho_\pi = 0.5$; $\rho_r = -0.5$; $m/y = 0.1$; $b/y = 0.5$; $\vartheta_\pi = 0.25$; $p = 0.04$; $r = 0.04$. For the Barro regime with $c_z = 0.1$ (Fig. 7.2b) the critical growth rate varies from -7.1% if $e/y = -7$ to -10.5% for $e/y = 7$.

FIG. 7.2 Minimum growth rate required for stability.

always be stable whenever the growth rate is sufficiently high. In a similar way it can be established that stability is also ensured if the real interest is sufficiently low (see Appendix 7.2).

Since these conditions are difficult to handle in more detail on the analytical level it may be useful to present some numerical results for plausible values of the parameters. A convenient device for assessing the stability characteristics of the model is to calculate the critical growth rate that is the minimum required for stability, n_{min} (see section 6.3). Then, the lower this minimum growth rate is, the more unlikely it will be for the system to be unstable.

Fig. 7.2 presents the results for the critical growth rate n_{min} in relation to the net creditor position e for the case with zero wealth elasticity and for the case with high wealth elasticity ($c_z = 0.1$). For all growth rates in the area above these curves the system is stable. In both cases the Blinder–Solow regime proves again to be significantly more restrictive than the other regimes, especially when the wealth elasticity is high. Further these figures bring out that the system in general becomes more stable if e/y is larger. This means that a country with large foreign debts will be more liable to instability than a net creditor country. This general rule is, however, violated for a certain interval with high e under the Tobin–Buiter regime (Fig. 7.2*a*).

Further it may be noticed that in Fig. 7.2*b* the Domar regime yields Domar's original condition for stability, namely that the nominal rate of growth should be positive (hence $n > -p$ and thus in this example $n > -4$ per cent). Finally, a remarkable result of the present analysis is that for the Blinder–Solow regime a high wealth elasticity of consumption turns out to make the system less stable. This confirms the conclusion of the previous chapter (as well as Chapter 2). For other regimes, however, our results seem to confirm the usual findings.

How the minimum growth rate depends on the other variables can be seen from Table 7.2, which presents the partial derivatives of n_{min} for the reference regime at three different levels of e in relation to domestic production y. The signs of most coefficients conform with what might intuitively be expected. Yet several observations may be made. First, it is important to note that a change in r leads to a practically one-for-one change in n_{min}. Secondly, unlike in the case with a purely exogenous interest rate, fiscal policy now appears to have some influence on the system's stability through the tax rates τ_2 and τ_1. However, the coefficients are very low. If, for example, τ_2 is raised by 10 percentage points the minimum growth rate falls by only 0.24 points (if $e = 0$). Monetary policy turns out to be totally ineffective again. Finally, these results confirm our observations from Fig. 7.2 that n_{min} goes down as e increases (and b decreases) and that a higher wealth elasticity pushes n_{min} up.

TABLE 7.2 *Partial derivatives of* n_{nim}

	$e/y = -2$	$e/y = 0$	$e/y = 2$
r	0.993	0.968	0.939
p	0	0	0
e/y	-0.005	-0.004	-0.004
b/y	0.005	0.005	0.005
m/y	0	0	0
τ_1	0.019	0.018	0.017
τ_2	-0.005	-0.024	-0.042
c_z	0.004	0.012	0.011
ϑ_π	0	0	0

Note: The parameter values are the same as in Fig. 7.2.

A somewhat remarkable result is that the reaction coefficient of the profit rate (ϑ_π) does not seem to influence n_{min}. In our numerical example this is due to the fact that the second Routh–Hurwitz condition, which is independent of ϑ_π, is conclusive to stability. Only when ϑ_π becomes very small does it appear to have an impact on n_{min}. This suggests that the interaction between growth and income distribution is a relatively 'fast' process in comparison to the dynamics of debt accumulation. This does not at all mean, however, that ϑ_π is unimportant; it can be shown to have an important impact on the shape and the duration of the adjustment trajectory.

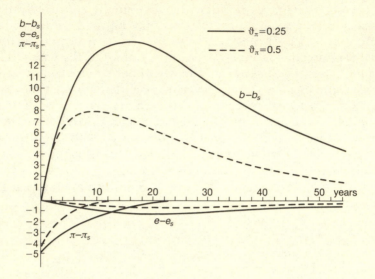

Note: This figure is based on a dynamic simulation of the linearized system (equation 7.11) starting from $e - e_s = 0$, $b - b_s = 0$, and $\pi - \pi_s = -0.05$. The natural growth rate is 6% and the interest rate 2%. All other variables have the same values as in Fig. 7.2a.

FIG. 7.3 The adjustment trajectory

This is demonstrated in Fig. 7.3, which is based on a simulation of the adjustment process starting from an initial situation characterized by a profit rate 5 percentage points below its steady state value π_s.

This figure brings out that the profit rate adjusts fairly rapidly to its steady state value. However, because during the first period the growth rate is below its equilibrium value government debt moves away from its steady state level reaching a peak of nearly 15 per cent (of domestic production) above b_s. That the accumulation of net foreign assets is much less affected is due to the fact that the lower profit rate and the growth rate have opposite effects on the balance of payments. Whereas the lower profit rate tends to create a deficit on current account because it increases consumption, the lower growth rate mitigates this effect because investment will be less. With the given parameter values, the first effect proves to be somewhat stronger so that the lower profit rate leads to a modest worsening of the international debtor position. When π approaches its steady state level the growth of public debt and foreign debt levels off, whereafter a long phase of steady decline of b and e sets in. In the case of a higher speed of adjustment of π ($\vartheta_\pi = 0.5$) the profit rate and the growth rate recover much faster, so that the amplitude of the movements in b and e is less wide.

7.7 Steady state equilibrium

Along the steady growth path all financial stocks must grow by the same rate as domestic product. As the growth of assets must be provided for by the government budget deficit and the surplus in the balance of payments on current account, these accounts will in general not be in balance. In nominal terms these accounts must satisfy:

$$\text{budget deficit} \quad : dB/dt + dM/dt = (n + p)(m + b)PK;$$

$$\text{current account}: dE/dt \qquad = (n + p)ePK$$

Where PK is the nominal capital stock, and B, M, and E the nominal stocks in absolute terms of public debt, money, and foreign assets.

Christ (1979) has pointed out for the closed economy that in the stationary fix-price models of Blinder–Solow and Tobin–Buiter equilibrium must be characterized by a balanced budget. But if one allows for inflation as in Christ this result is modified since then *real* stocks of financial assets need to be constant. This requires the government budget to show a deficit in order to satisfy the growing need for nominal assets due to inflation. It will be evident that in a growing economy the GBC must satisfy the increase in demand for nominal assets due to inflation as well as to real growth.

For an open economy the same reasoning can be applied to the BPC. In a zero growth, zero inflation economy the current account must be balanced. In a zero growth economy with inflation the current account must show a surplus when $e > 0$ or a deficit when $e < 0$ to supply the growing need of foreign assets or liabilities due to inflation, while in a growing economy it must supply the need due to real growth as well.

How the financial stocks and income distribution are influenced by the other variables in this model can be established from the total differential of equations 7.8, 7.9, and 7.10 subject to the steady state condition $b = \dot{e} = \dot{\pi} = 0$, which gives:[8]

$$0 = J \begin{bmatrix} \mathrm{d}e_s \\ \mathrm{d}b_s \\ \mathrm{d}\pi_s \end{bmatrix} + A\mathrm{d}x, \qquad (7.15a)$$

where J is equal to the J-matrix in equation 7.11, x a vector representing all other determinants of the system, and A the corresponding matrix of partial derivatives. Rewriting equation 7.15a we find the steady state effects:

$$\begin{bmatrix} \mathrm{d}e_s \\ \mathrm{d}b_s \\ \mathrm{d}\pi_s \end{bmatrix} = - J^{-1}A\mathrm{d}x. \qquad (7.15b)$$

In discussing this relation we shall follow the same procedure as before, first restricting the analysis to the simpler specific case with $\sigma' = 0$ and thereafter dealing with the general case on the basis of some numerical results. In addition, the analysis will be confined to the impact of the instrument variables of the government g, τ_1, τ_2, and p.

Solving equation 7.15 for $\sigma' = 0$ it is obtained that:

---

[8] In short-term analysis it is sometimes suggested that the so-called 'McKinnon–Oates condition' is sufficient for equilibrium in the case of perfect capital mobility and $\sigma' = 0$. This condition states that—for stationary equilibrium—the deficit in the government's budget should equal the deficit in the balance of payments on current account. Turnovsky (1976) has pointed out rightly that this condition is in fact a sufficient condition only in some very specific cases. More generally, conditions are required to hold for both variables separately. This is confirmed by the present analysis. This can be shown as follows. In our model the proper equivalent of the McKinnon–Oates condition appears to be $\dot{e} + b = 0$. Since also $\dot{\pi} = 0$ and all other variables are assumed to be constant, it can be seen from eq. 7.11 that this condition is fulfilled only if both $\dot{e} = 0$ and $b = 0$ or if the H-matrix satisfies: $[-1 \ \ 1 \ \ 0]' = -J[-1 \ \ 1 \ \ \mathrm{d}\pi/\mathrm{d}b]'$, where the prime denotes the transpose of the vector. On closer view this latter possibility should, however, be discarded for it is found to be satisfied only if $r = -1$, which is not only very unrealistic, but also in contradiction with the first-order conditions for stability above.

$$
\begin{bmatrix} de_s \\ db_s \\ d\pi_s \end{bmatrix} = \frac{1}{\text{Det}(J)}
$$

$$
\begin{bmatrix}
\vartheta_\pi \rho_\pi (n - \varepsilon_4) & -\vartheta_\pi \rho_\pi \varepsilon_2 & \varepsilon_2 \varepsilon_6 - (n - \varepsilon_4)\varepsilon_5 \\
-\vartheta_\pi \rho_\pi \varepsilon_3 & \vartheta_\pi \rho_\pi (n - \varepsilon_1) & \varepsilon_3 \varepsilon_5 - (n - \varepsilon_1)\varepsilon_6 \\
0 & 0 & (n - \varepsilon_1)(n - \varepsilon_4) - \varepsilon_2 \varepsilon_3
\end{bmatrix}
$$

$$
\begin{bmatrix}
-1 & c_1(y - \pi) & c_2 y_2 - (1 + e)\rho_\tau & c_2(1 - \tau_2) \\
1 & -(y - \pi) & -y_2 - (b + m)\rho_\tau & -(1 - \tau_2)m \\
0 & 0 & -\vartheta_\pi \rho_\tau & 0
\end{bmatrix}
\begin{bmatrix} dg \\ d\tau_1 \\ d\tau_2 \\ dp \end{bmatrix}. \quad (7.16)
$$

If the system is stable (hence $\text{Det}(J) > 0$ and $n - r > 0$) and $\tau_2 \geqslant \tau_1$ it can be assessed that the structure of these matrices is:

$$
\begin{bmatrix} + & - & ? \\ - & + & ? \\ 0 & 0 & + \end{bmatrix}
\begin{bmatrix} - & + & + & + \\ + & - & ? & - \\ 0 & 0 & + & 0 \end{bmatrix},
$$

and for the product matrix:[9]

$$
\begin{bmatrix} de_s \\ db_s \\ d\pi_s \end{bmatrix} =
\begin{bmatrix} - & + & + & + \\ + & - & - & - \\ 0 & 0 & + & 0 \end{bmatrix}
\begin{bmatrix} dg \\ d\tau_1 \\ d\tau_2 \\ dp \end{bmatrix}.
$$

Thus both tax rates τ_2 and τ_1 and the 'inflation tax' p have a positive impact on e_s and a negative impact on b_s. Government expenditure has just the opposite effects. These results are quite straightforward and need little further comment. An interesting result is that none of these instruments except τ_2 affects the steady state profit rate π_s. This is due to the fact that the interest rate is given, so that π_s only depends on the

---

[9] For $de_s/d\tau_2$ it is obtained that: $de_s/d\tau_2 = (n - \varepsilon_4)c_2 y_2 + \varepsilon_2 y_2 - \varepsilon_2(\tau_2 - \tau_1)\rho_\tau/\rho_\pi - \{c_1(1 - \tau_1) - c_2(1 - \tau_2)\}(n - \varepsilon_4)\rho_\tau/\rho_\pi$. Since $n - \varepsilon_4, \varepsilon_2, y_2 > 0$ and $\tau_2 \geqslant \tau_1$ this expression must always be > 0. Similarly it is found for $db_s/d\tau_2$ that: $db_s/d\tau_2 = \varepsilon_3 c_2 y_2 - (n - \varepsilon_1)y_2 + \{c_1(1 - \tau_1) - c_2(1 - \tau_2)\}\varepsilon_3 \rho_\tau/\rho_\pi + (\tau_2 - \tau_1)(n - \varepsilon_1)\rho_\tau/\rho_\pi < 0$.

natural growth rate, the given interest rate, and the tax rate on profits.

A similar structure of the product matrix is found for the general case with $\sigma' < 0$ for plausible values of the parameters. For $n = 6$ per cent and $r = 4$ per cent[10] it is obtained that:

$$
\begin{bmatrix} de/y \\ db_s/y \\ d\pi_s \end{bmatrix} = \begin{bmatrix} -33.2 & 24.2 & 5.2 & 0.6 \\ 43.5 & -33.7 & -9.0 & -1.9 \\ 0.3 & -0.2 & 0.05 & -0.06 \end{bmatrix} \begin{bmatrix} dg/y \\ d\tau_1 \\ d\tau_2 \\ dp \end{bmatrix},
$$

where e and b are expressed in ratios to y in order to ease the interpretation. Note that all coefficients have the same sign as in the $\sigma' = 0$ case above. The principal difference concerns the last row, which now shows positive effects on the profit rate of government expenditure g and tax on property income τ_2 and negative effects of τ_1 and p. These effects arise from the impact of these variables on e and thereby, since $\sigma' \neq 0$, on the interest rate. Apart from this indirect influence τ_2 has a direct effect on π, for at a higher τ_2 the (gross) profit rate needs to be higher in order to maintain growth equilibrium.

It should be noted that the absolute size of the coefficients in the product-matrix is very sensitive to the growth rate and the interest rate. For instance, if the interest rate is 2 per cent instead of 4 per cent a change in g by 0.01 would have led to an increase in public debt of only 0.06 instead of 0.44 as in the matrix above. And if the growth rate is 8 per cent instead of 6 per cent the change in public debt would reduce from 0.44 to 0.24.

7.8 A current balance regime

In all the foregoing analysis it was assumed that the government adopts a certain target for its fiscal policy irrespective of the outcome for the balance of payments. In this respect we followed the tradition of most GBC literature. However, this assumption does not seem very realistic, in particular for

[10] All parameter values are the same as in Fig. 7.2a. Further it is assumed that $\pi = 0.10$ and $\rho_\tau = -0.05$.

(small) open economies. In most countries the position of the balance of payments on current account is an important guideline of fiscal policy besides domestic considerations. For example, until the end of the 1970s budgetary policy in The Netherlands was formally directed at a structural norm of a 1 per cent surplus in the balance of payments on current account. Besides, it is well known for many countries that the urge for fiscal restraint is, in practice, much stronger in the case of a deficit in the current account than when it shows a comfortable surplus.

In this final section we shall examine the (extreme) case in which fiscal policy is fully directed at maintaining equilibrium in the current account. Assuming that the initial net stocks of foreign assets is nil as well, this policy constraint implies that $f = 0$ and $\dot{e} = 0$. If the government achieves this target by varying its expenditure g it can be seen from equation 7.5 that g must satisfy:

$$g = y - c - i. \tag{7.17}$$

Substituting this relation in the GBC the linearized differential system becomes:

$$\begin{bmatrix} \dot{b} \\ \dot{\pi} \end{bmatrix} = \begin{bmatrix} \varepsilon_1 - n & -\varepsilon_5 \\ 0 & \vartheta_\pi \rho_\pi \end{bmatrix} \begin{bmatrix} b - b_s \\ \pi - \pi_s \end{bmatrix}, \tag{7.18}$$

where $\varepsilon_1 = (1 - c_2)(1 - \tau_2)r - c_z,$

$\varepsilon_5 = (1 + b + m)\rho_\pi + \{(1 - c_1)(1 - \tau_1) - (1 - c_2)(1 - \tau_2)\}.$

The Routh–Hurwitz conditions of this system are:

I. $\text{Tr}(J) = -(n - \varepsilon_1) - \vartheta_\pi \rho_\pi < 0;$

II. $\text{Det}(J) = (n - \varepsilon_1)\vartheta_\pi \rho_\pi > 0;$ \hfill (7.19)

which implies after substitution for ε_1 that:

$$n - (1 - c_2)(1 - \tau_2)r + c_z > 0; \tag{7.20}$$

$$\vartheta_\pi \rho_\pi > 0.$$

From these results it can be concluded immediately that under this balance of payments regime the system is more

stable than under the original budgetary regime which required $n > r$ (eq. 7.14).

  The dynamics of this case is illustrated in Fig. 7.4. The
$\dot{b} = 0$ locus is discontinuous at $\pi = \pi_1$ because at that profit
rate the growth rate just equals the minimum growth rate
n_{min}. The position of the vertical $\dot{\pi} = 0$ locus is determined by
the profit rate at which the corresponding growth rate is just
equal to the natural growth rate n. As in that case the rate of
unemployment is constant the income distribution will be
constant as well. From the investment function (eq. 7.4) it
can be inferred that the steady state profit rate π_s depends on
n, r, τ_2, and ζ. As regards the stability of the system it can
easily be seen that the system is stable if $\pi_s > \pi_1$ and hence
$n > n_{min}$ (Fig. 7.4a) and unstable if $\pi_s < \pi_1$ (Fig. 7.4b).

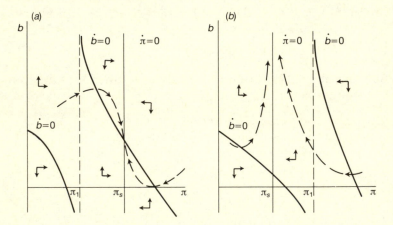

FIG. 7.4 Balanced current-account regime

Policy conclusions

On a very abstract level this model may illuminate some of
the recent experiences with fiscal policy in The Netherlands
and other European countries. As was described in the foregoing chapter, in the mid-1970s these countries were con-
fronted by several (external) shocks that on the whole had a
serious destabilizing effect on the growth of public debt. In
addition, in the beginning of the 1980s the real rate of interest
rose along with the international level of interest rates under

the influence of a changed mix of monetary and fiscal policy in the United States. The overall outcome of these shocks may be discussed with reference to Fig. 7.5. This figure draws the $\dot{b} = 0$ and the $\dot{\pi} = 0$ loci in the (b, π) plane. At π_s the growth rate equals the growth of labour supply ($\rho = n$). The asymptote at π_1 represents the profit rate at which the growth rate equals the critical growth rate ($\rho = n_{min}$). Let us assume that the economy was originally in its stable steady state equilibrium (b_s, π_s). Then, as a result of the fall in ζ and the rise in r, the $\dot{b} = 0$ locus shifts to the right as higher profit rates are necessary to ensure $\dot{b} = 0$. The effect of the changes in ζ, r, and n has a negative impact on π_s, while the changes in ζ and r tend to raise π_s. For simplicity let us therefore assume that these different effects neutralize each other, so that the $\dot{\pi} = 0$ locus is unchanged. As finally the exogenous fall in π implies a movement away from the original equilibrium, the initial position of the system after the 'shocks' is characterized by point A right of the original equilibrium.

Provided that the system is still stable ($\pi_1 < \pi_s$) the adjustment trajectory is described by the A–B curve, which shows that after a period of rising debt the system will eventually tend to a new stable equilibrium B where the profit rate has recovered to its original level and public debt has reached a

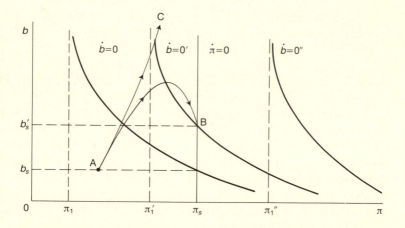

FIG. 7.5 Fall in profitability

higher but stable level. The specific shape of the adjustment trajectory can be explained as follows. As a result of the shocks the growth rate and thus the volume of investment fall to a lower level. Then, in order to avoid the emergence of a surplus in the current account the government has to raise its expenditure discretely. Because of the lower growth rate and the higher expenditure public debt starts to increase sharply. Later, as the profit rate and the growth rate recover this rising tendency is mitigated and may even turn into steady decline.

Next imagine that the rise in r and the fall in n are such that the system becomes unstable. In Fig. 7.5 this is shown by a further shift of the $\dot{b} = 0$ locus to the right. Then the adjustment process will follow the explosive A–C path. Although along this path the profit rate again tends to its stable level (π_s), public debt keeps growing till infinity. It may be noted that for government expenditure this trajectory entails that after the initial discretionary increase in public expenditure, the government has to bring down its expenditure continuously. This follows from the balance of payments target which implies that as private investment and consumption rise (because of the growing interest income), public expenditure must be reduced equivalently. Since debt grows without any limit it can easily be seen that sooner or later public expenditure will become fully 'crowded out' by the rise in private expenditure, and thereafter should even have to become negative, which is of course impossible.

How is this unstable process to be stopped? There are several options. The first and by far the most attractive option would be to raise the natural growth rate to such a level that the system becomes stable again. However, it is obvious that this option may be hard to achieve in reality. A second option is to raise taxes on wages. This may temporarily mitigate the 'crowding-out' of government expenditure by shifting the burden to wage-earners, but since it does not cure the instability of the system this cannot provide a permanent solution. A third option is to raise taxes on private property income. This is a much more attractive option, for it not only relieves the burden of the government but also reduces the instability of the system. If the tax rate is raised above the critical level

$\tau_2 = 1 - (n + c_z)/\{(1 - c_2)r\}$ (eq. 7.20) the process will even become stable again.

Although this last option is most effective from a long-term point of view, it is doubtful whether it will also be a politically attractive option because it leads to a *lower* growth rate of production and thus maybe even to a steeper rise in public debt in the short term.[11] This is illustrated in Fig. 7.6 which shows the adjustment trajectory for debt (b) and growth rate

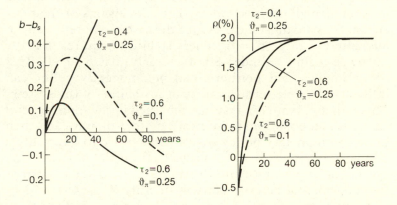

Note: This figure is based on a dynamic simulation of the linearized system (equation 7.18). Before $t = 0$ steady state equilibrium is characterized by $n = 2\%$, $r = 4\%$, $\tau_2 = 0.4$, and all other variables as in Fig. 7.2a. At $t = 0$, r rises to 5% thereby making the system unstable ($n = 2\% < n_{min} = 2.4$). If τ_2 is raised to 0.6 stability is again restored ($n = 2\% > n_{min} = 1.6\%$).

FIG. 7.6 Adjustment trajectories of b and ρ

(ρ) after an increase in r for the case in which τ_2 is left unchanged ($\tau_2 = 0.4$), and for the case where τ_2 is raised to 0.6 in order to restore stability. As this figure brings out the second (stable) alternative implies lower growth and higher debt in the 'short' run. The duration of this short run depends mainly on the difference between the growth rate and the

[11] The impact effect of τ_2 on b is obtained by differentiation of the GBC: $d\dot{b}/d\tau_2 = -(b + m)\rho_\tau - y_2$. If the sensitivity of ρ for τ_2 is substantial this impact might well be positive.

interest rate and on the speed of adjustment of the profit rate (ϑ_π). If ϑ_π is low this 'short' run may be quite long (as is shown by the figure). But even for higher ϑ_π the short run seems to last decades rather than years; this may be too long for governments with a really short time-horizon (for example because of periodic elections).

7.9 Conclusion

In this chapter we have analysed the dynamics of growth and debt for a small open economy. The conclusions of the present analysis are most clear-cut for the case of a purely exogenous interest rate ($\sigma' = 0$). Then stability requires for the reference regime (Blinder–Solow) simply that $n - r > 0$. This result implies that neither fiscal nor monetary policy can influence the long-term stability or instability of the system. This rather pessimistic result is modified in the more general case with an endogenous interest rate ($\sigma' > 0$), but even then fiscal and monetary policy instruments prove to have only a very small impact or no impact at all on the system's stability. The growth rate and the interest rate emerge again as the fundamental determinants of stability.

In general for other policy regimes less stringent conditions for stability were found. A necessary condition common to all alternative regimes was that n must satisfy $n - (1 - c_2)(1 - \tau_2)r + c_z > 0$, which implies that the government has at least one important instrument by means of which it might effectively influence the stability of the system, namely the tax rate on property income τ_2.

All policy regimes which are commonly considered in the GBC literature focus on norms for government outlays, or taxes, irrespective of their consequences for the balance of payments. In this chapter we have argued that this is inappropriate, because in practice the balance of payments on current account is an important guideline for fiscal and monetary policies, in particular for (small) open economies. Therefore we have examined a regime with a zero current balance target. The conditions for stability were then found to be $\vartheta_\pi \rho_\pi > 0$ and $n - (1 - c_2)(1 - \tau_2)r + c_z > 0$, which implies that in this regime the stability can be influenced effectively by the government through manipulation of the tax rate on interest income τ_2. Monetary policy, aiming at a certain target rate of inflation or depreciation, is once again ineffective in this case.

Appendix 7.1 Alternative regimes

This appendix establishes the stability conditions for the alternative policy regimes given in section 7.4. In all other regimes it is assumed that the target of fiscal policy is achieved by varying g. This yields the following conditions for g:

2. Tobin-Buiter $g = g_0 - (1 - \tau_2)(r + p)b$;
3. Christ $g = g_0 - (r + p)b$;
4. Domar $g = g_0 + \tau_1 w + \tau_2 y_2 - (r + p)b$;
5. Barro $g = \tau_1 w + \tau_2 y_2 + (\rho + p)(b + m) - (r + p)b$;

These functions have the consequences shown in Table 7.3 for the elements of the first two rows of the J-matrix.

TABLE 7.3 *Coefficient for alternative regimes*

New coefficient	Domar	Tobin–Buiter	Christ
$\varepsilon_1' =$	$\varepsilon_1 - \tau_2 r$ $+ \sigma'(b - \tau_2 b - \tau_2 e)$	ε_1	ε_1
$\varepsilon_2' =$	$\varepsilon_2 + \tau_2 r + (r + p)$	$\varepsilon_2 - (1 - \tau_2)(r + p)$	$\varepsilon_2 - (r + p)$
$\varepsilon_3' =$	0	ε_3	ε_3
$\varepsilon_4' =$	$-p$	$\varepsilon_4 - (1 - \tau_2)(r + p)$	$\varepsilon_4 - (r + p)$
$\varepsilon_5' =$	$\varepsilon_5 + (\tau_2 - \tau_1)$	ε_5	ε_5
$\varepsilon_6' =$	$\varepsilon_6 - (\tau_2 - \tau_1)$	ε_6	ε_6

The stability conditions for the regimes (2)–(4) are obtained by substituting the above new coefficients in the Routh–Hurwitz conditions, which yields for the Domar regime and for the Christ regime:

I. $n - p > 0$;
II. $n - (1 - c_2)(1 - \tau_2)r + c_z > 0$;

and for the Tobin–Buiter regime:

I. $n - \tau_2 r + (1 - \tau_2)p > 0$;

II. $n - (1 - c_2)(1 - \tau_2)r + c_z > 0$.

For the Barro regime where b = constant the system reduces to two dimensions. The new elements of the J-matrix are then:

$$\varepsilon_1' = \varepsilon_1 - \tau_2 r + \sigma'\{\tau_2(b + e) + (b + m)\rho_r - b\};$$

$$\varepsilon_5' = \varepsilon_5 + \tau_2 - \tau_1 + (b + m)\rho_\pi;$$

while ε_2, ε_3, ε_4, ε_5 are now equal to zero. For the reduced model with $\sigma' = 0$ this implies the condition $\varepsilon_1' - n > 0$, thus again:

$$n - (1 - c_2)(1 - \tau_2)r + c_z > 0.$$

These results are presented in Table 7.1 in the text.

Appendix 7.2 Stability of the general case

This appendix shows that the general model considered in section 7.6 is stable for a sufficiently low interest rate. Denoting the Routh–Hurwitz conditions by RH1, RH2, and RH3 it is obtained by differentiation from equation 7.12 that:

$dRH1/dr = -1 - (1 - c_2)(1 - \tau_2) < 0$;

$d^2RH2/dr^2 = 2\vartheta_\pi\rho_\pi(1 - c_2)(1 - \tau_2) > 0$;

$d^3RH3/dr^3 = -6(1 - c_2)(1 - \tau_2)\{1 - (1 - c_2)(1 - \tau_2)\} < 0$.

These results imply that RH1 is a negative linear function of r, RH2 a positive quadratic function of r, and RH3 a cubic function of r with a negative first term. These characteristics ensure that all conditions will be satisfied for sufficiently low (possibly negative) values of r.

8

Conclusion

This book investigates the dynamics of growth and debt on the basis of a disequilibrium model of medium-term and long-term growth. Particular attention is given to the dynamics ensuing from the government budget constraint.

The dynamics of government finance is usually analysed on the basis of a neo-classical-Keynesian IS/LM model. This model which concentrates on income–expenditure equilibrium neglects the distribution of income, and is essentially suited for short-period analysis. The evolution of public debt is, however, typically a long-period phenomenon. Therefore it is more appropriate to analyse the dynamics of public debt in the context of a growth model. Moreover, this model should also take account of the accumulation of debt and wealth in the private sector. In this book the dynamics of public debt is examined in relation to the distribution of wealth and debt between two distinct classes in the private sector. The last chapter also investigates the relationship of the dynamics of public debt with the growth of foreign debt and wealth.

8.1 Savings and growth

Starting from a simple generalized Pasinetti–Kaldor model with two social classes (workers and capitalists), Chapter 2 shows that the introduction of the government budget constraint raises serious difficulties with regard to the long-period solution of this model. In the presence of a government sector the steady state solution proved either to be unstable or to be characterized by a net *creditor* position of the government and the disappearance of the capitalist class. Apparently the traditional post-Keynesian model is too restrictive to provide a reasonable description of the long-term dynamics of the economy. Therefore it was necessary to develop a more sophisticated model.

Distribution effects

Although, according to Malinvaud (1986), the proposition of a higher propensity to save from profits than from wages is accepted by most macroeconomists, it still lacks a rigorous theoretical explanation. There seem to exist two opposing views, one starting from differences between the types of income (profits versus wages), and the other emphasizing differences between the agents who receive this income (workers versus capitalists or *rentiers*). The first approach is supported by Malinvaud (1986), who argues that changes in business income have a smaller impact on consumption than equivalent changes in wages income because of informational imperfections and liquidity constraints. This explanation of differential saving may be even more relevant in economies where savings by workers are institutionalized in obligatory savings schemes for pensions or social security funding. As premiums and transfers are only slowly adjusted to changes in the return of the investments, higher profits are not reflected in disposable income of households, and are thus automatically saved. The corporate or 'pension fund' veil is especially relevant in the short period. It is, however, hard to imagine that it will be an important factor in the long period as well. Sooner or later a structural change in profits will be recognized by households who will change their savings decisions accordingly.

For the explanation of differential saving we have therefore taken the other route emphasizing differences between the receivers of wages and profits. In this respect we follow the 'classical' view that differential saving is related to different types of agents in the economy.[1] As a first approximation we distinguish between two classes, namely workers with low

---

[1] In Ch. 7, which adds the foreign sector to the model, we have for practical reasons adopted a Kaldorian savings function with differential propensities to save related to types of income rather than to classes. This was necessary in order to reduce the dimensionality of the model.

propensity to save, and a corporate class of entrepreneurs and shareholders with a high savings propensity. This conception reconciles Kaldor's argument that differential saving has something to do with the organization of business with Pasinetti's notion of hereditary classes of workers and *rentiers*. In our model we assume that there exists a 'corporate class' with a distinct role in the economy and therefore with a different attitude towards saving and wealth. Workers are assumed to be risk averse and to save for their old age and inheritance only. For the corporate class saving and wealth is an aim in itself as it is a means of raising their power and status.

Of course, this division of the economy into two classes is schematic. A further improvement would be to disaggregate the economy into *n* agents or classes with different preferences towards saving and consumption. Besides the fact that this would tremendously complicate our analysis, one may doubt if it is very useful for the purpose of our analysis in which only two categories of income are distinguished, namely profits and wages.

Financial constraints

A (post-)Keynesian theory of investment can be built on the following principles:

1. The firm as organizer of investment: Investment projects do not exist as such, but only if embedded in the organizational and financial structure of a firm. Investment theory should therefore take account of the organizational limitations of growth and conflicting interests between managers, who desire expansion and perquisites, and shareholders, who desire maximum market value.

2. Imperfect markets: In the absence of perfect financial markets the investment decision cannot be separated from the finance decision. Imperfect capital markets imply rising costs of capital (cf. Eichner 1976), or even rationing of equity (cf. Greenwald and Stiglitz 1988*a*, 1988*b*). In this case internal savings, and thus current profits, and the availability of credit become primary determinants of investment.

3. Uncertainty: If future developments are uncertain the continuity or survival of the firm may be dominant relative to a first-best strategy of maximum growth or maximum profits. Therefore, investment strategies may be guided by rules and satisficing behaviour, rather than be derived from explicit maximization of some objective function.

In our modelling of investment we have emphasized the financial constraints. It is well known that in practice the flotation of new equity plays hardly any role in the financing of investment. In the absence of perfect equity markets firms have therefore to manage risks on their own, and must take account of the financial consequences when deciding on investment. In Chapters 3 and 4 we show that in the presence of financial constraints, arising from imperfect markets for risk sharing, investment can be explained in terms of internal savings and the desired rate of indebtedness. Thus investment depends on profits in two ways: as a source of finance (through the flow of internal savings) and as an incentive for taking risks (through the desired debt ratio).[2]

As a first step Chapter 3 investigates the determination of growth and investment on the basis of a model of a fully equity-rationed firm. This assumption is relaxed in Chapter 4 which introduces an (imperfect) equity market. In this chapter it is assumed that the market valuation of shares has a disciplining role with regard to managers. Following Odagiri (1981) it is assumed that risk of intervention by shareholders or take-over by others increases as the discrepancy between the actual market valuation and the maximum valuation becomes greater. Then, by discounting this risk in the managerial optimization procedure it is possible to establish a unique optimum growth strategy for the firm depending on the preferences of managers and shareholders, the chance of intervention by shareholders or take-overs, and the mean and the variance of profits, taxes, and the interest rate.

---

[2] In this respect our model is broader than Malinvaud (1980), who concentrates on the incentive role of profits: 'The main concern has been profitability as a precondition for risk-taking by entrepreneurs; the model cannot do much more than explore the consequences of such a precondition. Others will have to study the role of financial constraints' (Malinvaud 1980: 101).

8.2 Public debt and stability

Following a sequential analytical approach (cf. Malinvaud 1977) we have distinguished three levels of analysis, the short, medium, and long period. For each level we have analysed the dynamics of public debt, and its influence on the stability of the system as a whole.

Short period

Although we have not explicitly modelled short-period dynamics, it is shown that the distribution of wealth and debt may also have important consequences for short-period equilibrium. It is well known that a change in the price level changes the distribution of wealth between debtors and creditors, and will therefore have an impact on aggregate demand. Tobin (1980) pointed out that this may give rise to a 'reverse Pigou effect': that is, a general price rise causes expenditure to increase rather than to fall. Similarly our analysis suggests that a change in the interest rate may also have a reverse impact on expenditure and savings. This is due to the redistribution of income from the debtor sectors (government and the corporate sector) to the creditor sector (workers). Especially in the presence of a large public debt this may lead to a 'reverse Cambridge effect': that is, a higher interest rate leads to a *decrease* of aggregate savings. If this distribution effect is stronger than the conventional effect of the interest rate on investment, a higher interest rate may even yield a fall in aggregate expenditure (this may be called a 'reverse Keynes effect').

It is evident that these distribution effects may seriously affect the equilibrium-restoring role of the price level and the interest rate, and will therefore have a strong impact on the stability of short-period and medium-period dynamics.

Medium period

The medium period is characterized by sluggish prices and disequilibrium between aggregate demand and supply. In this context the decisive determinant of investment is the aim to adjust capacity to demand. This gives rise to a Harrod type of dynamics. Our analysis in Chapter 5 shows that the 'knife-edge' instability of Harrod's model is mitigated significantly if one takes account of a certain degree of price flexibility and feedback from a non-accommodating monetary sector. Nevertheless, even if this feedback leads to a stable equilibrium, it turns out to be stable only within a certain zone around this equilibrium, that is, it is locally stable but not globally. Numerical experiments indicate that this zone may take the form of an unstable limit cycle. Starting from a point inside this cycle the system will return to its equilibrium, but if it starts outside the cycle the system will recede from it for ever.

In economic terms this gives support to Leijonhufvud's proposition that Keynesian dynamics is characterized by a 'corridor': within this corridor the system is self-stabilizing, but beyond it the disequilibrium, or 'deviation-amplifying', forces become so strong that the system will never return to equilibrium by itself.

Whether a locally stable solution, and thereby a corridor, exists depends primarily on the response of investment to discrepancies between demand and capacity. If this acceleration factor is too strong the solution becomes unstable, locally as well as globally. There thus exists a critical value for the adjustment speed of investment beyond which the solution becomes unstable. In technical terms this critical parameter value represents the bifurcation point of the catastrophe manifold of the system (section 6.3). We have used the critical value of this parameter in order to assess the impact of different variables on the stability of the system.

Long period

The long-period analysis concentrates on the dynamics of growth, income distribution, and the accumulation of debt and wealth. As the medium-period results were not very encouraging as regards the intrinsic stability of the system, it is assumed that in the long period equilibrium between aggregate demand and supply is continuously being ensured by monetary policy. In the long period monetary authorities are thus assumed to have enough time to find the right policy to achieve full capacity utilization. The long-period dynamics is governed therefore by the interaction between labour market disequilibrium and the distribution of income, on the one hand, and the accumulation of assets ensuing from the budget constraints of the government, the workers and the corporate sector, on the other hand.

If the interaction between labour-market disequilibrium, wage growth, and investment is the dominant mechanism, it is shown that this may lead to a 'Goodwin' type of cycle. More interesting in the context of our analysis is that financial factors may also cause a long swing in economic activity. In the presence of financial constraints, in particular constraints with respect to equity finance, this cycle is governed by the interaction between investment, internal savings, and the evolution of the (desired) rate of indebtedness. Because investment now depends on the flow of internal savings as well as on the discrepancy between the actual and the desired debt ratio, a shock to the system, for example a fall in profits, will have a double impact on investment: first, through the change in internal savings, and second, through the change in the desired debt ratio. The analysis of the adjustment process for an individual firm (Chapter 5) reveals that this second factor especially may give rise to a lasting process of financial adjustment characterized by initial 'overshooting' of investment.

On an abstract level this may clarify some aspects of the developments after the oil shock in the mid-1970s. This shock not only affected the profitability of investment, but also changed the general state of uncertainty. As a result there was an adverse shift in business confidence leading to more prudential financial policies. Investment therefore fell not only because of the fall in internal savings, but because of the desire to reduce the rate of indebtedness as well. Notably this structural shift in the state of confidence may explain why recovery after the mid-1970s was so hesitant and why the recovery of investment in many countries lagged behind the improvement of actual profitability. These phenomena could not be explained by real factors alone. Financial constraints should be taken into account as well.

Open economy

In an open economy the domestic dynamics of wealth and debt should be considered together with the evolution of the external debt and wealth of domestic agents. In addition to the cumulating interest payments on public debt, net interest payments on foreign assets may now also produce a tendency towards instability. Through interest payments creditor countries tend to become even stronger creditors, and debtors ever larger debtors. Chapter 7 shows that for a small open economy the growth rate and the interest rate are the primary determinants of (local) stability. If domestic and foreign assets are perfect substitutes, the real interest rate in a small open economy is fully determined by the international interest rate. Hence, the stability of public debt depends crucially on the domestic rate of growth. Slowly growing economies will therefore be more liable to financial instability than similar economies with a high rate of growth. If, as a result of imperfect substitution, the domestic interest rate is dependent on the size of the net external position, this tends to increase the intrinsic instability for debtor countries. For creditor countries the risk of instability tends to be less.

The analysis of the open economy was restricted to the small open economy. It neglects the interaction between growth and asset accumulation in different countries. In this respect our analysis is still deficient. It would be interesting to extend the present analysis to a two-country model, or even to generalize it for more country models. This would require a synthesis of the analysis for the closed economy (Chapters 5 and 6) and the analysis of the open economy in Chapter 7. One interesting feature of an integrated world model is that changes in prices, exchange rates, and interest rates would cause distribution effects on a world scale as well. As a rise in the interest rate benefits creditor countries *vis-à-vis* debtor countries, it depends on the marginal saving propensities in different countries whether this leads to a rise or fall in aggregate expenditure.

Obviously, these models will be very complex and hard to deal with on the analytical level. Nevertheless, it would be very interesting to investigate how these models would behave in the long term. It is clear that a global steady state solution can exist only under very restrictive conditions. As steady growth requires all stocks and flows to grow at the same rate in real terms it is obvious that the net external position of any country must be zero in equilibrium, unless countries happen to grow at the same rate. Both conditions are very specific, and no obvious process seems to exist which would realize either of these conditions.[3] Hence, a steady state equilibrium seems to require international coordination of fiscal policies, i.e. the fiscal policy regimes should be consistent with a zero current account and a zero net debtor, or creditor, position in the long term.

Determinants of stability

There is an essential difference between the determinants of stability in the medium period and the long period. In the medium period, which is characterized by the disequilibrium dynamics between demand and capacity, all factors that tend to stabilize demand also have a stabilizing impact on the system as a whole. Thus all factors that raise the autonomous part of spending are intrinsically stabilizing. These factors include the autonomous inflation and money growth (which determines the equilibrium rate of growth). Further, all factors that strengthen the monetary feedback are stabilizing, in particular the degree of price elasticity and the sensitivity of the interest rate with respect to real money stock.

[3] There is no natural tendency towards a zero net external position. This can be seen as follows. In comparison with our model for a small open economy, the two-country case introduces one extra constraint, namely equilibrium between demand and supply on a world scale, and one extra free variable, the interest rate. Therefore the model is fully determined for any initial external position. Next assume that one steady state condition is satisfied, namely the net external position being zero. Then it is evident that this external position can remain zero over time only if the balance of payments in current account is zero as well. That is, if in both countries domestic demand just happens to equal domestic supply at the given international equilibrium rate of interest. This would, however, be purely accidental, and must be excluded on logical grounds. Therefore, steady state equilibrium is possible only if the real rate of growth is the same for both countries, or if fiscal policy in both countries deliberately aims at a zero external position or a zero deficit on current account.

In the long period the natural rate of growth and the equilibrium rate of interest emerge as basic determinants of (local) stability. Therefore all factors that depress the equilibrium interest rate tend to have a stabilizing impact on the system.

Thus in contrast with the medium-period dynamics all factors that reduce expenditure and increase saving are stabilizing.

A general conclusion of many IS/LM based studies on the stability of the government budget deficit is that a high wealth elasticity is essential for stability. However, our analysis, which concentrates on the long-period dynamics, tends to support the opposite conclusion, namely that a high wealth elasticity of consumption has a destabilizing impact on the system. This can be explained as follows. In short-period IS/LM models, characterized by under-utilization, a higher wealth elasticity enhances the feedback of public debt on consumption, and thereby on production and income, and thus finally on tax receipts. Therefore a rise in public debt may lead to reduction in the budget deficit if the wealth effect is sufficiently strong. In the long period when capacity is fully utilized, real tax receipts cannot be increased further through a rise in income. In that case, a stronger wealth effect only increases the impact of debt on the interest rate. Therefore a high wealth elasticity is generally destabilizing in our analysis, except in the small open-economy model considered in the final chapter where it turns out to be stabilizing again as it provides a check on ever-growing creditor positions (by stimulating consumption and thus deteriorating the trade balance) as well as debtor positions (by reducing domestic expenditure).

8.3 Policy conclusions

Discretionary behaviour of the government is often hampered by bureaucracy and many institutional and political constraints. This seems to be especially true for decisions on the government budget. Fiscal policy is therefore in our analysis conceived as rule-guided behaviour rather than as a continuous process of optimal decision-making. More specifically we have considered several well-defined budgetary regimes known in literature, notably:

1. Blinder–Solow regime, with fixed expenditure;
2. Tobin–Buiter regime, with a fixed sum of expenditure and interest payments net of taxes;
3. Christ regime, with a fixed sum of expenditure and interest payments;
4. Domar regime, with a target for the budget deficit;
5. Barro regime, with a target for debt as a ratio of national product.

A basic question we have tried to answer is which regime a government can best choose from the point of view of economic stability. The dynamics implied by these regimes have been investigated for the medium period, the long period, and for the case of the small open economy. In the medium term the Christ regime turns out to be the most stable regime, closely followed by the Tobin–Buiter regime. Both regimes are clearly counter-cyclical thanks to the fact that they imply an inverse relationship between expenditure and interest payments. As the interest rate is low in a depression and high during prosperity this produces a stabilizing variation in expenditure. The Barro regime, which aims at a constant debt ratio, performs by far the worst in the medium period. This is not surprising as this regime links government expenditure to two procyclical factors: tax revenue and the 'real erosion' of debt, through the growth of production. As a result a rise or fall in economic activity will be magnified by the consequential rise or fall in government expenditure. It should be noted that this interpretation of the debt target does not fully do justice to the tax-smoothing rule proposed by Barro (1979), according to which taxes do not have to be adjusted in case of temporary changes in production. Our debt regime (5) is thus more rigid than the regime originally proposed by Barro.

For the long period the results are different. Now the Barro regime proves to be the most stable regime; that is, with the smallest risk of a spiral of cumulating debt and interest payments. The second-best regime is the Christ regime which is obviously due to the strong feedback of debt service to expenditure. In the long period the Blinder–Solow Regime, which assumes fixed expenditure as well as tax rates, turns out to be the most destabilizing regime.

The results for the open economy are basically similar to those for the long period. The precise ranking of the regimes appears to depend on the net external position, but in general the Blinder–Solow regime performs worst again and the Barro regime best. These results reveal a sharp distinction between the stability of the budgetary regimes in the medium period and in the long period. This is especially true for the Barro regime which is the most stable regime in the long period while the most unstable regime in the medium period. Therefore it is impossible to establish a unique optimum regime for all periods and states of the economy. Nevertheless it is evident that a regime which links the room for government expenditure to the amount of debt service has a stabilizing impact on the economy in the medium period as well as in the long period. Therefore, of the regimes considered in our analysis the Christ regime, which implies a one-for-one linkage of expenditure to interest payments, may offer a reasonable 'second-best' solution from the medium-term as well as the long-term point of view.

In an open economy another factor must be taken into account, namely the evolution of the external position. As the change in foreign wealth depends on the excess of private savings over domestic investment including the government budget deficit it may be sensible to direct fiscal policy to a target for the balance of payments. In fact, the budgetary regime based on a structural deficit norm employed in for instance The Netherlands from 1961 to the mid-1970s was based implicitly on a norm for the balance of payments in current account.

Although it is attractive, on both political and economic grounds, to adopt certain rules or norms for fiscal policy, our analysis shows that the appropriate rule may vary with the state of the economy and the period considered. This means that a regime which performed well under certain conditions may become less appropriate if these conditions change. As a result formerly stable policy regimes may even turn into unstable regimes. In particular, we have discussed two such changes. First, it was shown that a structural rise in the real interest rate in relation to the growth rate—such as most countries have experienced in the 1980s—may affect the long-period stability of the economy, especially if the government holds on to a given target for expenditure (Blinder–Solow regime). But regimes with a target for the deficit or for the sum expenditure and interest payments may also become unstable then. Secondly, our analysis brings out that a structurally rising public debt is a significant threat to both the short-period and the long-period stability of the economy. In the short period the distribution effects ensuing from public debt tend to destabilize income–expenditure equilibrium (because of the reverse interest effect). In the long term a high debt leads to a higher interest rate which tends to destabilize the accumulation of debt. In formal terms, public debt can therefore be conceived as a slow variable which if it grows beyond a certain critical value may produce a 'catastrophe', i.e. it may cause a drastic change in the dynamics of the economy. Rules have therefore to be reconsidered regularly, and discretionary decisions may be necessary to change them. Thus not only does a change of the rules lead to a change of the system (Lucas 1976), but also a change of the system must lead to a change of the rules.

References

ASADA, T. (1987), 'Government finance and wealth effect in a Kaldorian cycle model', *Journal of Economics* (Zeitschrift für Nationalökonomie), 47: 143–66.

ASIMAKOPULOS, A. (1986), 'Finance, liquidity, saving, and investment', *Journal of Post Keynesian Economics*, 9: 79–90.

AUBERADA, J. (1979), 'Steady-state growth of the long-run sales maximizing firm', *Quarterly Journal of Economics*, 93: 131–8.

BAKER, A. J. (1978), *Investment, Valuation, and the Managerial Theory of the Firm*, Saxon House, Farnborough.

BARANZINI, M. (1975), 'The Pasinetti and anti-Pasinetti theorems: a reconciliation', *Oxford Economic Papers*, 27: 470–3.

—— (1982), 'Can the life-cycle theory help in explaining income distribution and capital accumulation?', in M. Baranzini (ed.), *Advances in Economic Theory*, Basil Blackwell, Oxford.

BARRO, R. (1974), 'Are government bonds net wealth?', *Journal of Political Economy*, 82: 1094–117.

—— (1979), 'On the determination of public debt', *Journal of Political Economy*, 87: 940–71.

BAUMOL, W. J. (1959), *Business Behavior, Value and Growth*, Macmillan, New York.

BLINDER, A. S., and SOLOW, R. M. (1973), 'Does fiscal policy matter?', *Journal of Public Economics*, 2: 219–337.

BUITER, W. H. (1983), 'Measurement of the public sector deficit and its implications for policy evaluation and design', *IMF Staff Papers*, 30: 306–49.

—— (1985), 'A guide to public sector debt and deficits', *Economic Policy*, 1: 13–60.

—— (1986), 'Fiscal policy in open, interdependent economies', in A. Razin (ed.), *Economic Policy in Theory and Practice*, Basil Blackwell, Oxford.

CALVO, G. A. (1985), 'Macroeconomic implications of the government budget', *Journal of Monetary Economics*, 15: 95–112.

CHIANG, A. C. (1973), 'A simple generalization of the Kaldor–Pasinetti theory of the profit rate and income distribution', *Economica*, 40: 311–13.

CHRIST, C. F. (1968), 'A simple macro-economic model with a government restraint', *Journal of Political Economy*, 76: 53–67.

CHRIST, C. F. (1978), 'Some dynamic theory of macroeconomic policy effects on income and prices under the government budget restraint', *Journal of Monetary Economics*, 4: 45–70.

—— (1979), 'On fiscal and monetary policies and the government budget restraint', *American Economic Review*, 6: 526–38.

COHEN, A. M. (1973), *Numerical Analysis*, McGraw-Hill, New York.

DARITY, W. A. (1981), 'The simple analytics of neo-Ricardian growth and distribution', *American Economic Review*, 71: 978–93.

DOMAR, E. D. (1957), *Essays in the Theory of Economic Growth*, Oxford University Press, New York.

EATWELL, J. L. (1971), 'Growth, profitability and size: the empirical evidence', in Marris and Wood (1971).

EICHNER, A. S. (1976), *The Megacorp and Oligopoly*, Cambridge University Press, London.

EWIJK, C. VAN (1982*a*), 'A spectral analysis of the Kondratieff-cycle', *Kyklos*, 35: 468–99.

—— (1982*b*), 'Stability in Keynesian and neoclassical growth models: a comment on Kuipers', *De Economist*, 130: 101–22.

—— (1986), 'Interest payments and the stability of the government budget deficit in an open and growing economy', *De Economist*, 134: 143–64.

FAZI, E., and SALVADORI, N. (1981), 'The existence of a two-class economy in the Kaldor model of growth and distribution', *Kyklos*, 34: 582–92.

FAZZARI, S. M., HUBBARD, R. G., and PETERSEN, B. C. (1988), 'Financing constraints and corporate investment', *Brookings Papers on Economic Activity*, 1: 141–95.

FISHER, I. (1931), *Booms and Depressions*, Adelphi, New York.

GABISCH, G., and LORENZ, H. (1989), *Business Cycle Theory*, Springer Verlag, Berlin/New York.

GOODWIN, R. M. (1967), 'A growth model', in C. H. Feinstein, *Socialism, Capitalism and Growth*, Cambridge University Press, Cambridge.

—— (1972), 'A growth cycle', in E. K. Hunt and J. G. Schwartz, *A Critique of Economic Theory*, Penguin Books, Harmondsworth.

GREENWALD, B. C., and STIGLITZ, J. E. (1988*a*), 'Financial market imperfections and business cycles', Working Paper 2494, National Bureau of Economic Research, Cambridge, Mass.

—— (1988*b*), 'Examining alternative macroeconomic theories', *Brookings Papers on Economic Activity*, 1: 207–60.

HAMADA, K. (1966), 'Economic growth and long-term international capital movements', *Yale Economic Essays*, 6: 49–96.

HARCOURT, G. C., and KENYON, P. (1976), 'Pricing and the investment decision', *Kyklos*, 29: 449–77.

HARROD, R. F. (1948), *Towards a Dynamic Economics*, Macmillan,
London.

HOOGDUIN, L. (1987), 'On the difference between the Keynesian,
Knightian and the "Classical" analysis of uncertainty and the
development of a more general theory', *De Economist*, 135: 52–69.

HOWITT, P. (1978), 'The limits to stability of a full-employment
equilibrium', *Scandinavian Journal of Economics*, 265–82.

JENSEN, M. C., and MECKLING, W. H. (1976), 'Theory of the firm,
agency costs and ownership structure', *Journal of Financial Economics*, 3: 305–60.

—— and WARNER, J. B. (1988), 'The distribution of power among
corporate managers, shareholders, and directors', *Journal of Financial Economics*, 20: 3–24.

JORDAN, D. W., and SMITH, P. (1987), *Nonlinear Ordinary Differential Equations*, Clarendon Press, Oxford.

JUDD, J. P., and SCADDING, J. L. (1982), 'The search for a stable money
demand function: a survey of the post-1973 literature', *Journal of
Economic Literature*, 20: 993–1023.

KALDOR, N. (1957), 'A model of economic growth', *Economic Journal*, 67: 591–624.

—— (1961), 'Capital accumulation and economic growth', in F. A.
Lutz and D. C. Hague (eds.), *The Theory of Capital*, St Martin's
Press, New York.

—— (1966), 'Marginal productivity and the macro-economic theories of distribution', *Review of Economic Studies*, 33: 309–19.

—— and MIRRLEES, J. A. (1962), 'A new model of economic growth',
Review of Economic Studies, 29: 174–92.

KALECKI, M. (1934), 'On foreign trade and "domestic exports" ', in
Kalecki (1971).

—— (1937), 'The principle of increasing risk', *Economica*, 4: 440–7.

—— (1943), 'Determinants of investment', in Kalecki (1971).

—— (1954), *Studies in Economic Dynamics*, Allen & Unwin, London.

—— (1971), *Selected Essays on the Dynamics of the Capitalist
Economy*, Cambridge University Press, Cambridge.

KEYNES, J. M. (1973), *The General Theory and After. Part II: Defence
and Development, The Collected Writings of John Maynard
Keynes*, xiv, Macmillan, London.

KLUNDERT, TH. VAN DE, and PLOEG, F. VAN DER (1987), 'Wage rigidity
and capital mobility in an optimizing model of a small open econ-

omy', Discussion Paper 168, Centre for Economic Policy Research, London.

—— and SCHAIK, A. B. VAN (1990), 'Liquidity constraints and the Keynesian corridor', Research Memorandum 429, Department of Economics, Tilburg University.

KREGEL, J. A. (1975), *The Reconstruction of Political Economy: An Introduction to Post-Keynesian Economics*, Macmillan, London.

KUIPERS, S. K. (1981), 'Keynesian and neoclassical growth models: a sequential analytical approach', *De Economist*, 129: 58–104.

LAING, N. F. (1969), 'Two notes on Pasinetti', *Economic Record*, 45: 373–85.

LEIJONHUFVUD, A. (1981), 'Information and coordination', in *Essays on Macroeconomic Theory*, Oxford University Press, Oxford.

LINTNER, J. (1956), 'Distribution of incomes of corporations among dividends, retained earnings, and taxes', *American Economic Review, Papers and Proceedings*, 46: 97–113.

—— (1971), 'Optimum or maximum corporate growth under uncertainty', in Marris and Wood (1971).

LUCAS, R. E. (1976), 'Econometric policy evaluation: a critique', in K. Brunner and A. H. Meltzer (eds.), *The Phillips Curve and Labour Markets*, supplement to the *Journal of Monetary Economics*.

MALINVAUD, E. (1977), *The Theory of Unemployment Reconsidered*, Basil Blackwell, Oxford.

—— (1980), *Profitability and Unemployment*, Cambridge University Press, Cambridge.

—— (1986), 'Pure profits as forced saving', *Scandinavian Journal of Economics*, 88: 109–30.

MARGLIN, S. A. (1984), *Growth Distribution and Prices*, Harvard University Press, Cambridge, Mass.

MARRIS, R. (1964), *The Economic Theory of 'Managerial' Capitalism*, Macmillan, London.

—— (1971), 'An introduction to theories of corporate growth', in Marris and Wood (1971).

—— and WOOD, A. (1971) (eds.), *The Corporate Economy*, London.

MAYER, C. (1988), 'New issues in corporate finance', *European Economic Review*, 32: 1167–89.

MEADE, J. (1963), 'The rate of profit in a growing economy', *Economic Journal*, 73: 665–74.

METZ, R. (1984), 'Zur empirischen Evidenz "langer Wellen" ', *Kyklos*, 37: 266–90.

MODIGLIANI, F. (1971), 'Monetary policy and consumption: linkages via interest rate and wealth effects in the FMP model', in *Con-*

sumer Spending and Monetary Policy: The Linkages, Conference Series No. 5, Federal Bank of Boston.

—— and MILLER, M. H. (1958), 'The cost of capital, corporation finance and the theory of investment', *American Economic Review*, 48: 261–97.

MOSS, S. J. (1984), *Markets and Macroeconomics*, Basil Blackwell, Oxford.

NICKELL, S. J. (1978), *The Investment Decisions of Firms*, Cambridge University Press, Cambridge.

O'CONNELL, J. (1985), 'Undistributed profits and the Pasinetti and dual theorems', *Journal of Macroeconomics*, 7: 115–20.

ODAGIRI, H. (1981), *The Theory of Growth in a Corporate Economy*, Cambridge University Press, Cambridge.

PASINETTI, L. (1962), 'Rate of profit and income distribution in relation to the rate of growth', *Review of Economic Studies*, 29: 267–79.

—— (1966), 'New results in an old framework: comment on Samuelson and Modigliani', *Review of Economic Studies*, 33: 303–6.

—— (1974), *Growth and Income Distribution: Essays in Economic Theory*, Cambridge University Press, Cambridge.

—— (1981), *Structural Change and Economic Growth*, Cambridge University Press, Cambridge.

—— (1983), 'Conditions for existence of a two class economy in the Kaldor and more general models of growth and income distribution', *Kyklos*, 36: 91–102.

PENROSE, E. (1959), *The Theory of Growth of the Firm*, Basil Blackwell, Oxford.

PLOEG, F. VAN DER (1983), 'Economic growth and conflict over the distribution of income', *Journal of Economic Dynamics and Control*, 6: 253–79.

RAU, N. (1985), 'Simplifying the theory of the government budget restraint', *Oxford Economic Papers*, 37: 210–29.

REIJNDERS, J. (1988), 'The Enigma of Long Waves', Ph.D. thesis, University of Utrecht.

ROBINSON, J. (1965), *The Accumulation of Capital*, Macmillan, London (1st edn. 1956).

—— (1962), 'A model of economic growth', in J. Robinson, *Essays in the Theory of Growth*, Macmillan, London.

SAMUELSON, P. A., and MODIGLIANI, F. (1966), 'The Pasinetti paradox in neoclassical and more general models', *Review of Economic Studies*, 23: 269–301.

SAWYER, M. (1989), 'Post Keynesian economics: the state of the art', mimeo.

SEOKA, Y. (1985), 'Steady state growth of the long-run sales-maximizing firm: comment', *Quarterly Journal of Economics*, 99: 713–19.

SHLEIFER, A. (1986), 'Do demand curves for stocks slope down?' *Journal of Finance*, 16/3: 579–90.

SKOTT, P. (1989), *Conflict and Effective Demand in Economic Growth*, Cambridge University Press, Cambridge.

SLATER, M. (1980), 'The managerial limitation to the growth of firms', *Economic Journal*, 90: 520–8.

SOLOW, R. M. (1971), 'Some implications of alternative criteria of the firm', in Marris and Wood (1971).

STEEDMAN, I. (1979), *Trade among Growing Economies*, Cambridge University Press, Cambridge.

—— and METCALFE, J. S. (1979), 'Growth and distribution in an open economy', in I. Steedman (ed.), *Fundamental Issues in Trade Theory*, Macmillan, London.

TAGGART, R. A. (1986), 'Have U. S. corporations grown financially weak?', in B. Friedman (ed.), *Financing Corporate Capital Formation*, NBER, Chicago.

TANZI, V. (1984) (ed.), *Taxation, Inflation and Interest Rates*, International Monetary Fund, Washington, DC.

—— BLEJER, M. I. and TEIJEIRO, M. O. (1987), 'Inflation and the measurement of fiscal deficits', *IMF Staff Papers*, 34: 711–38.

—— and LUTZ, M. S. (1990), 'Interest rates and government debt: are the linkages global rather than national?', mimeo.

TOBIN, J. (1960), 'Towards a general Kaldorian theory of distribution', *Review of Economic Studies*, 17: 119–20.

—— (1980), *Asset Accumulation and Economic Activity*, Basil Blackwell, Oxford.

—— (1982), 'Money and finance in the macroeconomic process', *Journal of Money, Credit and Banking*, 14: 171–204.

—— and BUITER, W. H. (1976), 'Long-run effects of fiscal and monetary policy and aggregate demand', in J. L. Stein (ed.), *Monetarism*, North Holland, Amsterdam.

TURNOVSKY, S. J. (1976), 'The dynamics of fiscal policy in an open economy', *Journal of International Economics*, 6: 115–42.

UZAWA, H. (1969), 'Time preference and the Penrose effect in a two-class model of economic growth', *Journal of Political Economy*, 77/4: 628–52.

WILLIAMSON, J. H. J. (1966), 'Profit, growth and sales maximization', *Economica*, 33: 1–16.

WILLIAMSON, O. E. (1988), 'Corporate finance and corporate governance', *Journal of Finance*, 18: 565–91.

WOOD, A. (1971), 'Economic analysis of the corporate economy', in Marris and Wood (1971).

—— (1975), *A Theory of Profits*, Cambridge University Press, Cambridge.

Index

adjustment process:
  and growth of firm 82–90,
    91–2, 195; creditor firm
    86–7; debtor firm 85–6;
    profitability fall 87–90
  and interest and wealth ef-
    fects 37–40
advertisement costs 52
agency theory 53 n.
aggregate demand, *see* demand
alternative regimes 187–8
arbitrage 160, 162
Asada, T. 41
Asimakopulos, A. 48
Auberada, J. 52, 60 n.

Baker, A. J. 52, 58 n.
balanced regime, *see* current
  balance
balance of payments con-
  straint 158, 166–7, 200
balance of trade 160 n., 161 n.
bankruptcies 95
Baranzini, M. 11 n., 44
Barro, R. 15 n., 199–200
  and Keynesian corridor 101–
    3, 110, 122, 125
  and long-period dynamics
    136–7, 142, 147, 156–7
  and open economy 163 n.,
    171, 173, 187–8
Baumol, W. J. 50 n.
Blejer, M. I. 126 n.
Blinder, A. S. and Solow, R. M.
  2, 199–201
  and Keynesian corridor 101–
    3, 105–6, 122–3, 125

  and long-period dynamics
    128, 129 n., 136, 142–4,
    147, 149, 156–7; reduced
    model of dynamics of
    growth and debt 142–4
  and open economy 164, 170–
    1, 174, 177, 186
  and Pasinetti paradoxes 11 n.,
    41
boundary conditions of savings
  propensities 32
bounded rationality 6
BPC, *see* balance of payments
  constraint
budget, *see* government
Buiter, W. H. 2, 11 n., 41
  and Keynesian corridor 101–
    3, 122, 126 and n.
  and long-period dynamics
    147, 157
  and open economy 171–2,
    174, 177, 187
bureaucracy, *see* government;
  policy

Calvo, G. A. 129 n.
Cambridge effect:
  normal 26–9 n., 36, 43, 45
  reverse 25, 33, 37, 193
capital:
  and long-period model, *see*
    long-period dynamics
  and open economy 161–2,
    166, 167
  and production 60–8
  see also equity; shareholders